THE ENVIRONMENTAL DIALOGUE IN THE GDR

Literature, Church, Party,
and Interest Groups
in Their Socio-Political Context
A Research Concept
and Case Study

Anita M. Mallinckrodt

Studies in GDR Culture and Society
A Supplementary Volume

UNIVERSITY
PRESS OF
AMERICA

All University Press of America books are produced on acid-free
paper which exceeds the minimum standards set by the National
Historical Publication and Records Commission.

Dedicated

in grateful memory

to my

extraordinary parents

whose modest agrarian values included a deep

appreciation for and of reading materials and

so, too, their daughter's world of writing

Table of Contents

A book becomes, and then is, many things to its author. For its readers, it is and may become something quite different. To clarify the former -- the author's premises and intentions-- these shared thoughts.

This book is, first of all, a response to colleagues who encouraged continuation of the interdisciplinary political science/ literary science approach begun with my 1984 study of GDR dime novels in their socio-political context. Specifically, this study was undertaken with scholars of literature in mind who sought a functional approach to their field, a way of looking at *how* the literature they study plays an institutional role within its political culture context. For political scientists, the study answered a challenge to examine the role of literature within its *political* culture and *political* socialization contexts, to look at *why* literature is an essential source of social-change signals.

Therefore, secondly, the book offers a new interdisciplinary research approach for GDR studies. It initiates a *political sociology of literature* with the help of systems/functional analysis. That conceptual framework, used as an aid for collecting information otherwise not generally available about the GDR, helps to analyze the significance of literature as an institution in the GDR's political culture, and, in turn, the context's influence on the role and functions of literature. In addition, by focusing on *interrelationships* within the GDR's socio-political system, the approach sheds light on the dynamics and process of social change.

Thirdly, this book is a study in *political communication*, specifically the environmental dialogue in the GDR in the 1980s. It examines the back-and-forth flow of political communication from party/state leaders to the general public and the feedback, or communicated reactions, from the public.

As a focus, a case study is offered of Hanns Cibulka's ecologically challenging diary *Swantow*, i.e., its context, content, and reception. This is followed by a survey analysis of selected dialogue highlights from 1983 through mid-1986 (post-Chernobyl), especially at the level of the institutions of literature and the church, interest groups, and SED party units. The survey concentrates on responses to *Swantow's* conceptual challenges and on discussions of related political culture values.

The study, thus, offers insight into environmental/ecological views of various interest groups and an abundance of primary source citations perhaps useful especially to American scholars undertaking more specific and in-depth studies of the interest groups discussed. Through chronological presentation, the survey suggests possible interrelationships between output (government actions and communications) and input (public demands and feedback). The feedback emphasis allows a focus on the dynamics of change in the GDR's socio-political system.

Within this context of premises and intentions, Chapter I of the book presents an overview of systems/functional analysis for literary scholars; for political scientists, it highlights recent developments in applying the approach especially to communist systems. Chapter II sketches the background of the debate about scientific, technological, economic, and social "progress" going on in the GDR at the time Hanns Cibulka, Gotha lyricist and diarist, published a controversial challenge to existing environmental/ecological policies and conditions.

Chapter III, then, contains a case study of that diary, *Swantow*, and Chapter IV surveys highlights of 3 1/2 years of subsequent dialogue which reflected and reacted to its conceptual challenges, as well as to the concept of progress in general. Although the study was complete by autumn 1985, it was reopened and expanded to include immediate dialogue reactions to the nuclear reactor accident at Chernobyl in the USSR in spring 1986.

Chapter V presents some summarizing ideas about the study itself and in conclusion offers theses which are also seen as further research topics. Comprehensive conclusions regarding ecology as a literary theme, or the GDR's environmental policy, decision-making process, and individual interest groups obviously remain outside the scope of the study.

An additional point requires clarification, that of translation. In an interdisciplinary study such as this, the question of when to translate is difficult to resolve. As a bilingual social scientist acutely aware of foreign language shortcomings among U.S. readers, I wanted to translate as much as possible to facilitate reader understanding; as a translator of non-belletristic materials, I did not want to insult literary scholars with inadequate rendering of precious nuances of language. Thus, various answers to the translation problems in this work were found.

For instance, translation of classical writers, such as Goethe and Hoffmansthal, is not attempted; instead, their poetic lines of German verse have been put into a footnote. Some of Christa Wolfe's unique formulations, too, are in footnotes, with an English paraphrase of their content in the text. In fact, that approach became the guideline for the entire book: (a) translations wherever necessary and feasible (with equivalent German words in parentheses where that might add specific understanding), but (b) English paraphrasing of content for literary or lengthy texts which should be left in the original for accuracy and context, and (c) inclusion of the original German lines as footnotes or as texts in Appendices for consultation by German-language readers.

An exception to this practice is found in the presentation of the case-study texts -- Hanns Cibulka's initial and revised *Swantow* -- in Chapter 3. Here, in addition to pages of paraphrased content for English-only readers, the chapter also reproduces key texts in the original German and in parallel columns. This was done to illustrate graphically the revisions in *Swantow* and to make them available for readers sensitive to changes in the German version.

Finally, sincere thanks to countless friends and colleagues in the US, GDR, and FRG who first challenged and then contributed so importantly, professionally and personally, to this book. And, as over many years, special appreciation again is due the librarians and archivists at the Central Institute for Social Science Research at the Free University in West Berlin. With so much extraordinary cooperation, I alone can be accountable for mistakes and shortcomings of this study.

Köln/Washington
July 1986

Chapter I

INTRODUCTION -- POLITICAL SOCIOLOGY OF LITERATURE

Decades ago sociologists together with their colleagues from
the humanities developed literary sociology as a way to analyze
the *societal* setting of literature. It seems time now for political scientists concerned with the *political* setting of literary
works to seek such cooperation in evolving a *political sociology
of literature*.

A significant stimulus to such an approach came from Maureen
Whitebrook in a 1983 article for teachers of political science.[1]
Whitebrook wrote that, similar to literary sociology, "literary
politics" should be concerned with literature's political background and context. Though thereby linking literature in a
cause/effect relationship to culture, her brief article did not
provide a specific approach for analyzing a given political culture and the literature within it.

In the GDR research field, political scientists who have
taken up Whitebrook's challenge to examine literature in its
socio-political context have used various approaches. The theory
of political socialization and political culture has frequently
been the point of departure and content analysis the methodology.
Nevertheless, the efforts remain fragmentary for political scientists know little about literature's functional role in society.

Recognizing that need as also their own, literary colleagues
are presently actively concerned about gaining more understanding
of the socio-political context of literature in the GDR. For instance, Heinrich Mohr, co-editor of *Jahrbuch zur Literatur in der
DDR*, says that while postwar FRG literary scholars were poorly
prepared to see the "new" literature in the GDR in a political
context, developments of the past decade are encouraging for
scholars now are focusing on "text and context".[2] In surveying
the US research field among Germanists, Patricia Herminghouse says
that although the centrality of literature in the political culture of the GDR is widely accepted, "we do not presently have all
the tools by which to guage parameters in the political and economic spheres which affect the functioning of this literary system. We urgently need a functional analysis of the total literary system..."[3] And Peter Hohendahl thinks such literary in-
vestigations seeking to situate individual work contextually would
be facilitated if literature were seen as an *institution*.[4]

Moving such concepts forward and together, political and literary scholars could develop a political sociology of literature
(what one might in German call *Literaturpolitsoziologie*) as a
fruitful new approach in both disciplines. To attempt such a

1

cooperation vis-a-vis the GDR seems most appropriate, for if literature has a political context anywhere, then surely there.

In beginning, as Herminghouse noted, a lot of background help
is available from literary sociologists. This is especially true
of GDR scholars who more easily make the conceptual socio-political connections Westerners are seeking. For instance, many researchers have discovered that the literature sociologists at the
University of Halle have done pioneering work. In two major em-
pirical studies[5] they mention many of the aspects which should be
examined in developing a socio-political institutional concept of
literature in the GDR. But they do not give answers to many essential (and essentially) *political* questions. Instead, they naturally concentrate on literary sociology themes -- reading behavior (*Leserverhalten*), social function of the arts, relationship of social and aesthetic factors to artistic effectiveness
(*Kunstwirkung*), influence of social and individual factors in the
process of art production and reception, the significance of aesthetic needs and interest in the effectiveness of art works, and
the role of social communication about the arts.

If, however, one takes what they intimate about literature's
political context, it at least is a good basis for further questions. For instance, the Halle scholars discuss at length what
they call art mediation (*Kunstvermittlung*). The first aspect is
reproduction, which includes the printing of a manuscript by a
publishing house. That, they say, involves "a series of selection procedures, agreements, and discussions between author and
editor, between editors and literary scholars".[6] Or, from the
publisher's point of view, the process concerns the important
third-party role which a publishing house plays in the "reciprocal
relationship between socialist-realistic literature and the socialist way of life".[7]

To understand the political dimension of this publishing process, as part of the institutional life of literature, one would
need to ask, for instance, how publishing house directors and editors are selected; does the Ministry of Culture itself first ap-
prove a manuscript the publishing house wants to publish or are
general political guidelines transmitted to the publisher from the
Ministry; if there are guidelines, are they firm or is there room
for compromise in the manuscript-selection process; is the role
which the literary scholars play strictly an artistic advisory
role; from where are they chosen; precisely what do they do; to
whom are the publishing houses responsible (for instance, League
of Culture, SED organizations, etc.,); does their varying accountability influence the openness of the manuscript-selection process; how are the pressruns determined; when a GDR-authored book
is published in the West before or after being rejected for publication in the GDR, to what extent are such decisions on both
sides based on literary standards or on the politics of the author

2

or his subject matter?

A second spect of art mediation in the GDR, according to the Halle authors, is distribution -- via bookstores, libraries, and personal exchange.[8] Here relevant political questions might include who determines how many copies of which books go to the book stores and to the libraries; who determines, and by what criteria, which books from abroad shall be purchased via license and/or which shall be purchased for limited library use (i.e., shall be put in the *Giftkammer*); what are the categories of selection for books to be sold outside of book stores, for instance, at kiosks, in department and office supply stores, and through book clubs.[9]

The sales efforts (*Werbetätigkeit*) of the publishing houses discussed in the Halle studies are also of great institutional interest, for it is said to include

> the organization of authors' readings, readers' discussions, and other events, as well as the sales publicity of book stores, the informational activities of libraries and their publicity to encourage reading, etc.[10]

Who, specifically, is responsible for organizing such readings and discussion; by what criteria are books and authors chosen for such activities?

A third aspect of art mediation is what the Halle literature sociologists refer to as *Literaturpropaganda*, or publicity for literature. As they say,

> Additional literature and art mediators are the schools, other educational institutions, and, not last, literature and art critics. The organizations, institutions, and media of art mediation are also subject to the social division of labor.[11]

Again, who selects the literature to be included in study plans for schools, the Ministry for Education, with or without suggestions from the Ministry for Culture? If reviews in the GDR daily press are intended to serve, among other things, management (*Leitung*) activities, as well as to inform readers about new publications and to give them a chance to respond,[12] how does this work in practice -- in a given period of time how much newspaper space is given to each of these tasks? How does this compare with literary reviewing in specialized cultural magazines such as *Neue deutsche Literatur* and *Sinn und Form*? Is a specific author reviewed differently in the journals than in the daily newspapers? What, indeed, is the political-guideline context within which the various mass media carry out their roles as art mediators? What is the impact on art mediation of Western reactions to books,

3

especially when heard in the GDR via Western radio broadcasts? In their transmission role, how closely do the social organizations, for instance the League of Culture, work with the Writers' Union or the regional Artists' Unions? What, essentially, is the interdependent relationship of the professional literary society to other aspects of literature as an institution, for example, to teaching, reviewing, public discussion?

The sales and information aspects, sometimes included in what the Halle literature specialists call "art communication", makes clear a basic fact about literature as an institution in the GDR-- it is not an elite affair based on profit, but rather intended as an "ideological mediator shaping conscience and personality".[13] Thus events which "take literature to the people" -- such as literary discussions in factories, book bazaars, "Book Week" -- are important. Who organizes these activities; how are the books selected?

Also of great significance for the institution of literature in the GDR is the contractual procedure of state financing and support of writers (*Auftragswesen*). As the Halle study explains,

> *The social commission to the artists include works resulting from contractual regulations with state organizations, social organizations, factories, and work collectives, but also works which arise entirely out of personal motives, assuming the artist understands him/herself as a medium of social needs.*[14]

Which writers, then, apply where? What are the selection criteria? Are Writers' Union members give preference over non-member writers? How often does it happen, as the Halle researchers suggest, that "over the years uniform commissions were given to always the same artists"?[15]

Such questions, and many more which could be asked, are *political*, that is, they have to do with structures and processes dealing directly with the *authoritative allocation of values for society*. In short, they ask "Who gets what and why?" about the opportunity to publish, the chance to be heard, the possibility of being financed, etc.

This context of GDR literature seems to be the basis for a widely prevalent intellectual view that GDR literature is taken seriously precisely because of its institutional politics -- GDR opinion leaders apparently see *what* appears in print by *whom* as cultural *policy* signals answering their question of "who will get what" in the foreseeable future; Western scholars often tend to read the signals similarly. At another level, however, that of GDR readers, the question of why literature in the GDR is taken seriously may elicit quite different answers relating to

4

individual psychological and intellectual needs.

While most of the political insights sought in the foregoing questions are undoubtedly available in existing individual studies, it would help in clarifying the *institutional* role of GDR literature if the facts were brought together and discussed within a context of socio-political system *interrelationships* -- for instance, (a) the possible influence of the Writers' Union on decision-making processes concerning the financing of writers, (b) the implication of such specific contract decisions on (c) literary production, or who writes what, and on (d) the GDR's politicl culture in terms of what books reach the public with what messages, then, (e) the feedback, or public reaction to such books, and, in turn, (f) the feedback of the Writers' Union into a new round of decision-making. Adding such a political dimension to what is already known sociologically about GDR literature could be most useful in future studies.

Admittedly, that is not easy. Foreign scholars often face serious problems when carrying out research in the GDR. On the other hand, however, the GDR is intellectually intriguing, for it is a society undergoing significant socio-political changes reflected in a vital and revealing literature. Examining that literature systematically, from a literary political sociology point of view, could disclose much more about the changes underway than can be uncovered through intuitive hunches.

1. Systems/Functional Analysis

As elaborated in earlier writings,[16] research models are useful for systematically studying political systems, even while the models' advantages and disadvantages continue to be vigorously debated. Obviously a model is not intended to reflect a specific country accurately, nor to encompass all the factors involved in its power relationships. But it can help organize facts and, if mechanistic cause/effect thinking is rigorously avoided, it can *suggest* interrelationships. A model carefully used can highlight a system's uniqueness or its similarities to other systems.

Among the models generally available, the often modified systems/functional approach, shown on the following page, remains relevant. It offers literary scholars a framework for visualizing the frequently overwhelming multitude of socio-political interrelationships which influence literature's role in a given society. For political scientists, the model's functions are proving useful in structuring currently popular "policy studies" (analysis of the series of decisions leading to a course of action or inaction)[17] and in examining "macro policy" via sophisticated data analysis (for instance, socio-economic and political input variables, their transformation within political institutions to outputs, and the

5

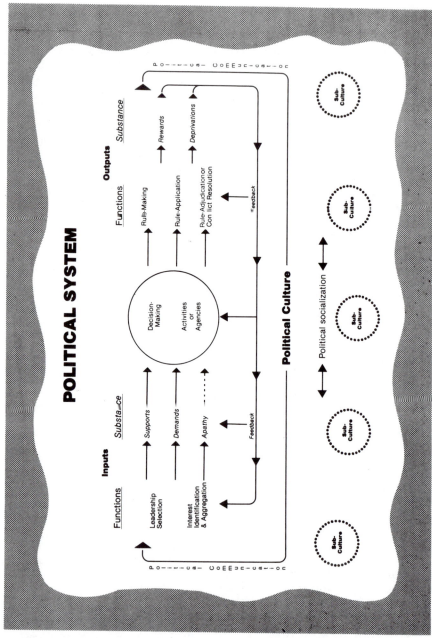

Fig. 1. Adapted by Mallinckrodt/Schaad from Irish and Prothro,
The Politics of American Democracy, 5th ed. Prentice-Hall, 1971.

6

resulting feedback loop which reaffects output).[18] And in the comparative politics field, Almond and Powell use the concept-- calling it a "systems-environmental approach"-- in their standard text *Comparative Politics Today*. Their adapted diagram is a circular input/output flow which includes influences from both the domestic and the international environment.[19]

For understanding socialist systems, the systems/functional model still seems more useful than the newer one called "corporatism"[20] or the older totalitarian, bureaucratic, or elite models. The systems/functional approach has the advantages of a broader conceptual framework, more independence from Western values and ideologies, and the possibility of focusing on change. In recent years, GDR specialists themselves, without referring to a specific research approach, have indicated the general relevance of systems/functional analysis. Political scientists, for instance, have written that

> the close and *dynamic interrelationships* between all its *elements* are characteristic distinctions of and prerequisites for development of the *political system* of Socialism at the present time. (Emphasis - AM).[21]

In other words, the systems/functional approach to the GDR encourages researchers to look at possible *interrelationships* between inputs into the system and its outputs (demands and supports which influence decision-making vis-a-vis specific policies).

For instance, one can focus on the input influences of institutions such as literature or the church and speculate about their impact, thus addressing a central question of political science-- what influences governmental actions, and how, in turn, does that process relate to political stability or change? It may be found, for example, that in "maintenance"-oriented political systems (rather than new, possibly revolutionary, systems with their goal of political "establishment"), socio-political changes offered from the top down are primarily changes of political *form*, whereas changes in *content* come chiefly, albeit slowly, as demands from the political culture base of the system up to the decision-makers.

Within the systems/functional framework one also can focus on the possible input influences of *interest groups*, an approach legitimized by H. Gordon Skilling's work on the Soviet Union.[22] It does not presume that interest groups in socialism are voluntary associations; instead, they operate in a very structured context and under the firm control of the ruling Communist Party. At the same time, this approach does presume that the state lacks total control. Rather, scholars speak of the "relative autonomy" of the state because there are influences *on* the government and different

7

points of view and influences *within* the government and party. In short, there is diffusion of influence, even if not of power. This possible multiplicity of influences on policy-making, as this study will show, is reflected in the *interest articulation* and *feedback* functions of the system. East European scholars themselves see an emphasis on such interest group functions as useful for understnding their system. For instance, Jerzy J. Wiatr, well-known Polish political scientist, some time ago accepted the so-called "pluralist", or interest group, approach as a realistic description of political relations in socialist countries.[23]

In addition, Western scholars are beginning to see participation in communist political systems, as through interest groups, differently than in the past. Donald Schulz, for instance, makes the case this way:

> *Until farily rocently it was commonly assumed that such forms of participation as existed in communist societies were not 'real', that this was 'illusory' or 'sham' or 'pseudo' participation...citizen involvement in communist societies was said to be 'mobilized' and controlled from above...Nor was it spontaneous; rather, such behavior was 'induced' or 'coerced' or 'manipulated'. Rarely, if ever, did it result in the perception or feeling on the part of the individual that he or she was involved in the policy input process....*
> *Recent studies have called the traditional assumptions and perspectives into serious question...results of these studies suggest that political participation is a much more subtle, complex, multidimensional, and mixed phenomenon than had previously been assumed.*[24]

According to that challenge, the definition of political participation in communist systems should encompass both autonomous and mobilized participation, both participation directed at policy formulation (input) and that aimed at policy implementation (output). Other analysts acknowledge that the process of internal debates within a ruling Communist Party and the specific input procedures of its party-led groups need much more study before the function of interest groups in communist societies can be adequately understood.

Within this context, attention to interest groups is particularly significant at present when some socialist countries are trying to increase both popular influence on political decisions and levels of political participation, while at the same time keeping firm control over the system's organizations and interest groups.[25] The GDR, for instance, sees its present stage of development -- advanced socialism -- as a phase in which the population's influence on the leadership of the society will increase. In this planned future development of socialist democracy, social

8

organizations are to be given new opportunities for interest-group input. The workers' experiences and consciousness, i.e., their individual and collective interests as expressed through their social organizations, are to be given more attention by decision-makers who integrate such interests into the generalized societal goals (*Gesamtinteressen*) of official resolutions and programs.

In addition to analyzing such input, the systems/functional approach helps researchers to also look at the *output* side of the political system. That, some scholars feel, is precisely where the essential differences of contemporary socialist systems can be seen most clearly -- for example, the broad scope of governmental action and its often restrictive nature.[26]

However, when attempting to apply the systems/functional approach to systems based on Marxism/Leninism, modifications are needed. For instance, in the GDR view the state, or political structure, is not separate from society but is a part of it,[27] i.e., the system is socio-political. Moreover, within the Marxist/Leninist concept of an integrated political economy, politics has primacy over economics.[28] Thus it seems reasonable when applying the model to the GDR to call it the *socio-political* system, as seen in the next sketches. In short, the socio-political system of the GDR includes those structures and processes which directly affect public policy and through which values are allocated for the society in an authoritative (legitimate) manner. Or, to put it more succinctly, politics is the system and process for deciding who gets what, when, and how.

The boundaries of that system are not static. Its ungeometric shape with boundary indentations suggest that outside processes push up against the socio-political system and at times penetrate it. One such obvious external force in the case of the GDR is its foreign relations. Observers have long, often speculative, lists of occasions when the GDR's socio-political system, with its decisions of who gets what, when, and how, is presumed to have been influenced by its own alliance system or by its major Western competitor, the FRG. This study, for instance, will show the significance of Western influence via media.

Moreover, in considering application of this analytical approch to the GDR, one also needs to think differently about the role of institutions within the socio-political system. In Western constitutional democracies, for instance, most scholars consider social institutions outside the boundaries of the political system per se. But that is not the case with the GDR where institutions such as the press or education are regarded as part of the state system. The church is another example -- in the West, where church and state are separated, the church as an institution is outside the political system but pushes into it when engaged in activities directly relating to public policy, such as the prayerin-school debate in the USA; in the GDR context, it might be suggested that the church is an in-*and*-out institution, overlapping the boundaries, as shown in the next sketch. GDR churches are neither public nor socialist organizations. Instead, they are individual social entities, i.e., private associations, which can only exist as an institution in the GDR through adherence to general rules governing the system per se ("the church *in* Socialism"). Those rules of the game include, for instance, limitations on public criticism of the system or an public activities threatening to the system. Acccording to the agreement reached between the GDR's church and state leaders in March, 1978, the two institutions will cooperate where possible without questioning each other's status. If there are differences of opinion, the state expects the church to tolerate its decisions.

And literature as an "institution" -- where does it belong? GDR scholars say inside the system; some Western scholars, beginning to look institutionally at literature's particular functions within the socialist system, seem to be moving toward that concept, as well. This study, too, assumes a within-system role for literature, without, however, accepting the contention that literature, as an institution, including everything from publishing to reviewing, is totally controlled by the SED, as some analysts contend. Specifically, as Fig. 2 on the next page shows, this study institutionally locates literature within the system's base, that is, within the political culture, and hypothesizes that:

> Literature's primary *political* function is found in its influence on the political culture, that is, its participation in the interrelationships of the political socialization process, i.e., the influencing of collective orientations toward the political system per se, political roles and structures, groups filling political functions, and specific political issues and problems.

2. Role of Political Culture

Social scientists are increasingly focusing attention on the psychological basis of the GDR's socio-political system, its *political culture*. Seen systematically, this "memory bank of a people" contains its collective orientation toward the political system as a whole, including images of the system as well as political values, expectations, and aspirations, or (in the concept of Almond and Powell) knowledge, beliefs, feelings, and judgements.[29] GDR scholars, too, have shown recent concern for the orientational base of their system, calling it the "mass consciousness" (*Massenbewußtsein*). W. Müller, writing in the *Deutsche Zeitschrift für Philosophie* in 1983, said that mass consciousness included citizens' attitudes and emotions (concepts, views, moods, feelings, customs, and traditions), as well as

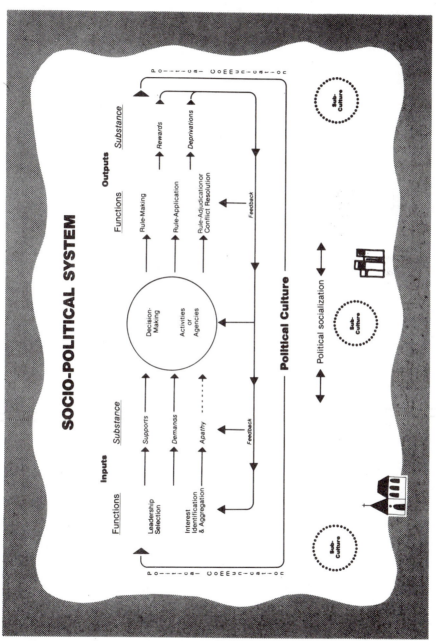

Fig. 2.   Adapted by Mallinckrodt/Schaad from Irish and Prothro.
The Politics of American Democracy, 5th ed.   Prentice-Hall, 1971.

consciousness regarding behavior. Influenced by values and norms, subjective consciousness, and individual experiences such as work and conditions of daily life, the mass consciousness, in Müller's view, reflects the central problem of the interrelationship of ideology and experience.[30]

In recent years this significant base of political systems has been the center of renewed and continuing discussion by Anglo-Saxon political scientists concerned with conceptual definitions and applications in the field of communist studies. At least three major reforms seem relevant to GDR research:

(1) The so-called 'classical' models linking political culture to political development[31] have been replaced by models using political culture to explain political change.[32]

Stephan White, for instance, wrote that political culture presumes dialectical change but not the nature or direction of the change:

Political culture, in fact, must be regarded as both 'causing' and 'caused': as a variable which mediates between the political system and its environment, providing 'a framework within which patterns of political belief and behavior, historically considered, can be located, and as a factor which will influence and constrain -- though not determine -- future patterns of development in a political system.

Moreover, White said, the political culture concept (dating back to Montesquieu, de Tocqueville, etc.) was especially helpful when applied to socialist systems -- it could, for instance, explain persistent historical specificity (the "Prussianism" of GDR socialism) and systemic similarities (uniqueness of the artists' role). In other words, the political culture approach did not presume homogeniety or unity, but instead allowed for the tug-of-war found in all systems between old and new influences on perceptions of the socio-political system.[33]

Some years later Barbara Jancar agreed, arguing persuasively that the "clasical view" of a linkage between political culture and political development was not tenable because it hypothesized a pluralistic, democratic outcome. Instead, a linkage between political culture and political change might lead to gradual congruence between the official political culture (the modern value system) and the mass political culture (the traditional value systems) through adaptation in both directions. This revised focus, therefore, permits the researcher to analayze sources of tension and to highlight uniqueness, rather than forcing attention on similarities by imposing Western values (pluralism, democracy).[34]

(2) The assumed discrepancy between elite and mass levels of political culture (sometimes also seen as "manifest" or "latent") has been relativized by inserting "or" -- official and/or mass culture -- to avoid implying that there are *ipso facto* two *distinct* political cultures.

Accepting that the political culture system was divided into the elites and masses, Lowell Dittmer, however, found that both originate *and* transmit political symbols, with the elites being more innovative. Cause and effect, therefore, are not sought, but rather interrelationships between and among communication channels, origins of innovation, and two-way flows of influence. In this sense, political culture is not just an inheritance (traditional culture) or an acquired framework (official culture), but instead is a set of identities generated by human activity and constant regeneration; it is a *process*, not mere imposition or manipulation.[35]

When Jancar entered the discussion, she agreed that it was essential to distinguish between official/elite and mass political culture without, however, implying that the official is not dominant. Insted, the definition should merely accept the fact that the official culture *may not be* that of the masses; socialist societies (such as the GDR, for instance), are *developing* political societies in which pre-socialist traditions are presumed to persist beyond revolution (*Umwälzung*), as contrasted to systems in existence for centuries.[36]

Such newer conceptualizations, with emphasis on the feedback function of the socio-political system, no longer see citizens as passive or manipulated objects of the domestic political culture. Rather, they are participants, attitudinally reacting to the objective conditions (societal, economic, political) of their life and place in the system.

(3) The old argument about whether political culture focuses on attitudes alone or also includes behavior can be temporarily resolved by emphasizing attitudes.

While attitudes continue to be difficult to assess for socialist systems, Jancar saw progress being made. Behavior, on the other hand, even if observable, does not always reflect real values. For the time being, then, one could study the values officially channeled into the political culture by the political leadership and hope one day to also assess how many have "taken" and how much tradition persists.[37]

Clearly, then, an understanding of the political culture base is essential for the understanding of a socio-political system. Historically, i.e., at least as far back as de Tocqueville, the concept has been recommended for analyzing political institutions

13

and policies, along with the relationship between political
thought, political culture, and political change.[38]

In addition, the more recent approaches give the political
culture concept a new breadth and dynamism, a scope adequate to
the five elements sociologist Volker Gransow proposes as essential
for analysis specifically of the GDR: three elements of the
dominant/official political culture (communist goal culture, industrial culture, and traditional German culture) and two non-
dominant political cultures (the oppositional 'better socialism'
and the alternative to socialism).[39]

Within this context, this study presumes that the psychological political culture base affects and is effected by the system
of interrelationships constituting the socio-political system of
the GDR. Moreover, literature as an institution is significant
within that base.

3. Literature in the GDR's Political Culture

In developing a political sociology approach to literature's
function within a political system, the researcher moves from the
general political culture context described above to literature as
an institution within it -- or more correctly, to institutional
aspects which are relatively clear at this time.

Central to this consideration are the GDR's own assumptions
about the importance and function of literary influences on the
political culture. As the GDR Germanist Joseph Pischel writes,
literature is a "specific intellectual, cultural organ of society",[40] or as others say "a conveyer" (Träger) of values. Put
another way, literature is part of the political socialization
process which influences the collective orientations constituting
the political culture, or base, of the GDR's socio-political system -- the values, expectations, aspirations.

The Halle literary sociologists have much to say about this
socialization process and literature's role within it. Values,
they write, are transmitted indirectly, or even "coded", to the
consciousness of social classes and groups (Schichten) through
works of art per se but also through literary criticism, public
response, and media policy. Indeed, literature makes an enor-
mously significant contribution to value critique, for it takes up
and considers new values which might gain currency vis-a-vis existing values of the 'Socialist way of life'. But while literature makes this contribution, on the other hand, its influence
should not be overestimated; values are constantly changing,
influenced by many factors other than literature. Moreover,
literary values do not create attitudes; instead, they activate
latent attitudes or strengthen existing ones. Nevertheless,

literature has a "mediation" role to play between general and individual concepts and so is "a key link in the development of socialist consciousness".[41]

Deputy Cultural Minister Höpcke characterized that role more specifically when he said that literature and art have an especial capacity to sensitize people:

> *The deep social meaning of this sensitization is found in sharpening the view of social questions, of progress and reaction, truth and falsehood, success of and dangers to the worker-and-farmer state, and of the contradictory relationship between new and old.*[42]

Such political socialization concepts become unusually clear when articulated for the base of the system, i.e., for reader-citizens at their workplaces. Specifically, in the GDR it is felt that since political culture attitudes are especially influenced through personal experiences and received communications, the workplace is central -- this, after all, is where most citizens daily spend the greatest number of active hours in closely structured small work groups:

> *The possibilities to enrich intellectual life in the firms through culture and art, to promote the talents and abilities of the workers, and to implement the resolutions of our party also in this area, are endless ....A song, recitation, film, picture, or charcters from books, television films, and theater plays are often able to express that which is desired more comprehensively and deeply than is possible with words.*[43]

Such efforts to influence the political culture through arts at the workplace take innumerable forms. There are the well-known organized visits of workers to concerts, museums, exhibits, theaters, movies, etc. Less well-known perhaps are the efforts regarding literature. For instance, in the early 1980s there were 633 libraries (usually maintained by the trade union), plus 176 branch libraries, and 2,531 book loan locations in plants (*Betriebe*).[44] The trend seems to be toward more readers and more reading, along with increased book purchases.

But SED leaders openly admit that not enough is done to support literature, especially in the little and medium-sized plants which employ about a fourth of all the workers in nationally-owned undertakings (*VEB*). More interest could be generated, party leaders say, if reviews were better and appeared not only in intellectual publications but also in the mass media.[45]

At the same time, much is undertaken to increase workers' interest in literature. For instance, book bazaars are set up at

15

workers' festivals,[46] and yearly the Confederation of Free German Trade Unions (*FDGB*) awards a prize for art works, including books, which best present the working class. This, then, is an opportunity for discussions in the plants and offices about art and its influence. In addition, various worker collectives have constant contact to authors and other artists, some of whom are honorary members of the collectives. In fact, it is reported that more than 3,000 trade union and work collectives have such contacts to artists and art institutions. Some authors have contracts to read in plants, thereby earning a bit of money and collecting reactions to their creative work. Then, too, songs and poems have their place at membership meetings of the basic SED units, and artists are invited to share in festive occasions within a factory.[47] In the party's view,

> *Our cultural life today is absolutely inconceivable without the planned development of these multifaceted forms of relationships between individual artists and plants or brigades, between artists' societies and plants, between readers and authors, and the public and theaters.*[48]

Fortunately, GDR publications also offer concrete examples of such contacts between workers and authors who visit plants to discuss their manuscripts or to read from published works. Such accounts of who reads what where are significant in assessing the institution of literature's potential impact on the political culture.

The Petrochemical Kombinat in Schwedt is illustrative of this interrelationship between writers and readers. For years the Kombinat had close ties to the Aufbau Verlag of Berlin and Weimar, and so held an annual "Book Week" which included "Publishers Day" where authors and workers came together to discuss current literature. Some 50 authors participated over the past 10 years -- including Helmut Baierl, Wieland Herzfelde, Renate Holland-Moritz, Wolfgang Joho, Hermann Kant, Wolfgang Kohlhaase, Lothar Kusche, Irmtraud Morgner, Dieter Noll, Herbert Otto, Alfred Wellm, Christa Wolf, Richard Christ, Christiane Groß, Heinz Kahlau, Richard Pietraß, Eva Strittmatter, Wolfgang Trampe. Through such encounters,

> *Authors are told about workers' experiences. They get to know the plant and its production tasks and problems vis-a-vis the struggle for better economic performance. In turn, the workers are introduced to new literary works, for instance, through readings. They develop their ability to judge literature, and thus their literary demands also mature.*[49]

Helmut Baierl, in a report to the annual FDGB Congress in 1982, expressed the author's perspective of such meetings in these words:

16

Many of our authors, including myself, could say that over the years they have had work contacts to brigades or simply to workers in plants, research centers, or on the streets.... And we indeed also have so much in common, we people from the arts and from production! After all, we are both making something new, bringing into the world what previously had not yet existed in this form.... My colleagues from the polishers brigade saw the Brecht House...and the Academy of Arts of the GDR. And during Book Week I want to invite them to Grotewohl House where I will read to them from my work about Rosa Luxemburg and Leo Jogiche. Before my time the colleagues naturally also were involved with culture, but now we are already quite 'expert'. And most important, of course, is talking with each other, learning to enjoy art.[50]

Still another example of contacts between writers and readers comes from the big Folk Festivals where "book bazaars" are tradition; there authors not only sell their newest books and autograph them but also discuss with readers.[51] Book stores, of course, also sponsor book bazaars and readings. In Berlin, the Authors' Bazaars are found in the Palace of the Republic during "The Day of the Arts".[52]

Further evidence, perhaps symbolic, of literature's importance to its GDR readers was seen on May 8 and 10, 1983 when the 50th anniversary of the Nazi book-burning in Berlin was commemorated. As Hermann Kant, chairman of the Writers' Union, reported to the meeting of that society several weeks later,

It was like a sample chosen from the huge reading public in whose center we live. On Sunday in two hours they had bought 120,000 Marks worth of books, and on Tuesday for two hours 50,000 listened and were not louder than 50....They are the best that can happen to literature-- they are people of a country in which books live; they are readers in a socialist country.[53]

In the early 1980s a new forum for bringing writers together with readers was introduced, a big conference called "Day of Contemporary Socialist Literature". The second such gathering was held in Karl Marx Stadt in 1984, attended by 24 authors and some 600 readers. According to reports, "well-known authors" (Johannes Arnold, Jurij Brězan, Herbert Otto) and "newcomers" (Angela Krauß, Gerhard Neumann) went into the big industries located in the district to discuss their writings with workers. Another feature of the forum was a three-hour colloquium in which authors, critics, book dealers, librarians, and cultural functionaries took part. Observers judged the meeting a success for, among other things, "the mature reader of our literature...spoke self-confidentially about his experiences in daily life and with literature".[54]

Special emphasis also is placed on creating appreciation for literature among GDR youth. For instance, the county organization of the League for Culture in Erfurt holds literary discussions in its youth clubs, in Eisenach a Readers' Coffee Hour (*Lesekaffee*), and in Nordhausen a series of discussions with young writers. (The Erfurt organization has also sponsored 23 annual conferences on Soviet literature.[55]) In 1982 and 1983 new Literature Centers were set up to supplement various programs already available for youth interested in literature. Intended to encourage youngsters between the ages of 14 and 25 to try their own hand at writing, one such center was organized in every county plus one in Berlin. Here aspiring writers schedule appointments with specialists (editors, established authors, literary scientists, journalists) to discuss draft manuscripts. The Centers also arrange public readings, literary workshops, lectures, and contacts for members with publishers.[56]

Such concrete examples illustrate the GDR's institutionalization of its literature within the socio-political system -- not just for intellectuals but also for workers. The examples also highlight the importance which the GDR assigns literature's functional role vis-a-vis the political culture, or "mass consciousness".

Consideration of such GDR views, along with those of Western scholars, suggest the following premises for political sociology studies of GDR literature:

1. Art/literature is political.

Based on the premise that art generally is "necessarily and ineluctably political", Benjamin R. Barber in 1982 coedited an insightful book entitled *The Artist and Political Vision*. In it he spoke for many other scholars who believe that literature

challenges or complements political vision, reenforces or spurns public mores, enjoins social integration or promotes social alienation. Art celebrates or defies, rejoices or despairs. It is neither detached, nor impartial, not isolated, nor pure.[57]

In a more recent innovative study within political science, Christine Schöfer argues that GDR literature is "politicized" but also "unquestionably constitutes an area of politics". The officially proclaimed role of literature is expressed and anchored in the cultural policy (*Kulturpolitik*) of the system. In Schöfer's view, "That means that the same cultural policy which can be viewed as an instrument of repression repeatedly reaffirms the authority of literature and the writers".[58]

18

2. Within the political culture, literature challenges and affirms.

Maureen Whitebrook in her stimulus to literary politics studies, noted that while most mainstream literature supports and upholds the established order, within the same culture it can act as a critique of society. In short, "works of literature reflect the values and attitudes of that culture; and as producers of the culture, works of literature also help to shape those values and attitudes".[59]

In an informative *Weimarer Beiträge* discussion with colleagues concerning the nature of GDR literature, K. Jarmatz emphasized the questioning role it plays. He wrote that, in striving for understanding of the particular dialectic of the GDR society, literature "is involved primarily because posible it provokes the right question; it asks questions".[60] At the SED's Academy for Social Sciences, Christel Berger wrote at length about how "individual and social values are formed, tested, sketched, discussed, and also eventually rejected" through central figures of literature, pictured positively and/or negatively.[61]

A specific exmple of literature's challenging/affirming role is provided by Margy Gerber. Her recent literary research shows that in the 1980s women authors in the GDR are challenging political culture values concerning women's emancipation. While classic emancipatory values remain, their realization is being relativized after several decades of experience -- confidence in individual achievements and the prospects of more emancipated male/female relationships seem to have been shaken.[62]

3. Literature should and can be looked at as a stimulus to socio-political change.

Increasingly U.S. social scientists focus on communications generally as a socializing force for socio-political change. Robert A. White, for instance, makes a persuasive case for "a research perspective in which the focus is shifted from communication as social control to its role in sociocultural change".[63]

The social change potential of GDR literature specifically was suggested in one of the early articles linking literature to political culture. In 1978, political scientist Arthur Hanhardt, Jr. proposed that in the changing GDR society literature had the "capacity to deal with tensions between the individual and the state in a socialist society that is itself 'unfinished'".[64]

More recently, too, Christine Schöfer made this point. The GDR's literature, she wrote, reflects and discusses socio-political developments from a non-official perspective. By questioning current official definitions and views, literature expands the limits of discourse about developments and so contributes to them, that is, to social change. In breaking through existing taboos, literature influences public discourse, firstly with readers.[65]

West German social scientists extend that premise, frequently contending that the questioning role literature plays is unique in the GDR's social change process -- there literature fills in, or substitutes, for the absence of public debate, as in the press. Irma Hanke, for instance, after studying hundreds of GDR novels, reasoned that literature in the GDR seemed to be a "substitute public voice" (Ersatzöffentlichkeit), functioning as "this society's understanding of itself".[66] Eckart Förtsch, too, observed that,

> The 'extra-literary' functions of literature, I suppose, increase in proportion to the virulence of crises and pathologica in life and to the extent that other channels of problem articulation (for example, the press and science) fall short. Literature takes over themes which otherwise would be concealed, postponed, or placed under taboo. Literature produces information and criticism of daily life, that is, critique from the everyday perspective vis-a-vis daily life and the factors which influence it.[67]

Hubertus Knabe, also viewing literature as a substitute for political discussion, found it to be a "seismograph of overall societal problems and states of consciousness".[68]

To such views Christine Schöfer, among others, replies that GDR literature is not "a substitute public voice"; instead, it is "a public voice". Seen functionally, as discussed earlier, literature is an inherent voice within the political culture of the socio-political system surrounding it. Its socializing content affirms and challenges what is not, is, or is not yet a public issue.[69] Obviously, therefore, literature's content often crashes loudly against the silence of public disinterest or the hush of official taboos. Such literary messages, "substituting" for audible public discourse, do not mean that the messenger is the substitute. Literature has its own voice, its publicness, in times of muteness as well as when a rare crescendo of other public views, surging up from soap boxes and lecturns, might thunder across a political system.

GDR scholars, as will be seen throughout this study, generally agree that literature is a stimulus to social change. For instance, in the Weimarer Beiträge discussion referred to earlier, Walfried Hartinger made the point that contemporary GDR literature was helping people to develop a "conflict capacity", that is, the ability to deal with value conflicts rather than with just problems of everyday life. Dieter Schlenstedt went a step further in

20

that discussion and said he saw a "critical socialist realism" (*sozialistischen kritischen Realismus*) developing within GDR literature through

> *artistic presentations not displaying their values positively, but rather provoking thought by presenting deficits -- a proclivity for problematic heroes who can stimulate reflection or also for suffering heroes who are offered to help one live one's own life.*[70]

In short, in Schlenstedt's opinion, the criticism was self-criticism, and that, he felt, could be seen as progress and accomplishment.[71]

These views, thus, reflected the unusual conference of literary scholars and philosophers in late 1984 which focused, among other things, on the premise that present conflicts were more comprehensible (*besser erfaßbar*) through literature than through the social sciences.[72] And, indeed, literary voices seemed to be responding to the earlier kudos (and implied challenges) from GDR philosophers. As Jürgen Kuczynski had written in 1980 to Hermann Kant, then head of the Writers' Union,

> *reading our contemporary novels will be much more important to future historians than most of the social science writings which we presently are producing. This is so because our novels describe accurately our advancing socialism, with all its contradictions and irritations, against the background of the new world which is unfolding. While our social scientists indeed speak of real socialism, in their concrete description of reality they often succumb to the tendency of embellishment.*[73]

Thus by the mid-1980s GDR literature was vigorously carrying out its socializing function -- stimulating social change by challenging, as well as affirming political culture values, attitudes, expectations, aspirations.

4. Critical literature may or may not constitute a "subculture".

If literature not only reflects but challenges the dominant political culture, it may be "socially critical", "political subcultural", or "anti-system" literature.

The first of the challenging literatures is the routine "social criticism" found in the political cultures of all sociopolitical systems. These are the widely-shared "loyal opposition" views, often institutionalized, which usually are referred to by careful political scientists as "social criticism", "dissent", or "protest".

21

If the opposition is not widely shared, it may be categorized as "subcultural". Although definitions vary considerably, according to Walter Rosenbaum, a political subgroup is an organized or unorganized "*aggregation of individuals* within a political system whose political orientations differ *significantly* from the *majority* within the culture, or at least, vary from the cultural orientations *dominant* in the society (Emphasis - AM)."[74] The distinction here seems to be the quality of the attitudinal deviation, as well as quantity. In H. Gordon Skilling's categories of opposition, such views accept the system per se but offer constructive criticism directed against a specific leadership, set of policies, or a specific policy.[75]

Finally, a non-loyal opposition, that is, fundamental rejection of the socio-political system per se, is in Skilling's terms "systemic opposition"..[76] Here the crucial distinction is the radicality of the deviational views.

An unusually suggestive illustration of this so-called oppositional landscape in the GDR was offered by its lyricist and song-writer Sascha Anderson in an interview following his legal emigration in August 1986. In his analysis of the cultural scene, Anderson explained that protesting artists of his generation (early to mid-30s) did not care about the political system, thus negating the label "anti-systemic". As he put it, "The GDR as a structure (*Gebilde*) does not interest me...I did not have to identify with this state structure (*Staatsgebilde*)". Instead, he identified himself with a circle of friends, a countryside in which he grew up, with certain developments or processes, "but never with the state structure". The charge that he was the center of "a new anti-movement in the GDR", Anderson asserted, "is precisely what it is not".

In addition to saying he ignored the GDR, the lyricist also did not indicate an "anti-systemic" preference for the West. About West Germany, he commented, "I do not think it is so much different here. I can imagine that I can work just as freely here as in the East". As for the idea of *Heimat* as a possible identification, "I absolutely would no longer accept it", he said. In short, Anderson changed residences to be near friends. Seen as a group, these GDR immigrant artists and writers were more interested in finding anonymity for their private lives than in taking an ideological position against one governmental system or for another.

At the same time, the values and activities Anderson said he and his generation represent also do not seem to fit into the wide-spread kind of loyal opposition usually tagged typical "social criticism" or "dissent" from the dominant political culture. Rather, this group of artists and writers is a minority within the GDR -- "Naturally the majority is those who have "adjusted".

Moreover, they are less interested in reform than in being left alone -- "I need anonymity in order to work". They wish to follow individual priorities rather than being concerned about a system which attempts to "inhale" them.

Thus, if not a fundamentally anti-systemic or an average dissenting group within the political culture, Anderson and his friends do seem to constitute a subcultural group. Within the context of their political self-image, they see themselves as "drop outs" (*Aussteiger*) from the dominant culture but still part of that culture -- in Anderson's words, "I think that an official culture also lives from the culture which is not integrated". This non-integrated, or political subcultural aggregation of writers and artists, is not homogenous. Instead, Anderson reports, they pursue "a very broad structure of individual cultural activities". Free of associations, organizations, and institutions, they have created their own media to avoid pressure from and rejection by establishment publishing houses. Through the production of cassettes, recordings of readings, and small pressruns of newspapers and books, they reach limited audiences. Such activities apparently are very individualistic undertakings, without a lot of contact among the initiators -- when ten such small newspapers, with a circulation from 30 to 100, had an exhibit in the Samaritan Church in Berlin in spring 1986, it was "the first time", according to Anderson, "that the authors of those media and their editors had been able to converse personally together (*untereinander verständigen konnten*)".

In Anderson's view, the next generation of critical artists and writers will be even more free. They will not ever have identified themselves with a system (*einsteigen*), as Anderson and his friends initially did, and so will not have to drop out (*aussteigen*). And the number of those who reject identification with the dominant political culture will increase.[77]

In recent years some Western researchers, including the author,[78] suggested that the official political culture of the GDR was being significantly challenged by political cultural subgroups focused on the ecology and peace issues. Involved were Öko groups, peace groups, and socially critical artists, many of whose members were using the institution of the church as a channel for interest identification and aggregation.

Since then, however, as this study will demonstrate, their views are more widely shared, and many of their orientations may no longer differ significantly from the majority within the political culture. Moreover, such groups now are increasingly utilizing the system's established interest groups as channels of social criticism. On the other hand, some of the critical artists, especially poets, continue to take more individual and more radical stands, as Sascha Anderson reported.

23

Thus, in the model used to orient this study, it seems tenable to relocate the institution of literature with a *portion* of it overlapping a subculture, as shown in Fig. 3 on the next page. The overlap, then, represents an aggregation of writers who may, indeed, differ *significantly* from the *majority* within the culture, or from *dominant* political culture orientations.

With that modified model of interrelationships, plus specific premises about literature's function in the GDR's political culture, a framework is in place for analyzing the environmental dialogue in the GDR. In it, the challenges to the dominant political cultural value of "Progress" have been numerous, as will be seen. Within that context, as hypothesized for this study, the institution of literature has been one socializer (along with the church and interest groups) of changing orientations toward the specific issue of environmental protection and ecological values in the GDR.

5. Summary

As sociologists have studied literature in its societal setting, so political scientists are beginning to look at it in its political context. This is the *political sociology of literature* approach.

In applying it, systems/functional analysis seems useful, for it helps to organize facts and suggest interrelationships. However, to optimally develop this approach to GDR studies, political scientists need to know more about how literary specialists see literature as an "institution" within the GDR's political culture. At the same time, political scientists can offer some initial suggestions for understanding literature's relationship to the sociopolitical system.

For instance, the institution of literature can be located within the political socialization process which orients citizens to the political culture of their system -- that is, collective values, expectations, aspirations (or knowledge, beliefs, feelings, judgments), that which GDR scholars are beginning to call "mass consciousness". Moreover, recent revitalized Western scholarly research into political culture offers useful concepts for differentiating between official and mass levels of political culture, assessing non-dominant political culture orientations, and considering the feedback processes within the system.

In the GDR, the potential impact of literature on the political culture is heightened when literature is taken to the workplace -- plant libraries, author readings/discussions/membership in collectives, trade union prizes for worker-oriented literature, literary presentations at SED meetings, and ties between big

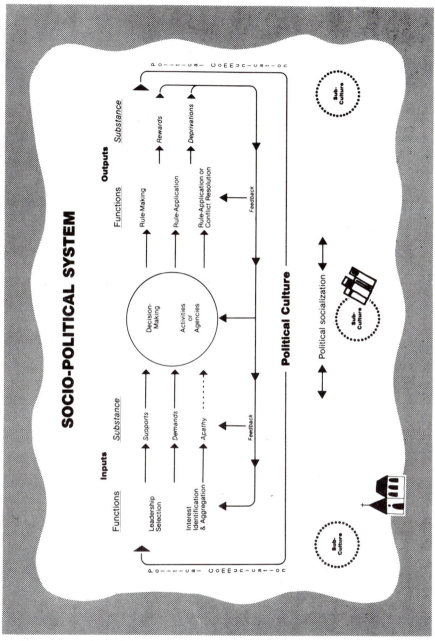

Fig. 3. Adapted by Mallinckrodt/Schaad from Irish and Prothro,
The Politics of American Democracy, 5th ed. Prentice-Hall, 1971.

25

industries (*Kombinate*) and publishing houses. Outside the factories, literature also is taken to the people, as at book bazaars
or public meetings between authors and readers. All this, and
much more which still needs researching, is part of literature's
institutional role in the GDR.

Meanwhile, scholars increasingly support the idea of viewing
literature in its socio-political context. Many make the general
case for its relationship to politics; some focus on the consequent need to see it institutionally/contextually; others emphasize its challenging as well as affirmative functions, i.e., literture as a stimulus to social change. On the one hand, some
analysts see literature's role as compensatory for the absence of
broad public debate on current issues while others contend that,
functionally, literature is always a public voice, whether or not
there is public debate.

GDR scholars, for their part, seem naturally to accept literature's role as a social change stimulus, particularly in writings of the 1980s. It is suggested by some that a self-critical,
realistic socialist literature is developing which helps people
cope with value conflicts, primarily through presentations of central literary figures. If literature challenges, then there may
be varying degrees of socio-political protest, ranging from typical social criticism, to subcultural, to anti-systemic articula-
tions and activities.

Within that context, this study hypothesizes that the GDR's
political culture increasingly reflects stimuli for political
change (illustrated by the ecology debate), and that literature
has a significant role in the multi-factor process of influencing
(not determining) change related as well as system affirming
values and norms.

Chapter II

"PROGRESS" AS A POLITICAL VALUE

For decades "progress" has been systematically disseminated as a value basic to socialism; more recently it is a value being scrutinized and redefined. In the GDR, differing understandings of the concept are at the heart of the environmental dialogue carried out at many levels of the system.

1. The Concept of "Progress"

Historians find that "progress" is one of the most universally significant concepts evolved in recent centuries. Cambridge professor J. B. Bury, writing in the 1920s, demonstrated that the idea of progress was not an ancient one, but rather born in the rationalist philosophy of the Enlightenment. In his work *The Idea of Progress*, Bury showed how the concept had been central to both social and natural science, as well as the arts. Thus it became a key value in the political culture of many industrial societies.

Taking the idea a step further in 1931, Charles A. Beard, in his introduction to a reissue of that famous Bury book, wrote that

of all the ideas pertinent to the concept of progress, to the interpretation of what has gone on during the past two hundred years and is going on in the world, none is more relevant than technology.

Assuming that it was technology's dynamic character which made it so significant for the idea of progress, Beard in the 1930s prophetically warned that "The solution of one problem in technology nearly always opens up new problems for exploration", and technology is producing other social effects which will make a return to an exact past impossible". As Beard then wrote,

In the idea of progress, accordingly, there is inevitably an ethical element. It implies that the stream of history flows in a desirable direction, on the whole; and at once we are plunged in the middle of ethics. Immediately a fixed point of reference, a bench mark, must be set up from which to determine whether the movement of history is in a desirable direction and, in the living present, what choices are to be made to accelerate the march toward the good.

In other words, "the idea of progress is both an interpretation of of history and a philosophy of action"[79] -- as, indeed, is heard in the current debate in the GDR.

27

2. Marxism/Leninism and "Progress"

Marxism/Leninism believes that it was Marxism which uncovered
the nature and motivation of progress. But in his introduction to
Kritik der Politischen Ökonomie, Marx cautioned that "the concept
of progress could not be understood with customary abstraction".[80]
Instead, the concept had several dimensions. Perhaps it could be
said here -- albeit greatly simplifying volumes of Marxist philosophy -- that the specific uniqueness of progress in Marx and
Engels' view was that objective laws of history (*Gesetzmäßigkeit*)
were involved in differing socio-economic formations replacing
each other. It was an *historical* movement to higher developments,
from old to new, from simple to complex; it was accompanied by
greater productive powers, more effective forms of economics, and
better forms of political leadership which led step-by-step to increased opportunities and freedom for people: "The forces which
determine sooial development are simultaneously the stimuli of
historical progress".[81]

Secondly, progress in Marxism/Leninism had a *social* dimension. Again simply put, it meant "change for the better" in social forces and material achievements, measured according to "the
material existence and developmental conditions of the working
class and the working masses themselves".[82] But while accepting
progress as an objective law of historical development, Marxism-
/Leninism warned against believing that social progress could be
linear and uninterruptable. To so believe, Lenin said, would be
"undialectic, unscientific, theoretically incorrect".[83] Neither
could progress be automatic or spontaneous. It would be achieved
or not achieved by the actions of people, especially organized into parties armed with scientific Marxist concepts.[84] And that
which would be achieved and defined as progressive would not only
be that which was "new" and "more", but that which served the people's need (in the socialist sense). Even under socialism, however, there would be problems cause by non-antagonistic contradictions. Thus, the concept of progress as "an interpretation of
history and a philosophy of actions", in Charles Beard's words,
became a key value in the political culture of socialist systems,
having both historical and social implications.

3. The GDR and "Progress"

Ever since the GDR was founded as a state, this message of
progress has been communicated unendingly into the political culture, through all channels available to the political leadership.
Replacing capitalist structures after World War II with reforms in
agriculture, education, justice, and industry, the GDR was said to
be laying the groundwork for socialism. Based on such prerequi-
site measures, the "construction of socialism" (*Aufbau des Sozialismus*) was declared by 1952. And by 1971 the GDR's development

28

was described as "advanced socialism" (*entwickelte Sozialismus*), a phase of historical development leading to communism.

Social progress, too, was emphasized. In its first (1949) Constitution, for instance, the GDR made that a goal of the new state:

> *Filled with the will to guarantee human freedom and rights, to fashion communal and economic life with social justice, to serve <u>social progress</u>, to support friendship with all people and secure peace, the German people has given itself this constitution.* (*Emphasis-AM*)[85]

Another illustration of the importance of the concept of progress to the GDR's socio-political system is found in the Party Programs of the SED. In the 1963 Programm, for example, progress is embedded in the context of the historical class struggle-- "There is no means of stopping historical progress" -- and its socio-economic dimensions -- "the social progress and standard of living of the people depends on how the Party, state, working class, collective farmers, and other workers utilize the basic economic and other laws of socialism".[86]

In the early phases of building socialism, the achievement of social progress in the GDR was especially seen as catching up with the standard of living in the West through use of science and technology (rather than, for instance, carrying out socially progressive experiments such as those in artistic and family life which had been tried briefly in the Soviet Union after the October Revolution). In short, social progress in the GDR was to be achieved through production (*Fortschritt durch Leistung*). This message obviously fell on fertile ground, for, as Hartmut Zimmermann has pointed out, "high regard for work, order and self-discipline" are among the traditional values prevailing in the GDR political culture.[87]

The 1968 version of the Constitution, reflecting an industrially growing GDR, spoke specifically of promoting science and education not only "with the aim of protecting and enriching society and the life of the citizens" but also of "guaranteeing the *constant progress of socialist society*" (Emphasis - AM)[88]. With the dramatic technological changes of the last decades -- especially in the fields of cybernetics and electronics -- specialists in the GDR, as in Western countries, began to speak of a "scientific-technological revolution". Viewing it as a qualitative change in production, GDR leaders said this revolution was a means for realizing socialism's goals of social and historical progress, i.e., for achieving the economic, technical, cultural, and social basis for a communist society.

This idea was incorporated, for instance, into the October 7, 1974 revised Constitution. Progress was implied, for the Constitution said that in a GDR involved in a phase of "advanced socialism", social and individual goals were served through the unity of the scientific-technological revolution and the advantages of socialism.[89]

In the 1976 Party Program there were references to "social" (*sozialen*) and "societal" (*gesellschaftlichen*) progress. For instance, the Program said that

> The socialist nation in the German Democratic Republic
> is historically rooted in the centuries-long struggle of
> the German people for social progress...[90]

In addition, the economic/industrial meaning of progress was spelled out by the use of words such as "growing", "intensifying", "productive upturn", "increases", "modernization", "expansion", etc. -- that is, *more* and *better* economic growth.

By 1981 the acceleration of the scientific-technological revolution became the priority of GDR economic and social policy. At the 10th SED Party Congress it was said that

> The possibilities of the scientific-technological rev-
> olution have now become immediate and major reserves for
> growth in our domestic economy's productivity and effec-
> tiveness.[91]

Especially education and research were expected to contribute to the acceleration of this progress.[92]

Moreover, in seeking to counter growing pessimism, a restatement of the Marxist view of progress was published in the mid-80s. Its basic component of optimism was emphasized in the title *Realistic Optimism* and its utility in the subtitle *Source of Strength in the Struggle for Freedom and Progress*. Acknowledging that questions of progress had become central to the ideological confrontation between socialism and capitalism, the author insisted that each generation had, indeed, experienced social progress under socialism and also reminded his readers that progress, of course, was a "zigzag movement".[93]

4. The Debate About Progress Begins: 1970s

The pessimism the above author referred to was being expressed by the early 1970s. The sanctity of the concept of economic and social progress, imbedded in the political culture of so many political systems, was being questioned. "So-called" progress, it was said, was not serving people's human and individual needs.

30

The first such challenges were heard in the West; then doubt in the GDR grew loud, too.

Club of Rome Report (1972)

A major impetus to the discussion of progress was the Club of Rome report on "The Limits of Growth". It concluded that

1. If the present growth trends in world population, industrialization, pollution, food production, and resource depletion continue unchanged, the limits of growth on this planet will be reached sometime within the next one hundred years. The most probable result will be a rather sudden and uncontrollable decline in both population and industrial capacity.
2. It is possible to alter these growth trends and to establish a condition of ecological and economic stability that is sustainable far into the future. The state of global equilibrium could be designed so that the basic material needs of each person on earth are satisfied and each person has an equal opportunity to realize his human potential.[94]

The Club of Rome report was not only a bombshell in the West. It disturbed Eastern Europe, too. The first reactions in the GDR, as reported in an analysis by Jan Kuhnert, came from so-called "professional imperialism researchers", for instance staff writers of *IPW-Berichte*. Initially seeing the Western report as an ideological weapon, such researchers said that in the world-wide systemic competition it intended to stabilize the imperialistic system and to deny transitional trends from capitalism to socialism.[95]

As so often, however, the GDR's "grand old man of ideas", Jürgen Kuczynski, quickly registered a dissenting opinion. In 1973, commenting on the theory of zero growth, he warned against naive and unscientific hopes for technologically-stimulated growth. Although writing about the capitalist system, Kuczynski's words seem to contain general and far-reaching warnings for GDR decision-makers, as well:

...one no longer can persuade with technocratic hopes. Whoever does not acknowledge that technical progress at present can solve social problems only if it is accompanied by social progress, whoever identifies scientific-technological progress with social progress, he/she really misunderstands the seriousness of the situation in the capitalist world.

About the socialist countries specifically, and their ecological policy especially, Kuczynski bluntly asserted that it was

31

dangerous "to minimize the problem of environmental protection, as so many did the problem of introducing the scientific-technological revolution".[96]

Literary Protests

At the same time, other voices disputing the sanctity of progress were heard within the literary world. In 1970, for instance, Christa Wolf had chosen satire as a vehicle for expressing doubts about aspects of scientific progress -- the delightfully humorous, though biting, story entitled *Neue Lebensansichten eines Katers* (based on E. T Hoffmann's *Kater Murr*). In it a cat, named Maximillian, says that the human animals inhabiting his world in an enlightened moment had invented "reasonableness", and through it now renounce all higher duties and find "practical" reactions to all situations.[97] For example, there was the "reasonableness" of the scientific vision of cybernetics sociologist, Dr. G. Hinze. As reported by Maximillian, this scientist advocated compilation of a comprehensive directory of optimal reactions for all human situations. Such a reference work, Maximillian comments dryly, was a remarkable idea; saving all the energy usually expended on needless human tragedies could have brought the scientific-technological revolution a whole decade earlier and enabled humankind to already live in the future.[98]

In 1972-73 Ulrich Plenzdorf's *Die neuen Leiden des jungen W* was a shattering reproach to a progress-centered *Leistungsgesellschaft* -- it suggested, among other things, that the achievement demanded of youth motivated efforts which might accidentally result in suicide. First excerpted in *Sinn und Form*, official journal of the Academy of Arts, the story then appeared on the stages of 14 theaters throughout the country, stimulated a questionnaire in the youth magazine *Forum*, and became the subject of a public discussion sponsored by the Academy of Arts (partially reported in *Sinn und Form*). In short, it was the institution of literature/art which published the story, made it public on stages, orchestrated the public debate, and provided interpretation of this major and early challenge to the GDR's political cultural values of "productivity" and "progress".[99]

Erwin Strittmatter, in 1973, tied the questioning of progress to the appreciation of and preservation of nature. He did so in a conversation with Heinz Plavius published in *Neue deutsche Literatur*, the official organ of the Writers' Union:

> I found, however, that through our economic and sociological struggles we somewhat lost sight of the fact that Humankind itself is a product of Nature and destroys itself if Nature is mishandled and misused through urbanized and pseudo-progressive arrogance...Our Marxist

32

classisists, for instance Engels, knew how the human being was interwoven with Nature, but we 'progress-intoxicated disciples' lost sight of this fact from time to time.[100]

Franz Fühmann, at the 7th Writers' Union Congress in 1973, made a similar point. Arguing against critics who assess literature vis-a-vis its ideological content, Fühmann reminded his colleagues that "The human being, that remarkable creation, is after all not only a social being; he/she is conditioned by society *as well as* by Nature, a contradictory yet indisolvable unity".[101]

By 1976 Joseph Pischel was motivated to publish a review essay about how GDR authors were reflecting "the relationship between Humankind and Nature". In that essay, Pischel acknowledged that the scientific-technological revolution had brought to the surface new questions for which the socialist society did not yet have ready solutions. Traditional images of nature and landscape no longer fit reality:

> *In the uncertainties of the search for a theme and imagery appropriate to the economic, social, and cultural changes within the interrelated structure of state, industrial landscape, and the relatively more primary natural landscape, it is seen that these philosophical and social problems -- which have to be solved during the establishment of communism -- have not yet conceptually become entirely clear within our general society.*

Indeed, Pischel concluded, "the philosophical question about the dialectical relationship of the natural and social conditions of human beings will remain a subject of conversation" among writers.[102] Gradually the natural scientists, social scientists, philosophers, ethicians, etc. would join in the GDR' search for new answers to the old questions about humankind/nature relationships and the newly recognized ecology/progress linkage, both of which were increasingly seen as being dichotomous.

Church Protests

The early 1970s also heard more church voices -- meant is the largest and most active of the GDR's religious bodies, the Evangelical Church[103] -- disputing the traditional sanctity of progress. In fact, following the state's recognition in 1960 of the church's relative independence in the GDR, religious leaders had increasingly expressed concern about the environment, science, and the future of humankind.[104] Thus by 1974 the *Landeskirche* in Saxony founded a study group for discussion of environmental questions and prepared a paper for presentation at the coming meeting

33

of the World Council of Churches. The GDR Federation of Churches' (*DDR-Kirchenbund*) committee on Church and Society put ecological problems on its agenda, too.

Typical of the concerns within the church circles were those expressed by Heino Falcke, chairman of the Church and Society Committee. Commenting on the past decade during which theologians had listened to and learned from scientists, Falcke said,

> One has become aware of what the philosophers say is the ambivalence of progress... Science, which was a motor of progress, was simultaneously sustained by hopes of progress; vis-a-vis the results of science, it suddenly strays from its own task and meaning... Science certainly can say what is...But science, indeed, cannot say what one should do, should leave alone, may do.

Moreover, in the view of such churchmen, everything was not the fault of the government. What was needed, among other things, was a "mass education process" to redefine current political culture values. As Falcke put it,

> we need only to think of the fact that our government, for example, absolutely does not have the freedom to give ecological reasonableness priority over economic priorities because the masses' expectation for increased consumption is so strong that it must be met.[105]

Mid-1970s Social Science Response

By the mid 1970s the debate concerning growth and progress in the GDR had become more sophisticated. Increasingly it was related to the current discussion about the values and norms of the socialist way of life (*Lebensweise*) central to the GDR's political culture. In addition, the West's Club of Rome report was being conceded more credibility; GDR social scientists were arguing that economic growth definitely had to be more closely related to specific socio-economic goals.[106] Thus the November 1976 conference of the GDR's social scientists, following the 9th Party Congress in spring, clearly reflected the public dialogue about progress. A key conference concern was the nature/ecology debate which touched key values and norms of the political culture, both at the official and mass level.

For instance, Kurt Hager, Politburo member and Central Committee secretary responsible for culture and science, opened the conference with a clear challenge -- not only purely scientific and technological problems were acute, but also "the relationship of Humankind and Nature are problems which urgently demand strengthened, goal-oriented common work". In the strengthening of such interdisciplinary social science efforts, the scientific councils (*Wissenschaftliche Räte*) would play an important role. They would orient the work of the social scientists, carry on theoretical and ideological discussions of basic questions, analyze scientific developments, develop research plans, and publicize the results of their work.[107]

Speaking to the conference on behalf of arts and culture, Hans Koch (of the Institute of Marxist/Leninist Cultural and Artistic Sciences within the Central Committee's Academy for Social Sciences) took up a core issue of the literary protest: "The interrelationships between the principle of socialist achievment (*Leistung*) and the cultural niveau of daily life is an area that should be researched more exactly". He said this was crucial because, among other things,

> *Here and there among us, too, the opinion is heard that culture and the arts are considered more important because, as 'an exercise in humanism', they are a humane counterweight to the scientific-technological revolution, to strictly economic and rationally utilitarian thought.*[108]

Helmut Bock, member of the Presidium of Urania, the adult education society, added that the debate needed more public input from a "popular science" point of view:

> *During the process of further developing our advanced socialist society, it is relevant in all areas of science to acquaint people precisely with the most _modern_ and _timely_ knowledge, including the developmental problems of the sciences.*[109]

Late 1970s Church Actions

By the late 1970s, ecological problems and their challenges to the concept of progress were routine concerns of churches. Their general complaint, according to numerous observers of the GDR church scene, was that one-sided concentration and specialization based on economic effectiveness had turned "the meaning of progress around to its opposite".

Particularly involved in the churches' environmental discussions were the Theological Studies Department of the Federation of Evangelical Churches (*Bund der evangelischen Kirchen*) in East Berlin, the Federation's Church and Society Committee mentioned previously, and the Church Research Center (*Kirchliche Forschungsheim*) in Wittenberg. The Research Center, originally seen as a forum for meetings between Christians and natural scientists, had elevated ecology to its "major task" by the late 1970s. Among other things, that meant regular publication of "Orientational Letters to the Humankind/Nature Conflict" which provided factual information the public wanted.

In addition, ecological problems were being discussed from a moral point of view at synodical meetings, church congresses (*Kirchentage*), seminars, lectures of the Evangelical Academies, and the programs of the student congregations (*Studentengemeinde*). By 1978 the GDR Church Federation for the first time called all the church groups involved with ecological concerns together in Buckow. The appeal was for new ecological criteria -- "Justice, Ecological Vitality (*ökologische Lebensfähigkeit*), Participation".[110]

The church in the GDR did not, however, spare itself criticism. It had come to feel that its own "Protestant work ethic", propagated over centuries, had contributed to the very problem it criticized. As *Glaube und Heimat* wrote in October, 1978,

> It was Christian thought which took from people their fear of intervention in Nature. It told them that intervention would not harm any gods. Environmental problems are the consequence, i.e.,...that the question of the relationship between Humankind and Nature has always been answered to the advantage of humans' right to life.[111]

Thus the church's words and deeds, gradually reaching growing numbers of GDR citizens, were a stimulus to intensified reexamination of political culture values and norms which for decades had affirmed, almost unquestioningly, the sanctity of progress.

Literary Debates Become Public

As the 1970s drew to an end, another example of literature's involvement in the ecology/progress discussion within the GDR's political culture appeared in print -- a February 1979 exchange of letters between Wilhelm Girnus and Günter Kunert. Suggestive of more confrontation to come, the critical, or "dissenting", author Kunert, writing about "symmetrical" shortcomings in environmental protection efforts in East and West,[112] was taken to task by Wilhelm Girnus, then the "literary establishment" editor-in-chief of *Sinn und Form*. The charge: Kunert had not distinguished between East and West and had failed to make clear that science and technology in the hands of progressive forces do not have the same negative results as in the hands of capitalists.[113]

The second round of the argument came in the July/August issue of *Sinn und Form*. In an open letter to Girnus, Kunert insisted that there certainly was a symmetry:

In opposition to all 'scientific' Weltanschauungen, it is to be feared that the same poison will emerge from the socialist automobile as from the capitalist one, and it does not depend at all on who is driving.

In addition, Kunert continued, there was an "asymmetry" regarding ecological information: "On the other side of the border one is rather conscious of the problem; on this side one suppresses it as adequately or as inadequately as one can. Between us: it is increasingly inadequate". After arguing his case with examples of automobile emissions, agricultural pesticides, liquid industrial wastes, and nuclear energy, Kunert concluded that

We just permit everything to go on and comfort ourselves with the imbecilic formula that humankind, which until now has survived everything, will also survive the present danger....Yet, in case wisdom is to be the final result, we have to ask ourselves if the cost of so-called progress has paid off. For my part, I, in any case, tend to be just a bit doubtful.

Girnus responded by first emphasizing that specialists in the GDR had discussed environmental problems and, in fact, had done so long before the mass media in the West discovered the term "environmental protection". Thus, the problem certainly was not one of inadequate information. Rather, said Girnus, the issue was that of carrying out laws already on the books and overcoming attitudes which blocked such implementation. Also not to be overlooked was the fact that specialists often disagreed about what measures were necessary. Then regarding progress as a concept, Girnus was strikingly harsh. He wrote Kunert,

Arrogantly you laugh about 'belief in progress'. In this scepticism you have colleagues and ancestors who are not a good omen: Spengler and the consequences...A certain Mr. Schicklgruber also thought he had to turn 'progress' off and that he could do so: the word 'progress' a typically deceptive vocabulary of Jewish liberalism. Denial of progress, of its possibilities, is the subterranean source of Nazi ideology. It is the ideology of confusion and the confused. Therefore its raging delirium and destruction. Categorical objection to the possibility of progress today leads logically to the fascist gas chamber.

Conceding that there, of course, could be no progress "without setbacks or retreats", Girnus added this significant invitation:

One could talk about what, in the various areas of human existence, one wants to understand as progress, how one could meaningfully understand this term.

And as a final admonition, Girnus said what many GDR leaders and non-literary specialists repeatedly would tell GDR writers -- "One thing I regret - you energetically beat the drum of criticism, but you do not indicate an alternative. Too bad. That is the proof of the pudding".[114]

This exchange clearly reflected the mood as well as central issues in the GDR's literary debate about progress: (a) skeptics' mounting pessimism and intensified criticism of 'so-called progress' vis-a-vis deep 'Establishment' displeasure with direct and indirect charges that socialist ecology was the same as capitalist ecology, (b) lack of positive, futuristic literary visions vis-a-vis unshakeable leadership belief in progress, and (c) dissenters' demands for more specific information and raised public consciousness vis-a-vis leadership charges that the protestors were unwilling to actively help solve environmental problems or to even grant that the system was seriously concerned about conditions which were leading to current misgivings about progress as a viable socio-political value.

"Establishment" Responses

In response to sharpening criticism, GDR leaders utilized many channels available to them for feeding affirmative information into the political culture debate about values and norms relating to progress. GDR citizens were reminded, for instance, that a Nature Protection Law had been passed as early as 1954 and a law regulating the use of nuclear energy and protection against radioactivity in 1962.[115] Also at the beginning of the 1960s a government center for radioactivity protection had been founded and in 1970 upgraded to the Governmental Office for Atomic Safety and Radioactivity Protection (*Staatliches Amt für Atomsicherheit und Strahlenschutz*).[116] In 1970 a new National Culture Law (*Landeskulturgesetz*) was passed, supplementing the earlier 1954 law. Next, in 1971 the GDR signed the RGW Treaty for Protection of Nature, with its provisions for long-range, cooperative planning, and set up the Ministry for Environment. Moreover, citizens could consult such legal provisions themselves in the collection of laws, *Atomsicherheit und Strahlenschutz*, published by the Staatsverlag in 1977.

Reminders also went out that the SED leadership had long ago warned the public of such problems. For instance, the effect which the environment, and the need to protect it, would have both on standards of living and economic productivity was discussed at the 8th Party Congress in 1971. In the Central Committee report to the Party membership, Erich Honecker had said that

An additional problem whose significance will increase in the coming years shall not go unnamed. Meant is

environmental protection, the fight against the pollu-
tion of air and water, the curtailment of industrial and
traffic noise. Certainly money is one thing we need.
Certainly we will progress only a step at a time. But
already now much could be practically improved if state
organs and economic leaders would mobilize all reserves
also in this matter and constantly keep in mind the
well-being of working people.[117]

In addition, the new SED Party Program, accepted in 1976, had reaffirmed the concern for environmental questions. It declared the
necessity of "maintaining Nature, as the source of life, material
wealth, health and joy, and of utilizing it rationally, on scientific bases."[118]

In 1979 a major publication by Paucke and Bauer -- *Umweltprobleme - Herausforderung der Menschheit* -- summed up many of
these views. In it the section on "Character of the Environmental
Problem in Socialism" made the point that, vis-a-vis the West, the
socialist system could more quickly put an end to the rape of
natural resources and gradually reduce the environmental costs of
capitalistic industrial procedures it had inherited. However,
while solutions to environmental crises were possible primarily in
socialism, the authors reminded readers again that it was essentially a matter of available resources. And that problem, in
fact, was urgent. Furthermore, the authors said, it was surely
time to go beyond pure economic reasoning to a broader "effectiveness" concept which included ecological factors. Implementation
of existing laws obviously remained a problem, too.[119]

5. 1980s Systemic Setting

Thus by the late 1980s currents of social change could be
sensed in the GDR's socio-political system, influenced in part by
various challenges to the concept of progress. Such currents
could be found especially within the political culture, the decision-making center, and among interest groups.

Political Culture Base

By 1980 nearly half of the GDR's citizens had been born after
World War II, that is, socialized in a socialist system. Although
systematic studies concerning the attitudes of GDR citizens toward
their system are rare, an astonishingly candid description of what
is "typically German" relative to other socialist political cultures was offered by Helmut Hanke of the SED's Academy for Social
Sciences. The East Germans, he said, were characterized by

industry, thoroughness, exactness, punctuality, love of
order and parsimoniousness, but also local narrow-mind-
edness, provincial insularity, pedantry and perfection-
ism, bourgeois life style and spirit of subjegation,
romantic musings and mystical speculations.[120]

Such GDR scholars as well as Western observers seem generally
to agree that the political culture of the GDR is significantly
influenced by (a) its pre-war German (Prussian) traditions, (b)
the war itself and the post-war construction period, (c) political
education in the principles of Marxist/Leninist philosophy, (d)
association with other East European socialist countries, and (e)
to an unknown extent, Western influence, especially via media.

Traditional Prussian/Protestant values had combined relatively easily with newly introduced Marxist/Leninist concepts of activism and rights equalling duties   Marxism/Leninism taught that
achieving the optimal, i.e., communist, society was a long-term
process, to be reached through performance and with the help of
science and technology.[121]   And, in fact, much has been achieved
in a system which, in the words of its national anthem, "arose out
of ruins".

Thus, it generally is reported, there is a wide-spread atti-
tude of appreciation in the GDR's political culture for the system's socio-political achievements -- jobs, education, health,
etc. GDR immigrants to West Germany expressed it in these words
in a sociological survey:

> *In the GDR one could live more quietly without being*
> *concerned that something would happen. One knew one*
> *could live without going under -- something one does not*
> *know here (FRG). One lived in a smaller but more se-*
> *cure world.*[122]

The appreciation for achievements is frequently accompanied by a
deep desire to maintain that status quo. Especially older generation citizens, who experienced the hardships of the war and post-
war construction period, value what is and so are said to be in-
tolerant of youth's desire for changes. Youth, on the other hand,
are increasingly impatient with and resentful of the status quo,
specifically the system's organizational restraints and agitation
for citizen activism. (It frequently is pointed out that, having
lived only in a socialist system, the youngsters are less Prussian
than their parents and so naturally less accepting of the old
values of authority and discipline.)

In the view of some analysts, the political culture values of
pride in accomplishment and appreciation of security relate, in
turn, to positive attitudes toward the collectivity of organized
work and consequently to close human relationships. Ralf

Rytlewski, for instance, found this appreciation especially within GDR parent/child relationships, the equality of women within the family, and the new emphasis on partnership as a lifestyle.[123] The GDR immigrants to the FRG referred to above also reflected this value of close human relationships -- they saw West Germans as less helpful and less friendly to children than East Germans; they did not feel accepted by West Germans and so did not feel "at home" in the West. The immigrants spoke of "basic differences in mentality" and characterized West Germans, among other things, as more demanding, less frugal, and less politically interested.[124]

A widespread value for active protest has not emerged from the dissatisfaction existing in the political culture of the GDR. Instead, a value has evolved which both GDR and Western scholars call "privatization". This development, in the view of former FRG diplomatic representative to the GDR, Günter Gaus, has made the GDR "a niche society". Gaus' colorful label has stuck and been widely elaborated by other observers of the GDR.

For example, after an extensive study tour of the GDR with fellow editors from *Die Zeit*, West Germany's renowned weekly, Theo Sommer reported that it was, indeed, a certain distancing from the state which molded life in the niches. But, he added, the niches "exist within socialism, not outside socialism. They are not incubators of opposition". In short, while one political culture value is the "carping" which GDR citizens do about their state, another value is that "they nevertheless support it", and a third is that they simultaneously try to achieve a sphere of meaningful privacy[125], albeit not as intensively as does the young generation of writers discussed in the preceding chapter.

One of the systemic aspects GDR citizens "carp" about a great deal is the lack of openness in the society. One GDR writer expressed the apparently wide-spread political culture value as the wish "that the people who have power would have less fear of innovation and change", while a dramatist saw the problem not as outright censorship but rather "ruffled areas" (*Knautschzone*).[126]

Indeed, critics of the "openness" of socio-political systems, West as well as East, increasingly seem to accept the theses that (a) in all political systems the mass media affirmatively support the system, (b) the challenges to systems are found at other levels (for example, belletristic or the non-mass, alternative press), and at the same time (c) "self-censorship" may be the major problem in most systems, regardless of official political culture values of pluralism of opinions, etc.[127]

GDR scholars, sharply criticizing the extent of self-censorship within their socio-political system, thus affirm "publicness" (*Öffentlichkeit*) as a political culture value. For example, Robert Weimann, writing in *Sinn und Form*, contended that

The more we distance ourselves from seeing socialist public discourse as the peaceful expression of a human community, and the less we understand public discourse as voluntaristic -- i. e., try to control the press in hurried campaigns -- the more urgent becomes the questioning of actual given historical conditions and social fundamentals.[128]

Increasingly the political leadership of the GDR seems to recognize that it has a communications problem which affects its image in the political culture. For example, Otto Reinhold, the first high-ranking SED leader to grant an interview to West German television, answered interviewer Günter Gaus' question about publicness (*Öffentlichkeit*) this way:

I believe that none of us in the party seriously question the fact that our presentation, the presentation of our problems, must be improved. Every political party constantly struggles with that, and I do not think it is that way only in the GDR.

At the same time, Reinhold pointed out to his Western audience that

We have an unusually large process of critical confrontations in many forms which are not always completely reflected, for example, in the press. I would like to just recall that during the last discussions of the (National Economic) plan, 735,000 suggestions were made ...of those, several hundred thousand were critical comments.

Agreeing that this was a kind of publicness which the GDR clearly practiced, interviewer Gaus conceded that it "perhaps is not seen correctly by us".[129]

Other Western observers, too, directly or indirectly, and from time to time, acknowledge that perhaps they have not looked deeply enough for evidence of dialogue in the GDR -- for instance, the above-cited editors from *Die Zeit*. After their study tour, they concluded that although the GDR could not be considered a democracy in the Western sense, there nevertheless were "astonishing possibilities" for GDR citizens "to say 'no' without negative consequences" and "many possibilities to express their opinions". The Western editors found those possibilities included "a highly developed petition system...a lively say-so of workers in the factories...and, as improbable as it sounds, even in the meetings before the managed elections".[130]

In other words, for Western observers the GDR's publicness is wider than sometime assumed; for GDR citizens their mass political culture values of "openness" is inadequately met by the system's input into their lives. Clearly, the well-educated GDR society increasingly knows more and so demands more information, especially about environmental problems, as will be seen. Furthermore, little can be concealed from the people because West German television and radio is an ever-present and inestimable influence. In addition to their own two TV channels, most East Germans can receive three additional German-language programs from the Federal Republic, plus radio broadcasts. That is an information menu available to few other peoples.

Another political culture value sometimes surprising to Western observers, but apparently rather natural, or *selbsverständlich*, for GDR citizens and their East European colleagues, is internationalism -- contradicting frequent assumptions of GDR isolation. For instance, a Polish social scientist found that GDR citizens had quite international values. Through a "secularization of life", K. Wasiak reported, the GDR had become a society interested in what is going on in a world which its people want to influence. He felt the appreciation/expectation of "existing social security" was a factor in the increasing satisfaction of GDR citizens with their own country, especially when combined with the perspective many of them have gained through participation in international cultural, scientific, and sports activities.[131] In addition to all such decades-long contacts with other socialist countries, in 1985, for example, twice as many GDR scholars and students also traveled to the West as had been able to do so ten years earlier; since 1975 the GDR had concluded 73 governmental agreements with Western countries in the fields of education, culture, science, and information.[132]

And regarding ecological concerns in the political culture, as seen earlier, environmental protection has long been a value. Indeed, environmental protection is a duty of GDR citizens, according to the 1969 Constitution and the 1974 revision:

> *(1) The land of the German Democratic Republic is one of its most valuable natural resources. It must be protected and utilized rationally.*
> *(2) In the interest of the welfare of citizens, the state and society shall protect nature. The competent bodies shall ensure the purity of the water and the air, and protection for flora and fauna and the natural beauties of the homeland; in addition this is the affair of every citizen. (Ch. II, Art. 15)*

But, as noted, by the 1980s this concept of the GDR's socialization was being challenged by Western media and GDR churches and writers. They were asking whether it was not precisely governmental effort toward economic achievements which were endangering those goals stated in the Constitution. Critics were arguing that environment and economy were not a unity; ecology and environmental protection were being sacrificed to the economy and to economic growth. In the view of many -- especially within the institutions of the church and literature-- that price was too high.

Although the church and literature as institutions had no real political power in this context, they had influence, especially the capacity to fill perceived information gaps and so to influence public opinion. In addition to criticizing official implementation of environmental protection, they were also critical of a related mass political culture expectation -- "consumerism". In fact, as some observers suggested, through their rejection of the current emphasis on consumption, these institutions were calling socialists back to their pure goals.[133]

According to the suggestive barometers of political culture found in church reports, the insistent demand for more and more consumer goods apparently was continuing. Church leaders spoke about the pressure of public expectations on the government, and church publications wrote about the need to change ways of life in "a society now oriented only toward well-being".[134] On the other hand, again as reflected in church reports, the value system of youth seemed to be changing; it was demanding "better" of society rather than just "more". For instance, church workers observed that youth

> *increasingly seek conversations with churches, not out*
> *of opposition but rather to have a free field for dis-*
> *cussions, to find orientation for their lives....*
> *Just as one is critical of parents, one is also criti-*
> *cal of the ideals of well-being in the West. Thus, to*
> *move there does not present a real alternative, for*
> *there one in any case has to do everything possible to*
> *acquire money in order to enjoy consumer goods.*[135]

Or as Hubertus Knabe reported in his study of ecological dissent in the GDR,

> *The ecology discussion in the churches and beyond shows*
> *that fundamental orientations, such as consumption,*
> *well-being, industriousness, order, family, etc., are*
> *beginning to also become brittle in the GDR.*[136]

In other words, by 1980 developments within the GDR's political culture base suggested that a tug-of-war was underway which could significantly affect socio-political change. Well-informed general studies showed that the contention was especially clear in the questioning of old orientations toward industrial progress and environmental protection, such as performance (*Leistung*), primacy of economic priorities, consumerism, and limited "publicness" (*Öffentlichkeit*).[137]

Decision-Making Center

While the political culture forms the base of a socio-political system, the decision-making activities and agencies are its center. In the GDR that includes the SED Politburo, Central Committee, and the Secretariat of the Committee, plus on the state side the State Council (*Staatsrat*), the Council of Ministers *(Ministerrat)*, and the Peoples' Chamber (*Volkskammer*).

Operational leadership and planning for the GDR's environmental protection is located primarily in the state organs which work closely with scientific institutions and social organizations to achieve implementation. The Council of Ministers passes environmental protection measures to be included in the economic plans and assigns responsibilities for carrying them out, for example, to the Ministry for Environmental Protection and Water Management. It, in turn, works through county councils (*Bezirksräte*) to coordinate environmental protection research and to present environmental plans to the State Planning Council for inclusion in the annual economic plans. Others having special environmental responsibilities include the state ministries for Science and Technology, Health, Material Resources, Agriculture, Forestry, and Food Processing Industries, Interior, Education, and Higher and Technical Education.[138]

It is this decision-making center which must provide evidence to the GDR population of the system's good performance. As in all modern societies, meeting the people's needs is a means of achieving and maintaining support for the system per se, for its incumbent leaders and/or governing party(s), and for current policies. (Indeed, as shall be seen later, by 1984 the question of how to achieve systemic stability was an issue of GDR intellectual debate.) Therefore, according to Western scholars and GDR specialists cited earlier, the GDR's decision-making center increasingly weighs conflicting group interests before resolving issues, rather than unilaterally passing along judgments of top SED leaders.

Several key principles shared by all the decision-makers influence their drive for good performance, including environmental protection. One is the principal of *democratic centralism* – after discussion has taken place, decisions are reached which then are binding on all levels of implementation. Secondly, to bring party influence (and/or control) to bear on the entire system, the placement of cadre in key positions is determined according to the procedure of *nomenklature* (similar to the procedure of political appointments to key positions in constitutional democratic bureaucracies). The candidates for these leadership positions are determined by those already in office, and so continuity is assured. Candidates have been selected, via the nomenklature system, for ability and party loyalty; their "election" then is a kind of referendum of choices already made by the decision-making center of the system. Because the SED strongly emphasizes education, many of the cadre who fill party and state positions have academic cre- dentials; they have gotten their initial positions, often in mass organizations or in Peoples' Assemblies (*Volksvertretungen*) at various levels, and then moved up through achievement. The nomen- klature procedure does not produce total homogeniety, or so- called input autonomy. Although there is agreement on basic values (such as the goal of economic growth and social progress), representatives of various institutions and ministries, and SED members themselves, advocate different priorities.

By the 1980s the awareness of environmental issues at this decision-making level became increasingly public. An example was the GDR's 1981-1985 central research plan for its social sciences. Published in the SED's theoretical magazine *Einheit*, one research emphasis (*Forschungsschwerpunkt*) dealt directly with ecology, in its ideological context: "Ecological Problems from the Viewpoint of the Confrontation Between Socialism and Imperialism Regarding the Future of Humankind" (an interdisciplinary research program of the Academy of Sciences). The specificity of this concern is seen even more clearly when it is noted that it is listed in the plan under the research complex dealing with (a) "Basic Questions in the Development of Scientific-Technological Progress", (b)"The Or- ganic Relationship Between the Accomplishment of the Scientific- Technological Revolution and the Advantages of Socialism", and (c) "Socialism's Unique Forms of the Relationship Between Science and Production".[139]

In addition, the Ministry for Higher and Technical Education in early 1980 announced a new two-year correspondence course (*Fernstudium*) of graduate studies in the field of Environmental Protection. The goal of the training program for university and technical school students was to better quality cadre in the tech- nical, natural, agricultural, and economic sciences for work in industry, construction, agriculture, forestry, nutrition, water resource management, and economics. Their training program would emphasize especially "rational utilization of natural resources" and "disposal and possible utilization of waste products in indus- try and agriculture".

Overall, the instruction would reflect "the complex character of environmental protection". It would integrate areas of study such as Marxism/Leninism and the fundamentals of socialist nation- al culture (*Landeskultur*), fundamentals of leadership, planning, and economics of environmental protection, basics of general ecol- ogy, selected problems of technological procedures in environmen- tal protection, basics of land, water, and air resource utiliza- tion, problems of noise abatement, environmental hygiene, and re- gional planning. In addition to specialized workshops, ten weeks of classroom work would include lectures, practice sessions, and integrated seminars (*Verflechtungsseminare*) dealing with the "complexity of the environmental protection phenomenon".[140]

Moreover, a new scientific discipline was being developed--environmental engineering (*Ingenieur-Ökologie*) which would concern itself with the "ecologicalization of production". Specifically, this meant the application of principles and mechanisms of ecological systems to production processes which at the moment were far from ecologically optimal.[141]

By 1981 the 10th Party Congress, held in a context of hardening international political and economic conditions, confirmed the goal of increasing economic growth for the GDR via increased productivity. It also continued the unity of economics and social policy as the "major task" (*Hauptaufgabe*), a dilemma, as will be seen. In addition, the goals of the five-year National Economic Plan, which the Party Congress approved, called specifically for environmental protection, primarily through use of modern technologies which would improve the working and living conditions of workers.[142]

In addition to the making of concrete decisions such as those above, a constant function of the GDR's socio-political system center is transmittal of communications to influence the political culture. For example, public media, endless public speeches, addresses to the SED faithful who in turn "pass the word" to the general public, etc., are used to publicize the decision-makers' perspectives.

By the 1980s environmental and ecological concerns were an increasing theme. A typical example was the SED's communication output about environmental protection in late 1980 via Party University (*Parteihochschule*) professors for Political Economy writing in *Einheit*. The authors not only reassured readers of socialism's successes, but said it was precisely the advantages of socialism which now motivated Western criticism of the East's absence or slowness of environmental protection and the human cost of its economic progress:

> *Where once bourgeoise economists denied a planned economy any vitality and day after day prophesized its destruction, so now -- in contrasting a 'social market' economy -- they concentrate on construing a contradiction between a socialist planned economy and humanism and freedom. Simultaneously they deny its capacity for effective economics under conditions of intensively expanded reproduction, as well as accelerated scientific-technological progress.*[143]

This theme of East/West asymmetry in the environmental protection issue, which had been the focal point of the Kunert/Girnus literary exchange in the early 1970s, would surface again and again. It

47

was a central point in the continuing debate about the nature of and the possibilities for social and economic progress.

The challenge from the West was a major point, for instance, in early 1981 when delegates from the major Communist Parties, East and West, gathered in Prague for an international symposium on "Communists and the Environmental Protection Movement". (An earlier 1972 international meeting had dealt with ecological/political relationships.) Excerpts from the opening speech and discussions published in *Problems of Peace and Socialism* made clear that a primary concern of the symposium was how communists should relate to Western environmental movements; the other issue was how to communicate with and about those movements, making clear the difference between the capitalist and socialist approaches to ecology. It was felt that

> *the urgent task of Communists' ideological work is found in...clarifying questions of scientific-technological progress, the position and role of science in capitalist and socialist societies, and the energy and other global problems.*[144]

Thus in the early 1980s, the concept of the GDR's decision-making center seemed to be that ecology must remain a subordinated priority because of the economic demands of the moment. Although the GDR's socio-political system had long been concerned with environmental protection, like many Western countries it, too, faced the common dilemma of environmental vs economic priorities, i.e., costs. On the other hand, in the decade of the 80s the decision-making center in the GDR would repeatedly make clear that questions of economics and environment could not be discussed outside the context of war/peace and armament/disarmament. Moreover, with the increasing international polarization of the environmental question, new security measures apparently were felt essential; reportedly the GDR Council of Ministers in November, 1982 ordered that environmental data be kept secret.[145]

Party and Interest Group Inputs

Mediating and/or transmitting between the political culture of the people and the central decision-makers of the GDR are a host of local level leaders and an unending number of interest groups. Their function is not only to serve the SED as channels for implemental output. In addition, they "register" movements within the political culture -- for instance, concerning environmental questions -- and transmit perceived demands and/or supports to the decision-making center of the socio-political system.

The key figures in all such groups which identify and aggregate group interests are the SED's cadre, or leaders. As noted,

their selection/election is influenced and guided by the party
bureaucracy, and only those groups which have SED approval can officially exist. Thus, citizens' independent ecology and peace efforts necessarily remain fragmented, failing to become "movements"
in the sociological or political sense. Many GDR citizens, therefore, also choose to work through existing and sanctioned groups,
such as those sketched below. (The following chapters will then
present evidence suggesting that challenges to the GDR's existing
political culture concepts of social and economic progress were
generated primarily within the institutions of literature and
church and these interest groups.)

Clearly, in the GDR's socio-political system the most important group transmitting input demands and supports into the center
of the system is, of course, the **SED** itself. Party units operate
everywhere -- at county (*Bezirk*) and district (*Kreis*) levels, on
the job and in the housing developments, and within the military,
state agencies, and mass organizations. Thus there are the basic
party units called GO (*Grundorganisation*), the BPOs in plants (*Be-
triebsparteiorganisation*), WPO in residential areas (*Wohngebiets-
parteiorganisation*), and APO at departmental levels (*Abteilungs-
parteiorganisation*). Their responsibility is to assure implementation of SED decisions within their spheres and, in turn, to reflect upward through the party's channels the reactions of citizens within the unit.

Very important in this whole chain of political party feedback from the top down and bottom up are the local Peoples' Assemblies (*Volksvertretungen*), sometimes also called Peoples' Representative Bodies. Among other duties, these local bodies at
county, district, town, and village level receive and act on complaints and petitions (*Beschwerde/Eingaben*) directly from the
citizens, including those concerning the environment.

In addition, advisory bodies and advisory commissions at various levels of the party and state hierarchies assess and select
interest group feedback for SED consideration. For instance, concerning environmental issues, there is the Advisory Council (*Beirat*) for Environmental Protection, founded under the 1970 National
Culture Law, to advise the Council of Ministers. The advisory
group includes representatives from other state organs, scientific
institutions, and social organizations.[146] Attached to the Mini-
istry for Environmental Protection and Water Management, the state
implementing agency for environmental work, is also an advisory
Kollegium. In the Ministry itself are cadre working closely with
social organizations[147] and, according to some reports, dealing
with increasing numbers of direct petitions and environmental complaints from the public.

Another major channel of feedback, for instance to SED Central Committee representatives, is the **National Front**. It is the

49

umbrella organization encompassing the system's non-communist parties (the so-called *bloc parties*): The CDU organizes and represents the interests of Christian-oriented people (in 1982, about 125,000 members), the DBD those of farmers (103,000 members), the NDPD the interests of former nationalist petit bourgeois and middle classes (91,000 members, and the LDPD those of the former urban petit bourgeois, or trade and craft sectors (83,000 members).[148]

More significant, however, in the life of the GDR's sociopolitical system are the **mass organizations** which also are part of the National Front. The three largest are the Confederation of Free German Trade Unions (FDGB) with 9.4 million members in 1985,[149] the Free German Youth (FDJ) with a membership of 2.3 million,[150] the Democratic Women's League of Germany (DFD) with 1.4 million.[151]

In the National Front, the **Chamber of Technology (KDT)** is increasingly significant. This mass organization for engineers, economists, and technicians, reportedly had a membership of 288,000 in 1985.[152] Founded in 1946 to support scientific-technological progress in the GDR, the KDT is responsible for rationalization/modernization advice and so is involved in around 10,000 projects, half of which concern more effective use of micro- and electronic technology.[153]

The KDT is organized at the county level and in the big plants. Through these various branches it translates research results into production practice, supports technical competitions of apprentices and students, participates in establishing technical standards, advises state and scientific-technological institutions, and carries on continuing-education programs for natural scientists and technicians, as well as special courses and self-study programs leading to diplomas. It publishes 30 technical journals and supports 12 professional organizations (*Fachverbände*) which reflect the numerous academic disciplines included within its membership.[154]

Indeed, scientists, speaking through such interest groups,[155] apparently are becoming increasingly vocal on ecological issues. Werner Gruhn, in his study of economic factors involved in environmental questions, observed that

Although education and research in the GDR places the economic utilization of scientific-technological progress in the foreground, ecological aspects are also increasingly taken into consideration in the works of GDR scientists....Nevertheless, maintenance of the environment usually is not presented as an independent value, but rather introduced into the consideration as an economic category.[156]

Moreover, such scientific specialists also participate in church discussion groups concerned with environment:

> So state officials responsible for the protection of nature gladly take part in informational evening programs of the church - or natural scientists report on the scope of their work (for instance, at a colloquium of pastors regarding nuclear energy).[157]

And, as noted earlier, many have an international perspective to problems, probably including environmental issues.

This intelligentsia (Intelligenz), according to an analysis by Gert-Joachim Glaeßner, is precisely the group in the GDR which is reformulating the concept of "progress". Indeed, the intelligentsia, in Glaeßner's opinion, functions as the avant-garde in the consequent reorientation of values, social aspirations, and life styles.[158] Significant proof of the intelligentsia's misgivings is found in its professional literature, according to Katharina Belwe and Fred Klinger. There it is candidly admitted that new technologies have not automatically brought only advantages, i.e., that progress is ambivalent. Indeed, "the frequency of articles which discuss the negative effects openly or between the lines makes clear that serious difficulties accompany technological change".[159]

Among the intelligentsia's **scientific institutions** which have special responsibilities for environmental protection are the Academy of Science, Academy of Agrarian Sciences, and the Building Academy of the GDR.[160] In fact, that responsibility seemed to be intensifying by the 1980s. This is suggested by the inclusion of two "areas of research concentration" concerning environmental-ecological issues in the central research plan of the GDR's social sciences for 1981-1985. The one research emphasis noted earlier was ideological, dealing with environmental problems in an East/West comparative context. The second emphasis was theoretical—included under the research complex dealing with "The Objective Laws of History and the Developed Socialist Society in the Gradual Transition to Communism" -- and was entitled "Scientific-Technological Revolution, Social Progress and Intellectual Confrontation". The research area was described as an interdisciplinary program to be carried out by the Academy of Sciences.[161] The impact of this five-year research program would be especially clear, as will be seen, at the later 1983 social science conference of the Central Committee, that is, three years into the projects discussed above.

Crucial in the GDR's ecological issues is its **League of Culture**. Set up immediately after the war ended in 1945, the League (Kulturbund, or KB) was intended to integrate the "old" intelligentsia into the challenges of building the new socio-political

system. Today the KB is involved in a spectrum of activities much
broader than just cultural and educational, and by 1980 it had organized some 147 clubs. Total membership for 1985 was reported as
nearly 264,000.[162]

Over the years, for instance, the KB's active committees and
work groups concerned with nature jointly held Landscape Days
(Landschaftstage), the first in 1966. There also was its organization, the Friends of Nature and Homeland, which had influenced
the Nature Reserve Law (Naturschutzgesetz) and the National Cultural Law referred to earlier. Overall, some 40,000 friends of
the environment are active through such KB organizations.

In 1970, as environmental complaints grew, so did requests
for a better organization. It was felt that a kind of lobby was
needed which could aggregate environmental interests and bring influence to bear on the political, economic, and social sectors.
Thus, in March 1980, the Society for Nature and the Environment
(Gesellschaft für Natur- und Umwelt, or **GNU**) was founded as part
of the Kulturbund. According to a very useful study of this new
organization, by Peter Wensierski, the GNU had 50,000 members by
the end of 1983.[163] The SED press reported that the members were
active in 1,880 specialist groups, ranging from ornithology to
dendrology.[164] Wensierski found that the membership represents
some 1,500 individuals, from gardeners to politicians and scientists. There also are group members, for whole institutes and enterprises can join. Church-involved environmental activities cooperate with GNU, as well.

Set up regionally, on the county level, GNU has the right to
make proposals to state agencies. Such proposals come from the
GNU's executive committee which includes individuals as well as
representatives of firms, institutions, and state agencies themselves. In addition, GNU pays special attention to young people
by organizing youth forums, vacation camps, and local youth.
groups. The GNU also carries out specific research projects
through its committees of specialists, maintains close relations
to industrial plants, and holds debates, colloquia, forums, excursions, exhibits, etc.[165] For instance, in recent years, GNU
and KB cooperation with state agencies has included recultivation
work in the protected reserve areas around the Fürstenwalde coal
mines and in industrially congested areas such as Eisenhütten-
stadt, Schwedt, Eberswalde-Finow, Fürstenwalde, and Rüdersdorf.[166]

Also significant as aggregators of specific group interests
within the GDR are its **professional societies** for artistic/cultur-
nal specialists -- authors, film/television personnel, musicians,
architects, theater artists, journalists, graphic artists, and
others. Through the relatively large number of cultural representatives on the SED Central Committee,[167] these professional societies have significant possibilities for influencing early

stages of decision-making. For instance, numerous "insider" articles and reports published in the West suggest that leading members of the Writers' Union ("leading" = "Establishment") have
considerable influence on the political decision-makers ("decision-makers" = "Politburo").

Aside from the internal politics of the Writers' Union (reported in speculative Western articles emphasizing who was
expelled and why and which works by whom are not published), it is
logical to assume that this official interest group of writers is
very concerned about influencing the issues of progress, ecology,
and environment. Indeed, the studies by Hubertus Knabe[168] and
Eckart Förtsch[169] show how widely the issue of "Humankind's
relationship to Nature" was discussed among writers.

On the one hand, then, the Writers' Union made its concerned
input directly into the system, while, on the other hand, its members individually also frequently took their disagreements directly to the public. For example, writers' frank discussions with
each other, as previously noted between Kunert and Girnus, provided evidence of their concern as well as use of *Neue deutsche Literatur*, the official organ of their Writers' Union, as a forum of
discussion.

At the local level the Artists' Unions, too, played an important role in aggregating the interests of writers. The societies
were active in exhibits, festivals, etc. that brought writers/art-
ists together with their audiences. The League of Culture, in
turn, helped facilitate such contacts by arranging discussions and
gatherings in its club houses where writers meet with medical
scientists, teachers, legal specialists, and other natural and
social scientists.[170]

And, of course, as has been seen, in the questioning of progress and the environmental protection issue, the **church** was one
of the most visible interst groups collecting and passing along
reactions of the citizenry. Since initial ecological interest developed in the early 1970s, some 40 environmental groups had organized within the context of the church by the 1980s.[171] Public
actions such as "Mobile Without Auto"", an annual affair since
spring 1981, increased public awareness of environmental issues,
as did lectures, seminars, etc.

Church leaders were aware that they and the church as an institution do not have political power per se. Rather, they accept
the socio-political system, favor evolution, and see themselves as
an influential factor for articulating innovative demands for reform vis-a-vis the state. As Erfurt theologican Heino Falcke put
it, the church must become "the attorney for emancipatory-innova-
tive causes...in that it stages a comprehensive learning process
within the church"; it must also become the interpreter of group

53

interests in specialist and political circles so that

the governing, who necessarily are bound by short-range, particular interests, are made so aware of their own general and long-range interests that daily politics at least keeps open the possibility of perceiving these interests.[172]

Thus, when the church leadership met with the GDR's state leadership in March, 1980, the clergymen emphasized, among other things, the need for more public information concerning environmental issues. While this was a point the churches repeatedly made, they had not waited passively for a state response. Instead, as noted, they made their own informative material available through the Church Research Center in Wittenberg and through church newspapers (with a circulation estimated by some to be about 147,000).[173]

By the early 1980s, then, the stage was set for an intensified environmental dialogue in which SED decision-makers, interest group spokespersons, church leaders and members, as well as writers would continue their search for new definitions of "progress" and related political culture values. A major voice in the dialogue would be that of Hanns Cibulka, speaking through his environmentally critical book *Swantow*.

6. Summary

Historically the concept of "Progress" dates back to the Enlightenment, as shown in the work of J. B. Bury, *The Idea of Progress*. In a 1931 reissue of the volume, Charles A. Beard warned that the development of technology, essential to progress, would bring with it serious problems.

Similarly, Marxism/Leninism, accepting progress as an objective law of *historical* development, also warned that *social progress* would not be linear and uninterrupted. Even under socialism there would be problems.

In the GDR the concept of progress had unceasingly been input into the political culture. Combined with traditional Prussian values of hard work, order, and self-discipline, it fell on fertile ground -- economic and social progress would be achieved through production. This was the message from the GDR's 1949 Constitution through all its official proclamations down to the present time.

By the 1970s, however, an energetic debate about the validity of progress was in full swing, triggered to a large extent by the pessimistic 1972 Club of Rome report "The Limits of Growth".

About the same time GDR literary voices, too, began to question progress. Among the first was Plenzdorf's, suggesting that a *"Leistung"* society demanded so much achievment of youth that suicide might accidentally result. Other writers tied their misgivings about progress to the destruction/preservation of nature. The church in the GDR also discovered and discussed anew the moral implications of progress/science/environment -- their price, their goals, their sense.

By the mid-1970s the progress debate in the GDR had become more sophisticated. Instead of just denying the Club of Rome's contentions, social scientists began to argue that progress, i.e., economic growth, had to be more closely related to specific socioeconomic, that is, people-related, goals, At the big November 1976 conference of GDR social scientists, there was a clear challenge to cooperate in a more interdisciplinary fashion and to examine closely the relationship between the socialist production principle (*Leistungsprinzip*), key to social progress, and the cultural standard of life.

In the late 1970s the church, too, intensified its concern, primarily through specific organizations and public discussions at Synod meetings, seminars, conferences, etc. While calling for more ecological justice, the church also exercised self-criticism vis-a-vis the so-called "Protestant work ethic" it had promulgated for centuries.

The literary debate became public, as well, in the late 1970s, highlighted by the exchange of communications between Günter Kunert and Wilhelm Girnus on the pages of *Sinn und Form*. In many ways it signaled the dimensions of the debate within the institution of literature -- on the one hand, criticism of so-called progress, on the other hand, criticism of literary pessimism and the failure to see that socialist ecology was not the same as Western concern for the environment.

Major natural and social science responses, some in book form, began to appear. They suggested that the time, indeed, had come for broadening the concept of "effectiveness" to include ecological, as well as economic, factors. Implementation of existing laws clearly remained a major problem.

In summary then, as the 1980s got underway, the political culture base of the GDR's socio-political system included significant support, primarily among middle-age and older citizens, for "productivity" as a value and appreciation for the system's performance in the areas of jobs, education, and health. At the same time, there was growing dissatisfaction among youth with behavioral norms such as regimentation and authoritarianism; the dissatisfaction among the general public was with the "pressure to perform" and the limited "openness" of public discourse.

Indeed, both the institutions of the church and literature had raised public questions about those issues and were also increasingly articulating doubts about the sanctity of progress as a key economic and social value of the political culture. Citizens now were often hearing critics (including those in the West) say that ecology and environmental protection were being sacrificed to the economy and economic growth.

The decision-making center of the GDR, early in the country's history, had made environmental protection a constitutional duty and had consistently reinforced the Marxist/Leninist principle of historical and social progress. At the same time, GDR leaders had also warned of pending environmental problems -- this point had been made as early as the 8th Party Congress in 1971. By 1980, ecology issues were incorporated in the central research plan for the social sciences; a new course of training in environmental protection was set up by the Ministry for Higher Education; the new profession of "environmental engineer" was introduced; and environmental protection measures were appearing in the five-year National Economic Plan.

Simultaneously, the GDR's leaders persistently used their channels of political communication to reinforce the now-challenged concept of socio-economic progress; they sought to clarify why, for the time being, economic growth had to be given priority over environmental protection by saying that without the former there could not be the latter. The discrepancy between East/West approaches to ecology was emphasized again and again, as incresingly was the linkage between environmental protection and peace.

The GDR's interest groups were also having their say in the debate over priorities for the 1980s. Scientists spoke through organizations, institutions, and professional journals; friends of the environment were especially active in the League of Culture and its newly organized Society for Nature and the Environment (GNU); artists spoke out through their journals and professional societies; religious leaders worked with citizens through church environmental groups.

The decision-making center had attempted to cope with the increased input of demands by creating a new structure to deal with them, the GNU. However, it was not at all clear by the 1980s whether this customary systemic procedure for dealing with an "overload" of demands would be adequate. Would the interest groups and the people they represented see this response to their demands as sufficient to warrant increased support for official programs and policies? After all, the rule-making action creating the GNU had not come until four years after the League of Culture had requested it. And while the GNU now was inspiring local groups to implement existing environmental provisions, some state agencies, on the other hand, were refusing to cooperate with church groups, and some arrests of people demonstrating for environmental actions were reported.

Thus, the GDR socio-political system entered the 1980s with (a) increased questioning within the political culture of the general concept of social progress and specific values relating to environmental/economic issues (apparently citizens experienced discrepancies between their daily socio-political experiences and generalized beliefs to which they earlier had been socialized); (b) increased demands for environmental protection being transmitted to the decision-making center by interest groups; (c) relatively moderate outputs to satisfy demands and some to control them.

Into this systemic setting would come *Swantow*, Hanns Cibulka's slim, little book, which once again would illustrate literature's reflection of and challenge to the political culture that had inspired it. It, too, would become a stimulus in the process of socio-political change underway in the GDR.

Chapter III

CASE STUDY: HANNS CIBULKA'S *SWANTOW*

As the 1970s turned into the 80s, a literary protest that had
been gradually building in the GDR reached a new peak with publication of Hanns Cibulka's diary *Swantow*. That work and the author's experience with it was a striking example of literature's
challenge to the sanctified concept of "progress", that is, an illustration of the institutional role of literature in the current
political culture of the GDR.

1. Cibulka's Background

Born in Bohemia, Cibulka served in Poland and Italy during
World War II and after the war settled in Thuringia. He was
trained as a librarian and heads the library in Gotha. In 1978 he
was elected to the board of directors (*Zentralvorstand*) of the GDR
Writers' Union. Writing poems and diaries, Cibulka is described
as a poet whose works reflect a bipolar tension effecting his relationship to reality -- one pole is that of nature's influence on
objective materiality; the other pole is memory's influence on
subjective activity. As a diarist, Cibulka conveys "concepts and
sensations, memories and reflections". In the author's works,
these two forms of writing, poetry and diary, are found to "alter-
nate with each other in an almost regularized exchange".[174]

One of Cibulka's earlier works which became relatively widely
known was the diary written on the Baltic island Hiddensee, entitled *Sanddornzeit*.[175] For a sensitive reader, this 1971 work
seemed to present humankind's burdensome, and at times moving,
"search for truth", or intellectual knowledge. An absorbed poetic
writer contemplating nature in soltitude, engages occasionally in
conversations with a natural scientist who interprets nature's
fragility and interdependence. Slowly the writer arrives at new
insights and goals for his own life and work, sharing his conceptual progress with his diary and its readers.

For instance, on the third day of his Hiddensee holiday,
Cibulka recorded in his *Sanddornzeit* diary a meeting with "Doctor
H" with whom he had become acquainted the previous year. Mutual
interests included their birth places (upper Silesia) and wartime
experiences ("he, too, had spent six years as a soldier and knew
the prisoner of war camps in Sicily as well as I did").[176] On the
fifth day of his recordings, Cibulka wrote that he was seeking
knowledge -- "what after all do we seek on all our travels if not
knowledge?"[177] And around the 45th day of his vacation the writer
perceived a new relationship between art and nature through conversations with the natural scientist, Dr. H.:

What surprised me about his studies was their unique
bridging of natural science knowledge and poetic in-
sight. It was a prose which described things not only
through abstract communication. Repeatedly the meta-
phoric punctuated his sentences...science and poetry be-
gan to touch each other once more.[178]

After defending the diary as a literary form where "poetry and
science can meet",[179] Cibulka then used his daily recordings to
laud the interrelationship and centrality of precisely that, art
and science:

The more our daily work is achieved through inorganic
energies, the mechanical, the impersonal which accom-
panies us everywhere, the stronger the human being must
reflect upon his intellectual, his cultural mission.
Concentration at the same time on scientific and on art-
istic energies constitutes the foundation of the human
vocation.[180]

Proceeding from that premise, the knowledge-seeking poet/diarist
discovered consequences for his own work. Exactly two months
after beginning his holiday, Cibulka concluded that the artistic
picture of nature must be more than mere description, that is, it
must be more than his initial diary entries. It must carry a message: "The poetic image must make statements which go far beyond
poetic description of our environment". Specifically, the poetic
image "must, like a bolt of lightening, open new horizons for the
reader". Further, "The image must illuminate, reveal, make the
reader see, expand his viewpoint...must again be a message" because the poetic image "gives back to nature on a higher level
that which an idea a world view, has gained from it".[181]

Only a few days later Cibulka seemed to signal what he specifically intended to do with his art/science "message" -- he
would protect, warn, remind the world's consciousness. How? Ten
days before the end of his holiday, Cibulka recorded a clue in his
diary when he commended *books and human thought* and wrote that
"through thought, powerful forces impact the world".[182] Retro-
spectively, then, this entire 1971 work by Hanns Cibulka, reporting a short island holiday, seemed to have been a prelude to his
later thought-provoking book *Swantow*, which would stir up a wave
of discussion in the early 1980s.

Indeed, *Swantow* represented long contemplation about the relationship between art and science. For years the author, along
with many of his countrypeople, had heard via Western media shocking reports of environmental pollution. Sensitive to nature, Cibulka thought about what he heard. And he looked anew at his environment -- for instance, during a 1977 vacation at a fish flawed
by crippled back fins and a cancerous growth on its underside.

Knowing what his next use of poetic imagery must convey, Cibulka's *Swantow* began to evolve —- a poem, diary-form descriptions and contemplations from a summer holiday on the island of Rügen in the Baltic, and troubled ecological insights. The author's unease, stimulated in part by past foreign media reports, increased through additional reading and study of environmental questions. As the manuscript grew, Cibulka's editor, Gerhard Wolf, with whom he had worked for 25 years, suggested revisions here and there.

In 1980, then, the book manuscript was submitted to the Mitteldeutscher Verlag in Halle (operated by the county SED organization), which had published previous works by Cibulka. There it passed the review (*Gutachten*) process, a significant procedure, for a publishing house director can find himself fired and off to another job if his competence in manuscript-selection is questioned too often. The review process, therefore, included recommendations not only from the author's editor and the publishing house editor (*Verlagslektor*) but also a third assessment from an outside specialist (*Aussenlektor*). For *Swantow*, this was the well-known Halle literary scientist, Prof. Dr. Dietrich Sommer. With these three recommendations positively supporting publication, Cibulka's manuscript apparently was sent on to the Ministry of Culture for final publishing permission.

Meanwhile, *Neue deutsche Literatur* asked the author to submit his manuscript for excerpted publication (*Vorabdruck*) in the journal. Thus the entire manuscript, as it had been given to the publishing house by Cibulka and his editor, was sent to *NDL*. There excerpts were chosen by the editorial staff. The work was published on 29 pages of the April, 1981 issue of the official journal of the Writers' Union,[183] in which, as noted, the author was active.

2. *Swantow*: The Initial Excerpted Version (1981)

Cibulka, of course, had not written for a vacuum. He had prepared a specific message, a challenge to aspects of the concept of "progress". It was intended for a specific socio-political system, indeed, one in which the value was central to the political culture.

Unlike the diary *Sanddornzeit* of a decade earlier, *Swantow* included Cibulka's poetic, as well as prose, thought. Thus it was at the end of one of the first poems appearing in the *NDL* excerpted diary that Cibulka suggested a major focus of his holiday contemplations —- technological developments endangering human life. The poem evoked moving images of rockets ripping through earth's casing, propelling the word 'progress' comet-like across the heavens. Everything which brings contemplative pleasure is allowed, said the poet in short staccato lines of verse, although, in fact, the rockets bind life and death together in hairbreadth proximity.[184]

Apparently this kind of "message" did not trouble the editors of *NDL* who freely chose to publish the diary excerpts. Since journal editors are not subject to pre-publication control, what they print is a matter of editorial choice (and sometimes also of editorial courage since they, of course, can be fired). The materials chosen for publication are intended to make a contribution to dialogue and discussion, especially for opinion leaders.

The excerpted version of *Swantow*, as it appeared in *NDL*, included a total of 20 diary entries, four directly concerning environmental questions. (See *Appendix A* for the German-language texts.) As will be seen, these entries were to become the focus of a post-publication debate which apparently contributed to revision of the full-length book published about 1 1/2 years later:

(1) The first environment-related diary entry presented in the excerpted version of *Swantow* concerned atomic power stations and the effects of radiation.[185] In this 3 August entry, Cibulka wrote that for days his thoughts had been occupied with the building of a dome over nuclear energy plants. "There is no technical necessity for building this dome", he wrote, observing that the thick concrete covering appeared to be concealing "a secret, a suspicious secret".

In the following three paragraphs, then, Cibulka quoted, from an unnamed source, a critical discussion of radioactive emissions from such plants. The report said, for instance, that "In normal operations an atomic power plant constantly emits radionuclides"; a large part of them are Krypton-89 whose slow disintegration rate means they remain in the environment, causing constantly increasing amounts of accumulated radioactivity. Additional radioactive substances enter the environment through waste water, and "one already knows how dangerous various nuclides are". The result of all this, the quote said, is "radioactivity which leads to an unspecific disturbance of the normal chemical order and the structure of affected cells. Impairments caused by such radioactive-damaged cells, which continue to multiply, are first visible after many generations of cells." After a brief reference to strontium, which "an organism, completely unkowingly, can absorb and store", the quoted material concluded with the terse assessment: "Contamination takes place in the darkness of technical measurability. The conclusion that 'what I cannot measure is not dangerous' is false".

(2) Several days later, on 6 August, Cibulka returned in his diary to the atomic energy theme. He introduced this second major ecological statement with the words, "Further into reading material on 'nuclear energy plants'". Again Cibulka quoted at length

from an unnamed author, this time from an uncritical one whose
thesis was "the complete lack of danger to the environment from
operating nuclear energy plants." She wrote, for instance, that

> *The shortage of plant experience had led to determi-*
> *nation of a minimum distance between large cities and*
> *nuclear power plants; in the USSR this initially was set*
> *at 35 kilometers. Moreover, long and thorough checks*
> *for harmful emissions in the atmosphere near the plants*
> *had shown, on the one hand, a total lack of danger from*
> *the operating plants to their environment, as well as*
> *the effectiveness of the previously discussed measures*
> *and, on the other hand, had established significantly*
> *more damaging effects on health from thermal energy*
> *plants using inflammable fossile fuels, especially ash-*
> *endowed materials and -- in an even higher degree--*
> *coal and oil with their high sulphur content.*[186]

(3) Five days later, on 11 August, the sight of an airplane
spraying collective farm fields inspired Cibulka to write a third
major ecological statement. His diary entry was a short 15-line
poem of environmental protest against contamination from nuclear
energy plants and a lengthy prose section condemning the increasing "chemicalization of life", as well as modern medical practices.[187]

The poem, speaking of nuclear energy plants measuring the
land "by the fathom cord of death", was followed by Cibulka's
question, "Are we not well on the way to disregard for basic laws
of nature and the interrelationship of all things?" For the next
paragraph, then, Cibulka -- using run-on sentences characteristic
of his diary style -- takes up the related theme of chemistry:

> *Our illnesses multiply in proportion to increases in the*
> *chemicalization of life. We already are paying too high*
> *a price for our dubious good living. From its modest*
> *beginnings, chemistry has become a Hydra monster; syn-*
> *thetic fertilizers, herbicides, poisoned air and water,*
> *radioactive fallout, and all that is to have no effect*
> *on a human being's health? The waiting rooms in the*
> *polyclinics are overfilled, the legion of doctors con-*
> *stantly increases, people ever more susceptible, soon we*
> *will face only an army of specialists, the general prac-*
> *tioner, as I remember him from my childhood, has become*
> *legend.*   .

Continuing this health theme for a page more in his diary,
Cibulka made these points, among others: (a) "The mass media want
to make us believe that we have a scientific age; we do not have
it"; (b) "What we lack until now is a science of humankind which
finally for once asks how the human should live and work, what is

really necessary for an existence worthy of human beings"; (c)
"The progress of medicine today proceeds primarily via the operating table, via the scalpel"; (d) "We live in an invisible trench,
under fire from all sides: water, air, nutrition, radioactive
zones"; (e) "In the last decades we have created many illnesses
ourselves, they are the result of our lifestyle...people are mur-
dering themselves, to be sure it is long-range murder"; and (f)
"The toughest of all revolutions is yet to come, the revolution
against ourselves, against our own lethargy, egoism, power in-
stinct...".

(4) Some weeks later, Cibulka recorded a fourth diary entry directly concerned with environmental issues. It was 27 August that
he again noted impressions stimulated by airplanes above his vacation island. This time Cibulka contended that such sights would
unconsciously influence a child toward aggression:

> The archaic landscape on Rügen is also fading. Giant
> metal birds soar through the air, military helicopters
> fly over the land at church-tower height, destroyers lay
> off the coast. The tension which such an environment
> induces does not leave human beings unaffected, they
> carry over to thoughts, feelings, behavior. This ele-
> ment of tension already sets in in the unconsciousness
> of children, turning into aggression.[188]

3. Political, Literary, and Public Reactions

A short time after the issue of *NDL* with the excerpted version of *Swantow* appeared in print, it was reviewed by a Reuters
News Agency correspondent. His review appeared in two West German
newspapers (see *Appendix B* for the text). It was published first
in the *Frankfurter Rundschau* on June 2, 1981, under the headline
"Alternative Tones from a GDR Lyricist"; on June 5 the same text
was printed in the *Bonner General-Anzeiger*, headlined "A Lyricist
from Swantow: Hanns Cibulka Generates a Discussion".

The lead paragraph of the review said that

> Through publication of a literary diary, the GDR author
> Hanns Cibulka has added a new dimension to criticism in
> and of the German Democratic Republic. And so, one
> hears from East Berlin, there then was also a serious
> confrontation about publication of the 30-page article
> in the latest issue of the monthly magazine of the
> Writers' Union, <u>Neue deutsche Literatur.</u>

Cibulka does not criticize the political-ideological system
of the GDR, the Reuters correspondent wrote, but rather applies
"European civilization criticism directly and correctly to the

'first German state of workers and farmers'". And so, the reviewer thought, Cibulka's diary sentences about "this not being a scientific era" and the "lack of a science of humankind" were

something like a death sentence for scientific socialism, which in the GDR is supposed to have ended exploitation of people by people. Cibulka is the first Alternative, the first Green in the GDR.

Another Cibulka diary entry cited in the review concerned the absence of adequate aid to the dying (*Sterbehilfe*), which the Reuters journalist assessed this way:

Thereby, for the first time in the GDR where the human being officially is the center of life, hard questions were asked about humanism. Ideological claims and the reality of political propaganda are not treated only as air. Cibulka condemns the burden of their 'Hydra monster', the nationally-owned chemical industry.

In addition to Cibulka's "chemicalization of life" charge, his six-line diary comment regarding military stimulation of childhood aggression was also emphasized in the review. This took up two paragraphs which, without a break, also included the first five lines of a following 25-line poem, as if it were one prose diary entry. The lines of poetry said, "Fatherland, who today can still say, I, Pilate, wash my hands in innocence". (See 27 August entry in *Appendix A.*)

At this point the reviewer reported that according to "informed East Berlin circles" there had been controversy about Cibulka's writing "not only before publication" but also that "the controversy about the provocative text continues". Going on with the text, the reviewer then in prose form quoted some of the remaining lines of the "Fatherland" poem -- "Countless are the apples of temptation. But this is my land, no theory that only the state holds in its hands. Others speak of leaving, I remain. I know...life, remains that which is always to be mentioned - earth, water, air" -- and concludes

The situation in the GDR and that of the people who live there is, thus, attacked at a level which itself would be very difficult to attack. Cibulka skips over the demand for more human rights and more political freedoms. Nevertheless, the GDR leadership suddenly sees itself subjected to a political criticism that goes to the roots. How difficult is is for them to suspect this Alternative, this Green, of anti-socialism in order to deprive him from the beginning of every following, is shown by the fact that the literary diary could appear in an official GDR organ.[189]

According to other "informed circles" in the GDR there is a version of events which differs from that reported by the Reuters correspondent: After the openly published ecological discussion between Kunert and Girnus in *Sinn und Form*, Cibulka's contribution to the same subject in *NDL* was seen as part of the continuing dialkogue about an important issue, that is, ecology.

Problems began after the West German newspaper reviews were, in turn, reported back to the GDR via West German radio.[190] That Western publicity about Cibulka's article came to the attention of the GDR Ministry of Economics, and Cibulka first learned indirectly that there was irritation (*Ärger*) about his writing. Disturbed by the author's publicized criticism of the nuclear power industry, economic specialists protested to the Ministry of Culture which, in turn, contacted the publisher.

In a discussion among the director and chief editor of the publishing house and the author, it was agreed to omit from the pending book those paragraphs about atomic energy which were quoted from US and USSR sources. Other changes were made for stylistic reasons or on the basis of what the author had additionally learned about his subject matter. The publishing house approved this version, as did the Ministry, and the technical work of printing the first pressrun of 20,000 copies went ahead in the Mitteldeutscher Verlag in Halle.

Meanwhile some public figures in the GDR published initial assessments of the excerpt. For instance, ten months after the *NDL* publication, Hermann Ley, Humboldt University professor of philosophy concerned with problems of modern natural science, reacted in print. In an article in the *Deutsche Zeitschrift für Philosophie*,[191] he took several other writers along with Cibulka to task. Ley said Cibulka's literary criticism of science and progress resulted from the author's "guilt complexes", "resentment", "'Oh, man!' feeling", "deformation of socialist consciousness", "self-pity", "naiveness", "resignation", etc. In short, "confusion festers in him".

In addition, Ley's article contained many of the objections repeatedly leveled at the GDR's progress-doubters. For instance, conceding that literary writing surely was not the same as social science studies, Ley asked in the first paragraph of his article why GDR writers, nevertheless, embraced positions characteristic of capitalist writing. Named as examples were Jurij Brězan, Inge von Wangenheim, and Hanns Cibulka. To Ley, a leading SED philosopher, it was incomprehensible that

> *socialist literature could not more often come up with the idea of examining the contradictory economic growth question within the context of the class struggle to assimilate the scientific-technological revolution.*

At the same time, Ley pointed out that some authors had been able to understand what was going on in modern technology and to present it understandably to readers -- for instance, Dieter Noll, Erwin Strittmatter, Hermann Kant, Peter Hacks, Alfred Wellm, Anna Seghers, Johannes R. Becher, Bruno Apitz, and Georg Maurer.

Cibulka, on the other hand, despite an admirable writing style, had serious shortcomings, in Ley's opinion. These included (1) failure to differentiate between East/West systemic contexts of environmental problems, (2) praise of the simple past without recognition that environmental pollution existed then, too, (3) lack of general and specific knowledge of global ecological problems and, instead, allocation of all guilt to a single discipline, i.e., medicine,[192] (4) neglect of the fact that the solution of one problem would, of course, produce others, (5) incomplete understanding of human behavior's complexity and the difference of socialization under socialism, (6) substitution of ecology for the international power question relating to class struggle and socialist revolution, and (7) succumbing to old conservative and reformist concepts of bourgeoise ideology ("What socialist practice of art does not have to take on is indicated in the function of the capitalist mass media").

In the same month that these specific critiques of Cibulka and other writers were published by Ley, the GDR's Deputy Minister for Culture, Klaus Höpcke, also went on record with *general* ideas about the current literary scene in the GDR. In the SED's official theoretical journal *Einheit*, Höpcke touched on some of the same issues raised by Ley.[193]

Proceeding from the premise that GDR literature "often takes on questions which at the present time move us greatly", the culture minister praised those authors who wrote about themes of (1) peace, (2) fascism, (3) the GDR's social development, (4) the worth of human beings and their position in society, (5) the relationship of freedom and responsibility in socialism, and (6) the individual's possibilities for realizing his/her "claim to happiness" in socialism. Then turning to "books in which a key-note of pessimism is sounded", Höpcke said that such works (names were not mentioned) fell short because they suggested humanity would not be able to achieve its "claim on happiness" and they ignored the role of the workers.

What was specifically missing in some GDR literature, wrote Höpcke, was an "orientation to reality" (*Wirklichkeitsnähe*) and a "truth of reality" (*Wirklichkeitswahrheit*), i.e., how the author "pushes forward to the essence of the phenomenon, how he discloses that essence from the viewpoint of socialist world change and makes it artistically experiential". The basic concept which some authors were forgetting was that "development proceeds in contradictions, and concepts of a situation without contradictions are

67

undialectical and not reflective of our world view". What was wished instead, in Höpcke's view, was "socialism-supportive critique...a criticism of inhibitions which harm the forward movement of socialism" but not "criticism of real socialism, uttered in the name of bourgeoise values and individualistic personal concepts, that is, anarchistic anti-order concepts."[194] Thus Höpcke, registering a general "establishment" literary critique against "pessimistic" writers, obliquely commented on Cibulka's overall challenge to progress.

Additional scholars took up and disagreed with other concepts reflected in Cibulka's work (though not citing it). For instance, Rudolf Woderich, publishing several months after Cibulka's excerpt, seemed to represent a wide-spread social science critique of literature's inability to see positive potential in technology and to recognize the essential relationship between increased production and improved standards of living which the literati were demanding.[195] Charging that the urgency of qualitative increases in production were "still not understood correctly" by "cultural practioners", Woderich was upset because the rationality of industrial production was "repeatedly the object of culturally critical attacks." Relying heavily on Soviet citations, Woderich underlined his charge that GDR cultural offerings continued to be permeated basically by pre-industrial ideals. In short, what was needed was a new aesthetic of industrial design. After all, the GDR's present culture rested on an industrial basis for which pre-industrial aesthetics were inadequate.

Despite the broadening discussion of the nature of "progress", which many writers probably applauded, it simply seemed to "turn off" others. Christa Wolf, for instance, may have been expressing that view when in 1982 she tartly wrote that with their "faster, better, and more" the industrial societies had subordinated "all other values to this 'value' of effectiveness...which has forced the mass of people into an unreal, illusory life and which has especially enlisted the natural scientists."[196]

Other more concrete public reactions also seemed related to Cibulka's concepts. For instance, of almost dramatic significance after publication of the *Swantow* excerpts was a 1982 church meeting in Magdeburg which discussed the security problem of atomic energy plants.[197] As noted, Cibulka had written extensively in his diary about this, and probably the word had gotten around somewhat that he was to omit these passages in the pending book version. Thus it was significant that GDR atomic scientists came to the Magdeburg meeting to explain the GDR's plans for expansion of nuclear energy facilities. Moreover, the place of the meeting was also newsworthy because, after being taboo for years, the theme of GDR nuclear energy plants had been addressed publically for the first time at a *church* meeting -- that had been in 1979 in Mecklenburg.[198]

Coincidentally, or perhaps "symbolically" since publication of Cibulka's book was pending, the distribution of the issue of *Der Parteiarbeiter* referred to earlier (p. 15) came about this time. Its guidelines for "cultural processes" in factories said,

> *Naturally the party functionary, if he wants to be informed in his discussions...must develop his own artistic understanding, must read, must take a position in discussions about the newest television film, a controversial book, a painting. (Emphasis -- AM)*

4. *Swantow*: The Revised Book Version (1982)

Published by the Mitteldeutscher Verlag of Halle/Leipzig in November 1982, *Swantow* by Hanns Cibulka appeared in a "Small Edition", about 4 x 7 inches in size. The white dust jacket of the slim 144-page volume was enhanced by a drawing of sea gulls flying over water and cliffs.[199] The first pressrun of 20,000 reportedly was sold out in three days.

Two tone-setting quotations from classical writers introduced the book. Both contained references to symbolism, one from Goethe and the second from Hofmannsthal.[200] And, indeed, as will be seen, Cibulka relied heavily on symbolism to make his prose points, sometimes telling the reader what the symbolism was but frequently also leaving relationships to the reader's imagination.

An example of the latter perhaps was the symbolic roles of the five people presented in the diary -- the writer Andreas (who thinks that "perhaps Swantow is nothing more than a renewed attempt to find a clue to hidden truths of life"), Andreas' woman friend Liv, through whom the truth seeking writer finds many answers, Pastor Krüger who focuses some of Andreas' spiritual searching, the minister's ingenuous wife Frau Krüger who offers uncompromising moral answers couched as "rule over one's self, duty, conscience", and Frau Krüger's brother, "the Doctor", whose natural science insights shed light on Andreas' ecological queries.

In the book-length version of *Swantow*, Cibulka's first major reference to these problems concerned the nuclear energy plant at Lubmin, south of the island Rügen, near Greifswald -- "Everything is quiet in a nuclear energy plant, deathly still", he wrote, "the energy is produced noiselessly."[201] This reference appeared as early as the fourth entry in the diary, 30 June. It was followed by a paragraph introduced as "reading material" (*Lektüre*). This paragraph quoted an unnamed source's discussion of radioactivity and a list of half-life rates, i.e., the time required for half of the atoms in a radioactive substance to disintegrate. Included were Iodine-120 with "1.7 million years" and Plutonium-239 with "24,000 years".[202] (This entry had not been in the *NDL* excerpt.)

69

In the diary several weeks passed before Cibulka returned to ecological issues. On 18 July, then,[203] he inserted into the diary the poem included in the excerpt, with its description of rockets and the observation that they bind "death and life in inseparble proximity" (see p.61). In the very next entry, 19 July, Cibulka announced progress in his search for truth: "suddenly one sees nature's small, insignificant-appearing creatures with other eyes."[204] And a week later he presented a bit of his "truth" via the symbolism of the wasp nest hanging inside his vacation cottage, near the front door -- "the wasps taught me anew the love for nature". What Cibulka specifically learned is found in his report of Frau Krüger's reaction to the author's lack of concern about the wasps. When she says, "You are living in ignorance of the danger", the author repeats her warning, "We live in ignorance of danger", pauses, and then adds "exactly that is the word." With this ambiguous "the word", Cibulka leaves it to the reader whether "danger" in nature is meant or "ignorance" of it.[205]

Having thus step-by-step developed his own ecological/moral concerns, Cibulka came to 3 August. In the original *NDL* version, this day's diary entry contained a major statement about atomic energy plants -- the critical quotation about the danger of radio activity (see p. 62). As noted, in the discussion between Cibulka and his publishers, it was agreed to omit that segment (probably the 'US source', see p. 66). In its place Cibulka inserted a brief reference to biological pollution of a Polish bay.[206]

Below and continuing on the next page are the 3 August entries. On the left is the original text as it appeared in the 1981 *NDL* excerpt, with those sentences later omitted underscored with a broken line; to the right is the parallel material from the revised 1982 book version with its newly introduced sentences solidly underlined:

Ein Gedanke, der mich seit Tagen beschäftigt: der Kuppelbau bei den Atomkraftwerken.
Es gibt für die Kuppel keine technische Notwendigkeit. Vielleicht ist es eine Erinnerung an die Kohlenmeiler des Waldes, an die alten Kuppelgräber. Solche Zeichen kommen von weit, reichen tief, sind immer das Ergebnis einer umfassenderen Anschauung. In solchen Formen können sich aber auch uralte Tabus andeuten. Daten und Namen kann man löschen, Formen tauchen immer wieder auf, geben dem Menschen zu denken. Es scheint, als umschließe auch heute noch der Rundbau, die Kuppel aus meterdickem Beton, ein Geheimnis, ein bedenkliches Geheimnis.

„... Im Normalbetrieb gibt ein Atomkraftwerk ständig Radionuklide an die Umwelt ab. Bei einem mittleren Atomkraftwerk werden jährlich 80 000 Ci über den Kamin in die Umgebung abgeblasen. Ein großer Anteil dieser Radionuklide ist das Krypton-89 mit einer hohen Halbwertzeit. Wenn jedes Jahr die

70

gleiche Menge Krypton-89 in die Umwelt gelangt, steigt die Strahlenbelastung ständig an, denn das Krypton vom Vorjahr ist immer noch vorhanden und nur zu einem winzigen Teil zerfallen.

Über das Abwasser wird ebenfalls eine Vielzahl radioaktiver Substanzen abgelassen. Von einigen Nukliden weiß man bereits heute, wie gefährlich sie sind.

Im Normalbetrieb eines Atomkraftwerkes wird die Bevölkerung vor allen Dingen mit Strahlen im niedrigen Dosisbereich belastet. Diese Strahlung führt zu einer unspezifischen Störung der Normalordnung des Chemismus und in den Strukturen der betroffenen Zellen. Strahlengeschädigte Zellen, die sich weiter vermehren, zeigen erst nach vielen Zellgenerationen einen sichtbaren Schaden. Der zeitliche Abstand zwischen der Bestrahlung und dem sichtbaren Schaden kann viele Jahre betragen. Bei Erbschäden beträgt die Latenzzeit oft mehrere Generationen.

Inkorporierte Alpha- und Beta-Strahlen können meßtechnisch nicht erfaßt werden, da ihre Strahlung wegen der geringen Durchdringungsfähigkeit im biologischen Gewebe nicht bis zur Oberfläche des Körpers durchdringt. Zum Beispiel kann Strontium völlig unbemerkt vom Organismus aufgenommen und gespeichert werden. Es gibt praktisch keine Möglichkeit, seine Existenz im lebenden Körper festzustellen und nachzuweisen. Die Verseuchung erfolgt im meßtechnischen Dunkel. Falsch ist der Schluß: Was ich nicht messen kann, ist ungefährlich."

39

Merkwürdig: die wahren Hintergründe der Dinge leuchten für mich immer erst dann auf, wenn ich über sie schreibe.

Wäre es denkbar, daß der Mensch eines Tages nur noch die abstrakte Sprache der Wissenschaft versteht, das bezifferte Programm, und nicht mehr die Sprache der Poesie?

Zbignew hat geschrieben, sagt Liv. Sie reicht mir durch das Fenster den Brief.

Ich öffne den Umschlag. Eine bedenkliche Nachricht, sage ich, die Gdansker Bucht ist biologisch umgekippt. Die polnische Regierung hat das Baden verboten, auch das Betreten des Strandes ist untersagt.

Das kann doch nicht wahr sein, sagt Liv.

Zbignew ist vor Ort gewesen. Er schreibt, daß auch die Buchten von Szczecin und Lübeck durch Eutrophierung bedroht sind. Lies selbst.

63

Nach dem Lesen des Briefes sagt Liv: Die Natur schlägt zurück, wer weiß, wie lange wir an der Ostküste unserer Insel noch baden können.

Merkwürdig: die wahren Hintergründe der Dinge leuchten für mich immer erst dann auf, wenn ich über sie schreibe.

Wäre es denkbar, daß der Mensch eines Tages nur noch die abstrakte Sprache der Wissenschaft versteht, das bezifferte Programm, und nicht mehr die Sprache der Poesie?

The diary entry for 6 August,[207] coming just a few days later, included a firm statement about the writer's responsibility to truth, illustrated through the symbolism of the paper he uses to record his thoughts:

> *Does it suffice if we always write only up to the margin of the page? To leave the white page behind, to write over into the margin, to also make the unarticulated audible. In the unarticulated, the terribleness, the intolerable of our times is consummated.*

In the original excerpted version of this entry, however (see pp. 62-63), two lengthy paragraphs, introduced as "Further into reading material on 'nuclear energy plants'", had followed. They presented an unnamed source's uncritical assessment of dangers to the environment from operating nuclear energy plants (possibly the 'Soviet source' referred to in the negotiations over content, as discussed on p. 66). Those paragraphs were omitted from the final book version and replaced with two conceptually suggestive sentences:

> *Whoever wants to write must be part of his time but also must have the strength, if necesary, to live against his times.*

> *Perhaps Swantow is nothing more than a renewed attempt to track down concealed truths of life.*

On the following pages, then, are the original paragraphs of the 6 August entry (left) and the revised book version (right), with broken underlines indicating sentences omitted and solid underlines showing those added·

Genügt es, wenn wir immer nur bis an den Rand des Blattes schreiben? Das weiße Blatt hinter sich lassen, über den Rand hinaus schreiben, auch das gesagte hörbar machen. Im Ungesagten vollzieht sich das Schreckliche, das Unerträgliche unserer Zeit.

45

Weiter in der Lektüre „Kernkraftwerke". Die Verfasserin spricht von einer vollkommenen Gefahrlosigkeit der in Betrieb befindlichen Kernkraftwerke für ihre Umgebung. Sie schreibt: „Die völlige Ausschaltung des schädlichen Einflusses auf die Umgebung erfordert bei der Projektierung, beim Bau und Betrieb Maßnahmen, die schwere Havarien, bei denen Spaltprodukte nach außen gelangen, sicher ausschließen, bzw. Maßnahmen, die eine radioaktive Verseuchung der Umgebung verhindern. Der Mangel an Betriebserfahrungen führte u. a. dazu, daß ein Mindestabstand der Kernkraftwerke zu großen Ortschaften festgelegt wurde. Daher gibt es in den Projektierungsvorschriften aller Länder Normen für die Mindestentfernung der Kernkraftwerke von großen Ortschaften. In der UdSSR war dies anfangs auf minimal 35 km festgelegt worden. Das hat insbesondere auch die Entwicklung der Kernkraftwerke als reine Kondensationskraftwerke und nicht als Heizkraftwerke bestimmt.

Eine lange und gründliche Kontrolle des Luftraumes in der Umgebung von Kraftwerken auf schädliche Auswürfe hat einerseits die vollkommene Gefahrlosigkeit der in Betrieb befindlichen Kernkraftwerke für ihre Umgebung sowie die Wirksamkeit der oben erwähnten Maßnahmen gezeigt und andererseits für die Gesundheit bedeutend schädlichere Auswirkungen durch Wärmekraftwerke mit fossilen Brennstoffen nachgewiesen, insbesondere bei ascherreichen festen Brennstoffen und – in noch höherem Maße – bei Kohle und Erdöl mit hohem Schwefelgehalt."

46

73

Genügt es, wenn wir immer nur bis an den Rand des Blattes schreiben? Das weiße Blatt Papier hinter sich lassen, über den Rand hinausschreiben, auch das Ungesagte hörbar machen. Im Ungesagten vollzieht sich das Schreckliche, das Unerträgliche unserer Zeit.

Wer schreiben will, muß in seiner Zeit stehen, er

74

muß aber auch die Kraft haben, wenn es not tut, gegen sie zu leben.

Vielleicht ist Swantow nichts anderes als der erneute Versuch, den verborgenen Wahrheiten des Lebens auf die Spur zu kommen.

The next diary entry concerning ecological problems was dated 11 August.[208] It began with the description of the small airplane spraying farm fields and the poem about nucler energy plants measuring the land "by the fathom cord of death" which had been part of the excerpt (see pp. 63-64). However, much else had been omitted and added.

First of all in the revised book version, the account of the deformed fish which had so impressed Cibulka (see p. 60) was added after the poem, as well as a lengthy protest against water pollution including primarily Western examples. "For decades," Cibulka wrote, "people have dumped industrial and urban wastes directly into the oceans". Contaminated coastal areas he cited were those of the United States, Sicily, Japan, Norway, and Canada, along with lakes in Switzerland, Hungary, and West Germany.

Next the "chemicalization of life" criticism was presented, but without the earlier "Hydra monster" description of the chemical industry. Instead, there were these new thoughts:

I know very well what advantages chemistry has brought humankind in the last hundred years, but I also see the Janus face of the chemical industry. Unforseen side effects appear, chemical poisons are introduced into the food chain; even in the fat of Arctic seals, in the plankton of oceans, 10 ppm of DDT were found. The nitrate concentration in vegetables increases, hemoglobin changes appear, environmental poisons in mothers' milk, cancer-causing substances even in the blood of newborn children. The biological structure of humans, the nervous system is simply not capable of adapting to changed environmental conditions.

The next sentence was the original thought about "over-filled waiting rooms", but without the initial specific reference to "polyclinics". Added was the information that, "The breakdown of the biological process in human cells is already indicated in several cities in the USA". And, continuing on with the initial description of physicians as an "army of specialists" confronting patients, Cibulka now wrote that they represented "a clinical ecology."

Gone altogether from the book text was Cibulka's initial charge that "there is no science of human beings" and that "progress in medicine leads primarily to the scalpel and operating table". Added was the idea that "Environmental pollution kills without knife, bullet, it needs no ax, no concussion, it has its own methods to end life without sting, without venomous tongue".

Thus, clearly, several significant themes of the original version of *Swantow*, which had been commented on in the Western

newspaper review, had been omitted in the book revision -- Cibulka's disbelief in "a scientific age" and his contention that there
was no "science of humankind which finally asks how humans should
live and work". Omission of both these themes seemed to reflect
the author's intellectual reconsideration of his earlier views and
of the reactions to them, i.e., (a) GDR criticism of writers who
in their ecological discussions water down or ignore basic principles of Marxism/Leninism regarding science and social progress, as
well as the nature of humankind and society and (b) Western criticism which saw such an approach as anti-systemic critique.

In addition, a third omitted theme that had figured prominently in the original excerpt was Cibulka's attack on medical
practices. As noted earlier, it had been featured in the Western
newspaper account and also had drawn angry protest from Hermann
Ley. Not surprisingly perhaps, in the revised version of *Swantow*
much of the responsibility for illnesses then was assigned individual life styles. Also perhaps not astonishing, in the context
of "establishment" critique of the excerpt, was omission in the
final book version of Cibulka's pointed question, "Which poli-
tician today still speaks of the power found in self-denial?"

The following pages show the significant editing of the original 11 August diary entry (left) and the revised book version
(right). As previously, broken underlining indicates omissions
and solid underlining additions:

. . . .

MIT der Klafter des Todes
vermessen
die Schnellen Brüter
das Land.

Im Wasserbett
Kernstäbe,
Primärkreislauf,
abgeblasen
über den Kamin
die Radionuklide.
Der Mensch
im Strahlengeviert.
In den Abwässern
staut sich die
Schuld.

Sind wir nicht auf dem besten Weg, die grundlegenden Gesetze der Natur und
das Zusammenwirken aller Dinge zu mißachten?

48

Der Mensch
im Strahlengeviert.

Im Abwasser
staut sich die
Schuld.

Der Doktor hat uns gestern einen Fisch gezeigt, den man unweit von Zudar gefangen hat. Seine Rückenflosse war verkrüppelt, an der Bauchseite hatte er ein Karzinom.

Sind wir nicht auf dem besten Weg, die grundlegenden Gesetze der Natur und das Zusammenwirken aller Dinge zu mißachten? Seit Jahrzehnten schütten die Menschen die Abfälle der Industrie und der Städte direkt in das Meer. Die Weltmeere werden angereichert mit radioaktiven Substanzen, Schwermetallen und Chemikalien, mit organischen Lösungsmitteln, Spurenelementen, chemischen Kampfstoffen, aber auch mit Detergenzien und Insektiziden. Die halbe Weltproduktion an Quecksilber erreicht heute den Ozean. An den Küsten der USA werden selbst Fässer mit radioaktivem Müll, eingegossen in Beton, Stahlbehälter mit Nervengas und Gelbkreuz im Ozean versenkt. In jedem Liter Meereswasser, ganz gleich wo wir ihn schöpfen, an den Küsten Siziliens oder in Japan, in einem norwegischen Fjord oder in Kanada, überall finden wir meßbare Mengen von

Unsere Krankheiten wachsen in dem Maße, in dem die Chemisierung des Lebens zunimmt. Wir zahlen bereits heute einen viel zu hohen Preis für unser zweifelhaftes Wohlleben. Aus den bescheidenen Anfängen der Chemie ist ein hydraköpfiges Ungeheuer geworden; künstliche Düngemittel, Herbizide, Ver-

Radioaktivität, die vom Menschen erzeugt wurde. Aber auch die Gase, die die Industrie Tag für Tag in den Himmel bläst, fallen zusammen mit dem Regen ins Meer. Der Bleigehalt der Luft hat sich in den letzten zehn Jahren verdoppelt. Die Menschen setzen das Meer dem Einfluß unberechenbarer Substanzen aus; aus dem Hinterhalt treffen sie das Leben.

Kein Wunder, wenn eines Tages das Meer zu revoltieren beginnt. Haben wir vergessen, daß auch die Flüsse und Seen atmen und leben? Aber ihre Wasser riechen schon lange nicht mehr nach Wasser, ich kenne Flüsse, die stinken wie eine Abdeckerei; der Zürichsee, der Balaton, aber auch der Tegernsee sind lange schon tot oder am Sterben. Wer heute auf die Selbstreinigung der Gewässer hofft, ist ein Narr. Eines Tages wird uns das Meer seinen blinden Spiegel entgegenhalten, aber dann wird es zu spät sein. Die Schreie der Menschen werden ungehört an den Küsten verhallen. Das Meer wird der Schauplatz unserer künftigen Katastrophen sein. Ist das moralische Gewissen der Menschen wirklich am Zerfallen?

Wir zahlen bereits heute einen viel zu hohen Preis für unser zweifelhaftes Wohlleben. Ich weiß sehr gut, welche Vorteile die Chemie in den letzten hundert Jahren den Menschen gebracht hat, ich sehe aber auch den Januskopf der chemischen Industrie. Unvorhergesehene Nebeneffekte treten auf, chemische Gifte werden in die Nahrungskette eingeschleust; selbst im Fett arktischer Seehunde, im Plankton der Weltmeere wurden 10 ppm DDT nachgewiesen. Die Nitratkonzentration im Gemüse nimmt zu, Hämoglobin-

giftungen der Luft und der Gewässer, radioaktiver Niederschlag, und das alles soll sich auf die Gesundheit eines Menschen nicht auswirken? Die Wartezimmer in den Polikliniken sind überfüllt, die Legion der Ärzte wird immer größer, der Mensch immer anfälliger, bald werden wir nur noch einer Armee von Spezialisten gegenüberstehen, der Hausarzt, wie ich ihn aus meiner Kindheit noch kenne, ist zur Legende geworden.

48

Die Massenmedien wollen uns glauben machen, wir hätten ein wissenschaftliches Zeitalter; wir haben es nicht. Was uns bis heute fehlt, ist die Wissenschaft vom Menschen, die endlich einmal danach fragt, wie der Mensch leben und arbeiten soll, was zu einem menschenwürdigen Dasein überhaupt notwendig ist. Wie wäre es sonst möglich, daß ein Drittel der Menschheit krank ist, nicht nur physisch. Wir leben, wie die Blinden unter den Blinden, gehen ins Krankenhaus, um uns heilen zu lassen, hoffen auf Heilung, sehen aber nicht, daß auch die Medizin bereits am Stock geht. Der Fortschritt der Medizin führt heute vorwiegend über den Operationstisch, über das Messer. Wir leben in einem unsichtbaren Schützengraben, von allen Seiten liegen wir unter Beschuß: Wasser, Luft, Ernährung, Strahlungsfelder.

Bei unserem gestrigen Spaziergang sagte mir der Doktor: Wir brauchen keine neuen Operationssäle, keine neuen radiologischen Kliniken, was uns not tut, ist eine gesunde Lebensführung nach innen und nach außen. Die Mehrzahl der Krankheiten, an denen wir heute leiden, sind das Ergebnis unserer Lebensweise, unserer Umwelt. Bereits hier müßte der Kampf der Mediziner beginnen und nicht erst am Operationstisch. Eine Vielzahl von Krankheiten haben wir uns in den letzten Jahrzehnten selbst in die Welt gesetzt, sie sind das Ergebnis unserer Lebenssucht. Der Mensch hat sich selbst versklavt.

„Du mußt dein Leben ändern" – heißt das nicht auch, sein Bewußtsein ändern, den Kampf gegen sich selber aufnehmen, unnachgiebig sein, ohne Konzession?

veränderungen treten auf, Umweltgifte in der Muttermilch, krebsfördernde Stoffe selbst schon im Blut neugeborener Kinder. Die biologische Struktur des Menschen, sein Nervensystem ist gar nicht in der Lage, sich so schnell auf die veränderten Umweltbedingungen einzustellen. Die Wartezimmer sind überfüllt, die Legion der Ärzte wird immer größer, der Mensch immer anfälliger. Der Zusammenbruch der biologischen Prozesse in den menschlichen Zellen deutet sich in einigen Städten der USA heute schon an. Bald werden wir nur noch einer Armee von Spezialisten gegenüberstehen, einer klinischen Ökologie, der Hausarzt, wie ich ihn aus meiner Kindheit kenne, scheint Legende geworden. Die Menschen leben in einem unsichtbaren Schützengraben, von allen Seiten liegen sie unter Beschuß. Die Umweltverschmutzung tötet ohne Messer, ohne Kugel, sie braucht keine Axt, keinen Schädelbruch, sie hat ihre eigene Methode, Leben umzubringen, ohne Strachel, ohne Giftzahn.

Bei unserem gestrigen Spaziergang sagte mir der Doktor: Wir brauchen keine neuen Operationssäle, keine neuen radiologischen Kliniken, was uns not tut, ist eine gesunde Lebensführung nach innen und nach außen. Die Mehrzahl der Krankheiten, an denen wir heute leiden, sind das Ergebnis unserer Lebensweise, unserer Umwelt. Hier beginnt der Kampf der Mediziner, nicht erst am Operationstisch.

»Du mußt dein Leben ändern« – heißt das nicht auch: sein Bewußtsein ändern, den Kampf gegen sich selbst aufnehmen, unnachgiebig sein, ohne Konzes-

Warum haben wir nicht den Mut, uns gegen die eigenen Lebensgewohnheiten zu stellen? Die Natur hat gar nicht mehr die Kraft, all das zu erneuern, was wir täglich in uns und in unserer Umwelt zerstören. Der Mensch mordet sich selbst, allerdings ist es ein Mord auf Zeit.

Wie oft schon hat man uns gesagt, daß sich das Wissen in den letzten dreißig Jahren nicht nur verdoppelt, daß es sich auf verschiedenen Gebieten verzehnfacht habe. Was aber haben wir mit diesem Wissen angefangen? An unserer inneren Front haben wir Waffenstillstand geschlossen, verstopfen uns die Ohren, machen kleine schlaue Umwege vor uns selbst, doch die Wahrheit können wir auf die Dauer nicht vor uns her schieben.

Es ist und bleibt die Aufgabe des Menschen, dem Wunder Leben gerecht zu werden, dafür zu sorgen, daß es im Wunder bleibt und nicht dahinsiecht. Was haben wir durch unsere egoistische Lebensweise nicht alles schon zugeschüttet? Die schwierigste aller Revolutionen steht uns immer noch bevor: die Revolution gegenüber uns selbst, gegen unsere eigene Trägheit, den Egoismus, den Machtinstinkt, eine Revolution, die uns lehrt, ganz anders über den Menschen zu denken als bisher.

49

Die Wahrheit ist den Menschen nicht nur zumutbar, sie ist bereits heute Voraussetzung für seine weitere Existenz.

Welcher Politiker spricht heute noch über die Kraft, die im Verzicht liegt?

sion? Wann werden wir den Mut aufbringen, uns gegen die eigenen Lebensgewohnheiten zu stellen? Die Natur hat gar nicht mehr die Kraft, all das zu erneuern, was wir täglich in uns und in unserer Umwelt zerstören. Der Mensch mordet sich selbst, allerdings ist es ein Mord auf Zeit.

Wie oft hat man uns schon gesagt, daß sich das Wissen in den letzten dreißig Jahren nicht nur verdoppelt, daß es sich auf verschiedenen Gebieten verzehnfacht habe. Was aber haben wir mit diesem Wissen angefangen? Haben wir an unserer inneren Front Waffenstillstand geschlossen? Wir verstopfen uns die Ohren, machen kleine schlaue Umwege vor uns selbst, doch die Tatsachen können wir auf die Dauer nicht vor uns herschieben. Der Mensch ist für sein Denken und Tun voll verantwortlich. Keine Regierung, kein Volk, auch nicht der Einzelne kann sich aus dieser Verantwortung entlassen.

Es ist und bleibt die Aufgabe des Menschen, dem Leben gerecht zu werden, dafür zu sorgen, daß es ein Wunder bleibt und nicht dahinsiecht. Was haben wir mit unserer egoistischen Lebensweise nicht schon alles zugeschüttet? Die schwierigste aller Aufgaben steht uns immer noch bevor: die Revolution gegenüber uns selbst, gegen unsere eigene Trägheit, den Egoismus, das Machtdenken, eine Revolution, die uns lehrt, ganz anders über den Menschen zu denken als bisher.

Die Wahrheit ist den Menschen nicht nur zumutbar, sie ist bereits heute die Voraussetzung für seine weitere Existenz.

The 27 August diary entry was another with significant changes. Originally it also included an idea highlighted in the Western press review and strenuously objected to by Hermann Ley--unconscious influence of weapons on the aggressiveness of children (see p. 64). In the revised version,[209] precisely that one-sentence contention about children was omitted. Instead, three paragraphs appeared criticizing U.S. military policy and discussing the relationship between the costs of correcting environmental pollution and monies spent on armaments:

> From year to year the environmental burden in the world increases. Industrial states need billions to restore ecological balance; the United States of America, however, is on the way to a new, high level of armaments.
>
> The destructive capacities of modern weapons have taken on shocking dimensions. In World War II the biggest bomb had a detonation force of ten tons of TNT, the atomic bomb of Hiroshima a magnitude of 13,000 tons, the current atomic warheads possess an incomprehensible destructive power of 25 million tons of TNT.
>
> Is humankind on the precipice of its destruction? For the totality of life we will have to take up anew the struggle for universal disarmament in all countries of the world so that life again becomes a gift which one accepts with complete joy and does not pass on to one's children with misgivings.

As noted, in the 1980s discussion this ecology/peace relationship had become a major argument in defense of the GDR's environmental protection policies.

On the next page, then, are the two versions of the 27 August diary entry, with the original on the left and the revision on the right:

Das archaische Landschaftsbild ist auch auf Rügen im Verblassen. Metallene Riesenvögel ziehen durch die Luft, Kampfhubschrauber fliegen in Kirchturmhöhe über das Land, vor der Küste liegen die Zerstörer. Die inneren Spannungen, die eine solche Umwelt auslöst, gehen an keinem Menschen spurlos vorbei, sie übertragen sich auf sein Denken, Fühlen und Handeln.

Von Jahr zu Jahr nimmt die Umweltbelastung in der Welt zu. Die Industriestaaten benötigten Milliarden, um das ökologische Gleichgewicht wiederherzustellen; die Vereinigten Staaten von Amerika aber sind auf dem Weg zu einer neuen Hochrüstung.

Die Vernichtungskapazität der modernen Waffen hat erschreckende Dimensionen angenommen. Im zweiten Weltkrieg hatte die stärkste Bombe eine Sprengkraft von zehn Tonnen TNT, die Atombombe von Hiroshima eine Größenordnung von dreizehntausend Tonnen, die atomaren Sprengköpfe von heute verfügen über die unvorstellbare Vernichtungskraft von fünfundzwanzig Millionen Tonnen TNT.

Steht die Menschheit vor ihrem eigenen Abgrund? Wir werden den Kampf um die Totalität des Lebens, um eine universelle Abrüstung in allen Ländern der Welt von neuem aufnehmen müssen, damit das Leben wieder zu einem Geschenk wird, das man voller Freude annimmt und nicht mit Bedenken an seine eigenen Kinder weitergibt.

Auch in dieser Nacht steht über Swantow ein Sternen-

27. August

Das archaische Landschaftsbild ist auch auf Rügen im Verblassen. Metallene Riesenvögel ziehen durch die Luft, Kampfhubschrauber fliegen in Kirchturmhöhe über das Land, vor der Küste liegen die Zerstörer. Die eine solche Umwelt auslöst, geht an keinem Menschen spurlos vorbei, sie überträgt sich auf sein Denken, Fühlen, Handeln, schon im Unterbewußtsein der Kinder setzen sich diese Spannungselemente fest, schlagen um in Aggressivität.

Auch in dieser Nacht steht über Swantow ein Sternenhimmel, der seit vielen tausend Jahren zu unseren Weisheiten, aber auch zu unseren Verbrechen gleichmäßig schweigt.

The entry of 28 August was interesting, too.[210] Cibulka had written about the artistic process and concluded that it might also include coincidental influences. The final sentence of those contemplations was brief -- "One dare not forget that even the clear heavens still have a veil." It was omitted, obviously not as a direct reference to environmental issues but perhaps because it was perceived to be a symbolic one.

Similarly, the two sentences replacing that thought about a writer's creative process may also be interpreted in different ways. Cibulka wrote in the final version that

> *Just the word coincidence alone expresses something else: Something comes your way in life that is more than you wanted. Perhaps that which comes our way is also law.*

One possible interpretation would be to hear Cibulka say that the moral obligation he felt to articulate ecological issues was binding on him (was law, or *Gesetz*) even though his discoveries of truth about the problem had not been planned but had come coinci- dentally to a sensitive writer contemplating his natural environment.

This change in the texts is shown in the comparison on the next page of the original (left) and the revised (right):

Meine Gedanken über das Schreiben sind nichts anderes als die Selbstbefragung eines Menschen. Ich bin kein Theoretiker.

Beim Schreiben eines Gedichtes gibt es für mich drei unterschiedliche Phasen:

Die intuitive Erfassung im geistigen Raum. Hier wird das Gedicht vorbereitet, umrissen, auf seine Weise fixiert. Nicht erst im Vers, bereits im vorsprachlichen Raum, wo das Formlose formhaft wird, begegnet man der Poesie.

Die gedankliche Konzentration. Man fühlt sich aus der Zeit herausgehoben, vergißt, daß man einen Körper hat, man geht nur noch den Gedanken nach, den Metaphern. In dieser Phase des Schreibens muß man seinen Gefühlen, seinen Erfahrungen die Härte und Dichte eines Kristalls geben. Aber auch ein undefinierbares Ordnungsprinzip hat seine Hand mit im Spiel.

Zu der dritten und letzten Phase würde ich den Unbestimmtheitsfaktor zählen. Ich könnte sagen: Der Schriftsteller muß bei seiner Arbeit auch dem Zufälligen gerecht werden.

Allein schon das Wort Zufall drückt im Kern etwas anderes aus: Da fällt dir im Leben etwas zu, das mehr ist als das Gewollte.

Vielleicht ist auch das, was uns im Leben zufällt, Gesetz.

Meine Gedanken über das Schreiben sind nichts anderes als die Selbstbefragung eines Menschen. Ich bin kein Theoretiker.

Beim Schreiben eines Gedichtes gibt es für mich drei unterschiedliche Phasen.

Die intuitive Erfassung im geistigen Raum. Hier wird das Gedicht vorbereitet, umrissen, auf seine Weise fixiert. Nicht erst im Vers, bereits im vorsprachlichen Raum, wo das Formlose formhaft wird, begegnet man der Poesie.

Die gedankliche Konzentration. Man fühlt sich aus der Zeit herausgehoben, vergißt, daß man einen Körper hat, man geht nur noch den Gedanken nach, den Metaphern. In dieser Phase des Schreibens muß man seinen Gefühlen, seinen Erfahrungen die Härte und Dichte eines Kristalls geben. Aber auch ein undefinierbares Ordnungsprinzip hat seine Hand mit im Spiel.

Zu der dritten und letzten Phase würde ich den Unbestimmtheitsfaktor zählen. Ich könnte auch sagen: Der Schriftsteller muß in seiner Arbeit auch dem Zufälligen gerecht werden. Man darf nicht vergessen, daß auch der klare Himmel noch einen Schleier hat.

Several other entries in the diary are worth noting because
they also contained salient aspects of Cibulka's critique of
science and its relationship to progress and humanity's well-
being. One of these entries contained the author's negative por-
trayal of medical doctors.[211] In some ways the 6 September depic-
tion (not included in the excerpt) was just as harsh in its implications as the omitted segment excerpt about the medical profession per se, which had irked Hermann Ley.

In the book pages, then, Cibulka portrayed an individual doctor exemplifying irresponsibility and presented him through Nurse
Liv's account about a doctor for whom she had worked. The lengthy
entry began when the vacationing Liv had to go to the city hospi-
tal to present herself at the personnel department. That evening
after supper she told Andreas the long story of her differences of
principle with the doctor who formerly was her superior, principles which had motivated her resignation from the job.

It all began, Liv related, when she recorded near-death experiences of a patient and passed them along to a psychologist
relative who, in turn, started the process of having the account
published. Liv's superior, the head doctor (Chefartzt), objected
because he perceived the account as criticism of his clinic, as
well as unscientific "fiction, mystification". Highlights of the
ensuing confrontation included this conversational exchange between them:

The Chefartzt says to Nurse Liv, "Did you ever even once
think about the fact that you are an employee of a state institution?...That obligates!" "Surely", she responds, "but it also is
an obligation to truth". "Our state has made an exemplary training available to you", the doctor continued, "Income possibilities
are good, it provides your daily bread." "Nevertheless", Liv
counters, "one cannot buy the attitudes of a person to some things
in life with bread or money".

Liv's story then ended with her willingness to leave her job
and the head doctor's acceptance of her resignation. Cibulka's
comment consisted of one sentence -- "I do not know any human
society in which there are not also elements of despotism".

Another reference in the book version of *Swantow* to responsibility for "truth" and to the illusion of progress came in the
entry of 9 September,[212] which had not been part of the excerpt.
After Andreas read aloud to Liv the poem he had been working on,
she warned him that people like a "technical director" and others
"in these circles" would react negatively to such texts. Andreas
insisted that was unimportant. When he sat at his desk, he said,
technical directors did not exist. Rather, as a writer his words
could have meaning only if he confronted the facts of life. To
which Liv replied,

*I know what you want to say with your verse: the views
of danger, the not-wanting-to-understand of many people,
unexpectedly we were all jolted out of our dreams of
progress....don't forget, a truth uttered at the wrong
time can also have dubious consequences for you. One is
suddenly a branded person whom others avoid.*

Assuring Liv that he was not as pessimistic as she, Andreas argued that there was movement forward, but that it all took much time
-- "In science, too, there are conceptual errors which cannot be
revised even after thousands of years".

And so perhaps with this sentence and others added in the
final version of *Swantow* to explain the responsibility and role of
writers, Cibulka put his experience with the revised text in perspective for sensitive readers.

5. Theoretical Limits of Critique

Assessing the official reactions to and discussions of concepts in Cibulka's excerpted *Swantow* text, as well as the revisions undertaken, some of the basic principles of Marxism/Leninism
which were to remain relatively untouched in the ecology/environ-
ment discussion now seemed clear (that is, there would be official
protest and criticism if they were denied or ignored.) By late
1982, they seemed to include these tenents and theories:

-- Social and economic progress *is* possible through science
   (the theory of "historically objective laws of scientific
   development").

-- Under socialism, science serves humankind and society (the
   dialetical interrelationship between production and science and the "scientific-technological revolution").

-- There is, indeed, a "science of humankind" which asks "how
   humans should live and work, what is essential to a human
   existence with dignity" (the theory of Marxist humanism);
   there is a science of dialectical materialism for relationships of humankind and society (Engels, "the science
   of real people and their historic development").

-- Despite ecological problems in socialism, capitalism is
   the greater exploiter of nature (the theory of "the historical progress of socialism" and the class struggle between the two world systems).

In addition, atomic energy, defined by the GDR as economically essential to its future economic development, apparently was largely
outside the realm of critique, too.

On the other hand, ecological criticisms which did not con-
tradict Marxist/Leninist fundamentals apparently were acceptable.
For instance, even if the belief in social and economic "progress
through science" was sanctified, one could question whether the
price of progress, in the sense of "well-being" or "standard of
living" had been too high.

Similarly, even if science generally, or fields of natural
science specifically, should not be condemned for having served
socialist society inadequately, individual scientists might, indeed, be taken to task for personal irresponsibility. In fact,
the absence of individual responsibility vis-a-vis environmental
protection was a favorite critique, as was the relationship between military defense costs vs the costs of desired improvements
in environmental protection.

In the accelerated discussion of the next several years, such
fundamental principles of Marxism/Leninism would be repeatedly re-
called and newly elaborated from many disciplinary points of view.
And even more significant, the list of "acceptable" environmental
critiques would expand.

In fact, after Cibulka's controversial and early contribution
to that debate, it might logically be suggested that the initial
excerpted version of *Swantow* was a "trial balloon" of the literary
community (editors of *Neue deutsche Literatur* plus the writer himself). Through its publication, they provoked reactions which
suggested clearer parameters for the spreading and intensifying
ecological debate. In this sense, Cibulka's search for "the hidden truths of life" through *Swantow* had perhaps not been without
success.

6. **Summary**

The writings of the sensitive, nature-oriented poet and
diarist Hanns Cibulka reflected and accelerated the 1980s ecological debate in the GDR. In his 1971 diary, *Sanddornzeit*, Cibulka
had signaled that he would use his message about the unity of art
and science to protect, warn, and remind "the conscience of the
world".

And so he did, in a controversial second dairy entitled
Swantow, first excerpted in *Neue deutsche Literatur* in April 1981.
It contained several entries very critical of existing environmental protection and expressed doubts about the "progress" of science and technology. Four of the excerpted diary's 20 entries
directly concerned environmental questions -- two about atomic
power plants and the effects of radiation, one regarding "the
chemicalization of life" and modern medical practice, and another
concerning socialization of aggression.

86

According to Western press reports, based on "informed East Berlin circles", there were controversies about the article in the GDR before and after its publication; according to other directly informed GDR sources, the controversy was a reaction to that Western media comment. Consequently, text changes were negotiated before the final book revision was published.

Meanwhile, an initial and major public comment on the *Swantow* excerpts came ten months after they appeared in *NDL*, from a natural scientist and philosophy professor. Hermann Ley did not accept Cibulka's "scientific pessimism" and certainly not his broadly-aimed critique of the natural sciences. Furthermore, if artists were going to write about science, Ley insisted, they jolly well should do their homework first. Equally unacceptable was Cibulka's failure to differentiate betweeen socialist and capitalist approaches to ecological problems.

The same month Deputy Minister of Culture, Klaus Höpcke, wrote about the GDR literary scene generally. Without mentioning writers by name, Höpcke criticized pessimistic books, thus referring obliquely to Cibulka's challenge to the concept of progress. Other articles of similar tone, dealing with various conceptual aspects of the *Swantow* critique but not directly with the excerpts, followed in literary and cultural journals. Especially significant, too, was a church meeting held in Magdeburg after publication of Cibulka's excerpts -- at it the security problems of atomic energy plants, a point severely criticized by Cibulka, was discussed with GDR atomic scientists.

After all of this, the book version of *Swantow* appeared from the Mitteldeutscher Verlag in Halle/Leipzig in November, 1982. Gone were Cibulka's initial discussions of atomic energy plants; included was a listing of the half-life rates of radioactive substances. References to air and water pollution now included exampleos from the West. Disbelief in science per se was omitted, as was the generalized criticism of the medical profession; appearing instead was a personalized story about the inadequacy of an individual doctor.

The public reactions to and discussions of Cibulka's excerpted *Swantow* suggested that ecological criticism was acceptable, and indeed could be quite pointed, if it did not deny or ignore basic Marxist/Leninist concepts of social and economic progress through science and of science serving people, not profit. As will be seen, this would also be the context for later reactions to and reviews of the book version of *Swantow*.

Thus, a suggestive question arises: Was the *NDL* excerpted version of *Swantow* a literary trial balloon testing those current parameters of the ongoing ecological debate and dialogue in the GDR?

Chapter IV

THE ECOLOGICAL DEBATE FEEDBACK: 1983-1986

In the years following publication of Hanns Cibulka's
Swantow, the dialogue in the GDR about ecology and progress intensified at many levels -- for instance, within the institutions
of church and literature, interest groups and the decision-making
structure, and thus the political culture, as well. Reactions to
the April 1986 nuclear reactor accident at Chernobyl, in the Ukraine, of course, were a high-water mark.

A chronological examination of highlights in that dialogue
sheds light on factors which may have stimulated awareness and
socio-political change in the GDR, as well as on their possible
interrelationships. This process of feedback -- that is, reactions communicated by word and deed -- is what Karl Deutsch
called "the nerves of government".[213] Their impulses, or signals,
of satisfaction or dissatisfaction reflect sudden change, growth,
and evolution. In short, feedback *from* within the system tells
decision-makers what is really going on, which may differ from
what they expect or wish. Reacting to such feedback signals, they
can make corrections and changes and, in turn, communicate the response *to* the system. In the GDR in the early 1980s this dynamic
process of feedback and political communication was very active.

1. 1983

Official statements in the early months of 1983 about ecological and environmental problems suggested some emphases of the intensified debate about progress. For instance, the growing concern about environmental issues in the advanced socialist society
of the GDR was pointed up in the Theses for the Karl Marx Year,
which **SED** leaders formulated for the year-long observations of the
philosopher's centennial death-anniversary.

Three of the theses contained ecological challenges to the
GDR's socio-political system -- solution of "global problems such
as protection of the natural environment" (#19), solution of "basic current problems such as...rational utilization of nature and
environmental protection" (#23), and organizing "careful management of all natural resources" (#25). Moreover, the Theses contained about two dozen references to "progress", mostly "societal"
(*gesellschaftlichen*) and "social" (*sozialen*) with a few mentions
to "historical" or "humankind's" progress.[214]

Another opportunity for the SED leadership to communicate a
message of optimism and reassurance about progress came when the
GDR held a widely publicized international conference to honor the

Marx anniversary year. Sponsored by the SED Central Committee, the conference's theme, "Karl Marx and Our Time", attracted representatives from 145 Marxist parties and movements around the world. In a major speech by SED leader Erich Honecker, the international audience was assured that for the GDR, as an advanced socialist society, "Scientific and social progress are two sides of the same coin". Thus, the country's flourishing economy, said Honecker, "must provide the means to permit healthy progress in many other spheres within the framework of our far-reaching goals. This includes measures to protect the natural environment".[215]

About the same time, however, a prominent voice in **literature** again warned about the human price of so-called scientific "progress" -- Christa Wolf in her Frankfurt lectures, excerpted in *Sinn und Form*:

> *The kind of progress in art and science to which we have become accustomed - exceptional record achievments - can be had only through depersonalization...The price of this kind of progress, which the institution of science has long produced, I thought, was gradually too expensive to me.*

A follow-up statement by Wolf expressed an even more fundamental critique of science per se, not unlike what Cibulka had said. Responding to accusations of "scientific enmity", Wolf at first thought that charge was an "absurd misunderstanding", but then

> *I paused: could I still be friendly toward a science which has distanced itself so far from the thirst for knowledge - from whence it came and with which it nevertheless still secretly identifies? -- I think we have to stop taking seriously the labels which it pins on us.*[216]

Soon thereafter Jürgen Kuczynski, economic historian and philosopher, again threw his weight into the discussion. Using the pages of the Writers' Union journal *Neue deutsche Literatur*, he applauded critical authors and chastized defensive social scientists whom, he said, reflected "scientific unease about the contradictions in our life". Returning, perhaps unconsciously, to a Cibulka symbolism omitted from the final version of *Swantow* ("One dare not forget that even the clear heavens still have a veil"- see p. 82), Kuczynski argued that although

> *we consider it eminently important to deal with the veil over and the polished-clean parts on the surface of the capitalist world...turned around, we should in all urgency guide the attention of our citizens to the dull spots on the surface of our socialist system.*

Such "spots", Kuczynski wrote, possibly thinking of environmental

90

pollution, not only can be overcome in socialism but must also "be eliminated as quickly as possible".[217]

Of significance, perhaps in part as response to Cibulka's criticisms and that of others, was the page-long interview with the **state** Minister for Environment, Dr. Hans Reichelt, published in *Neues Deutschland* in early February. Assuring readers that the SED and government "have always placed great importance on environmental protection", Reichelt offered many concrete examples. For instance, he cited VEBs where environmental protection measures were being intensified and others written into the economic plans. In addition, he reported that some 1,200 themes relevant to ecology were being researched and coordinated by his Ministry, and that specific projects were included in factory plans and those of regional and local governmental units, as well. The overall impression was that of a socio-political system exerting great efforts to solve its environmental and ecological problems.[218]

Daily application of the system's rules regarding the environment -- an output function -- was also being helped along by the GDR's **mass organizations**. For instance, in May 1983 the League of Culture's relatively new Society for Nature and Environment (GNU) launched a big media campaign for forest protection. Under the motto "Everything for the Protection of Our Forests", practical projects were undertaken, along with broadly-based information programs to heighten public awareness of the need to protect and maintain the forests. This message was carried along the system's many political communication channels, such as media, conferences, podium discussions, lectures, etc.[219]

Interesting, too, in this period of accelerated dialogue within **professional societies** and academic disciplines, was an article in *Deutsche Zeitschrift für Philosophie* entitled "Ethics and the Future of Humankind". Never before, wrote the author, have the prospects for human life been so dependent on goal-oriented humanistic thought and behavior. Since ethics, therefore, is becoming increasingly important, it is essential that it be oriented to historical and social criteria, i.e., the social progress of the working population. Ethics must speak to the enormous and real worldwide threats to human civilization, dangers said to be caused by scientific-technological progress per se, or, indeed, even by human work.[220]

Similar in tone and significance in the GDR's dialogue at this time was the book referred to earlier, *Realer Optimismus* (see p. 30). Also conceding the centrality of progress-related questions in current international discussions, this book from the SED's publishing house made a strong case for the credibility of optimism within the Marxist/Leninist philosophical context -- "the certainty of being able to realize great goals and ideals".[221]

Although the Protestant **Church** in the GDR was very much involved during 1983 with celebration of the Martin Luther Year,
ecology was by no means neglected. Since environmental protection
had been defined as a moral and Christian issue, this concern was
high on the discussion agendas at the seven regional church conferences (*Kirchentage*) which took place during spring and summer
months.[222] In addition, the church contributed to general awareness through its public actions. Church groups in Rostock organized a protest against the building of a highway in a natural pre-
serve area, and a nationwide bicycle cavalcade of young Christians
made its way to Potsdam for a week-end of discussions under the
slogan "Christian Responsibility for Creation".[223]

    Another **interest group** was heard from in late September, the
economic specialists. A large economic science conference of more
than 700 participants was held to assess fulfillment of the 1981-
1985 goals of the central research plan for the social sciences.
Thus the conferees included not only economists, but also natural
science and technical university teachers, plus representatives of
party, state, military, and social organizations.[224] The highlight of their meeting was the address by SED Secretry for Economics Günter Mittag. One of his major themes was that the socialist economy was developing its productivity more dynamically and
regularly than was capitalaism; another was that the GDR economy
had no alternative to constant growth in productivity and national
income because that "is and remains the basis for social progress
in all areas". At the same time, Mittag referred only briefly to
the GDR's environmental problems. Probably thinking of air pollution, he said that, despite "the measures essential for environmental protection", brown coal remained the GDR's cheapest and
most effective source of energy.[225]

    How deeply the ecological debate had disturbed certain levels
of society was suggested by two articles appearing in quite different journals in October 1983. For instance, the **SED**'s *Einheit*
offered as its special theme a new *philosophical* discussion of a
very old subject, the "meaning of life and work" in a Marxist/-
Leninist socio-political system. One of the articles in that 27-
page section was unusually interesting because of its literary
references and it authorship. Prof. Reinhold Miller (head of the
research department in the Institute for Marxist/Leninist Philosophy at the SED's Academy for Social Sciences) said he was writing
about "the meaning of life" because in the present period (a) so
many people felt threatened by international confrontation, and at
the same time (b) the progress of science and technology was opening up so many new possibilities for improvement and extension of
human life. Much of the "meaning of life", wrote the philosopher,
was found through a person's social involvement, in leaving behind
evidence which suggested "that he had done something valuable"
during his life. And precisely this, in Miller's view, was a significant theme in current GDR literature which made clear that

that which one can do to be "valuable" depends on systemic opportunities and context.[226]

Almost as an elaborate footnote to philosopher Miller, the
cultural journal *Weimarer Beiträge* published an article by Leipzig
professor Günther K. Lehmann. It openly confronted the ecological
question via a new definition for "meaning of life" from the *aesthetics philosophy* point of view. Offering opinions on many of
the issues raised by Cibulka's writing, Lehmann, for instance,
argued that the West does not have the answer to environmental
protection. Its anti-technology/science/industry concepts were
inappropriate, its pre-industrial idylls based on antiquated
concepts of nature. On the other hand, Lehmann wrote,

> In the Marxist view of nature, one can readily recognize
> an 'ecological' concept which, based on development of
> productive forces, is completely capable of sustaining
> real socialism and its aesthetic culture.[227]

At the same time, he conceded, even in socialism daily aesthetic
values applied to nature were incomplete and in the process of
evolving. Thus, for instance, fondness for the traditional fig-
urine of a garden dwarf (*Gartenzwerg*), which "in its own way simu-
lates an idyll of nature and satisfies a need", does not exclude
gradual development of aesthetic appreciation for modern industrial forms and designs. In short, "every discipline – including
aesthetics – is confronted, directly or indirectly, with the basic
question of scientific-technological progress in socialism".[228]

Meanwhile, within **literature**, Cibulka and *Swantow* continued
to be part of the dialogue. Throughout the GDR the author held
more than 100 readings –– at League of Culture meetings, universities, libraries, church youth groups (Protestant and Catholic), in
factories, before work collectives within state agencies, and with
natural scientists. Some were especially contentious discussions,
dealing with the priorities of military defense vs environmental
protection expenditures or those of agricultural production vis-a-
vis environmental protection measures. The stack of letters from
readers in Cibulka's file also continued to grow, finally total-
ling several hundred. One offered unusual insight into how GDR
readers/citizens saw the role of literature in their society:

> I don't know if an echo from a reader is important to
> you, but I would like, nevertheless, to sincerely thank
> you for Swantow. I must admit that at first I had prob-
> lems with the beginning pages. It seemed as if a diary
> awaited me which would tell a love story, share observa-
> tions of nature, and go somewhat into a reverie about a
> patch of safe and sound environment. As I said, it ap-
> peared so, and I am glad I did not succumb to the danger
> of putting the book aside after reading the first pages.

*That you share with readers your concern about the world
certainly would not be important if innumerable people
did not share this concept, be able to see it affirmed
in literature, and have the experience (apparently com-
monly called 'reading experience') that someone else has
formulated what one feels, experiences, about which one
contemplates, usually unfortunateely without results.
For that you are to be thanked, also for the courage
which is involved. And it appears as a stroke of luck
for you and the reader that this not exactly comfortable
piece of literature became public. Of course, you know
that art's effectiveness is limited, that no book or
painting until now has been able to hinder war or stop
catastrophies, even though the producers of art wish for
nothing with more longing. But to ask questions such as
you raised, to put into words what must be said (repeatedly, if need be), from that the reader gains strenth,
even if at first it is in the mentioned sense of affir-
mation. This much I at least have to tell you, in the
hope that such encouragement helps to remove possible
doubt about what art can accomplish. Books such as
Swantow are important because they leave a trail and effect individual considerations. I put the book down,
knowing that through it the danger had not grown less.
And yet, suddenly, there was a hope, a belief (or what-
ever it should be called) that humankind would come to
its senses, that the apparently unstopable descent into
the abyss, nevertheless, could be halted, in contrast to
all experiences and observations which we daily make
anew.*

Literary critics, too, continued to write assessments of
Swantow. Monika Melchert, for instance, writing in a late summer
issue of *Sonntag,* found it a "thoughtful, a quiet book". She lik-
ed the author's closeness to nature and his style of "brief and
pointed" descriptions. Regarding its controversial theme, Melchert found that *Swantow's*

*admonitions and warning words are not, however, written
from an anti-industrial, contra-technicl progress position, but rather out of a deeply felt responsibility of
people vis-a-vis nature and thereby -- and above all--
vis-a-vis human life. That makes this little book valuable.*[229]

Gerhard Dahne, writing in *Neue deutsche Literatur* which originally excerpted *Swantow* 2 1/2 years earlier, provided readers
with a literary text analysis of a book he found positive because
readers "begin to talk with each other. *Swantow* is a diary which
excites". Equally so was the reviewer's conclusion, read in the
context of official criticism of *Swantow.* Despite humankind's

inability to give up the struggle for a better world, including the entire societal project for which people want to work and live within a socialist context, Dahne asserted that

> the absurd is also part of the world. To name it by name, to have made it tangible, that characterizes the artistic potential of the Swantow diary.[230]

Interestingly, both of these assessments appeared later in the year in an annual anthology of book reviews published by the county SED's Mitteldeutscher Verlag in Halle/Leipzig. The introduction to that anthology (entitled "The Scolded Metier") called for better book reviewing in the GDR (less descriptive and more thought-provoking) and offered its 1983 collection as examples of what could be done. If those facts are added together -- two positive reviews of Swantow included in an anthology of 'better' reviews printed in Cibulka's publishing house -- it might be suggested that the 'institution' of literture offered its colleague Hanns Cibulka a vote of confidence despite (or because of) the publishing problems he had had. In this case 'institution' included the book reviewers, the organizations Writers' Union and League of Culture whose publications had originally printed the reviews, the editors who selected the reviews for inclusion in the anthology, and the publishing house (SED enterprise) which had first published Swantow and then the anthology.[231]

The literary and reading world in the GDR was also beginning to talk about another work on the theme of progress which had been published in 1982 -- the science fiction novel Andymon (subtitled "A Space Utopia"). It was coauthored by two freelance natural scientists: Karlheinz Steinmüller, a physicist and computer specialist, known for several short stories of fantasy, and his wife Angela, a mathematician and electronic data processor. Together they had written a novel for Verlag Neues Leben whose theme was humankind's improveability (if not perfectability) and capacity to live humanely within the scientific-technological world.

The setting of their story at first was a great spaceship, designed "once upon a time" by Earthpeople. It was a kilometer-long cylinder, equipped with state of the art hi-tech, robots programmed with humane values, and a sperm bank containing specimens of all races known on Earth. Around the year 2000, when Earth was destroyed, the ship was hurtled into endless space with its cargo of Earth treasures. Its goal: to reach a new planet where all that had been positive about human life could be continued.

After thousands of flight years, the first sperms were incubated, i.e., were "born". Each child was reared by a robot nurse, Ramma, programmed with principles of developmental psychology. Educated by their "Genius Universal Robot" teacher, Guro, the

95

children from age 5 on learned the collective natural and social science knowledge of the human race. The Totalscope taught them Earth's history through sensory experiences; the Nature Park enclosed within the spaceship taught love for flora, fauna, and animal life representing all of Earth's continents. Periodically new groups of children were born in the spaceship.

When half the flight time was behind them, the young spaceship crew sent out a pathfinder space capsule to survey their new planetary home. It was a shock -- not only was Andymon uninhabited but uninhabitable! It was endless desert, as they had learned Earth was before life developed there. If the spaceship's restless passengers were to live on Andymon, they would have to force climatic changes on the barren planet. Algae mutations were thus developed in the laboratory and "sown" onto Andymon, producing an evolution that was dangerous and difficult.

The drama of this story by the Steinmüllers was not only the technological problem-solving required to settle the new planet, but also the clash between human psychologies influenced by generational differences. On the one hand, there were the "work, work, and more work" motives of the older pioneers and, on the other, the "quality of life" wishes of the younger.

The "messages" of this fascinating story were basically these, all relevant to the GDR's progress debate:

(1) Nature is glorious but not to be conquered; its limits must be accepted.

(2) Humankind's intellectual abilities are great and should be developed, but their limits also recognized.
"What, after all, do we know? A bit about nature, about technology, least about how one designs a society, not to mention how our own psyche functions."[232]

(3) Technology has limits; its priority may and should be questioned.
"The plans which we had drawn up years ago for the settlement, grand global plans and computer scenarios, concentric growth of human influence, had one and all and anew after every correction proved to be too rigid. I myself, an enthusiastic champion of these plans, now had to admit that it was not possible to plan ideas and goals in detail. Everything remained fluid."[233]

(4) Humankind is precious, its social relationships and democratic decision-making crucial.
"You not only scorned the ship's constructors by erasing their knowledge, but you also despised us by presuming to know our interests better than we know them."[234]

96

This seemed to some editors and readers to be a rather different kind of science fiction. *Andymon* did not, for instance, deal with more- or less-advanced creatures or interplanetary wars. Instead, it simply transferred familar Earth humans through time and space to continue their humanistic evolution elsewhere. In addition, the authors were not conventional literati, but rather natural scientists contemplating relationships between humans and nature from the viewpoint of physics, mathematics, and cybernetics. Thus *Andymon* was neither pessimistic, naive, or nostalgic. At the same time, however, the authors did not give science/technology a clear green light either. They said it had its limits, and its goals must be questioned. *Andymon* thus seemed to be a laudable exception within the momentarily unexciting East European science fiction field, a book which contributed importantly to the dialogue about progress in the GDR.

Some years later the Steinmüllers, contrasting their 1982 work with earlier science fiction, would point out that instead of presenting "the ideal future primarily in technical details with social aspects only as a background", in *Andymon*

> *we attempted to counter this 'static' Utopia with a 'dynamic' one. The society there is free of exploitation, the protagonists who settle a planet are unburdened by social birth-marks. But what they accomplish is only a beginning, the start of a development whose future is open. We presume that there will never be an end to all contradictions and so an end to development of humankind. Therefore, unlike many previous novels, we do not need external confrontations with exploitative orders or natural forces. We develop our story line primarily through internal conflicts.*[235]

By late 1983, then, the input into the political culture regarding the value of progress had been heard from **literature**, and the **church** had again added its voice at a synodical meeting in Mecklenburg in November where environmental protest petitions (*Eingaben*) were discussed and a statement issued about "the concerns and fears of many citizens about increasing strains on our environment".[236] And at a meeting of the League of Culture in late November the **interest group** GNU earned praise for its three short years of activitity and achievments in sensitizing GDR citizens to their own responsibilities for the environment. Not surprisingly, since that meeting came a month after new Pershing and Cruise missiles had been stationed in the FRG, spokespersons used the occasion to emphasize the relationship between peace and environmental protection -- if one did not have to pay so much to defend the former, there would be more to use for the latter.[237]

The other side of the GDR's socio-political system, the **state** output side, was especially active in environmental affairs in early December:

(1) The annual economic plan (*Volkswirtschaftsplan*) for 1984 was passed, calling for implementation of

> *measures to keep water and air clean, as well as to utilize and harmlessly dispose of waste products and reduce noise, especially in the areas of coal and energy plus the chemical industry...Priorities are the stipulated projects in the GDR's capital city, Berlin, congested areas such as Leipzig, Karl-Marx-Stadt, and Halle, as well as the Erz Mountains.*[238]

This evidence that resources were to be made available for national and regional plans (which include investments for environmental protection) was significant if central planning is seen as the most important instrument in socialist systems for goal-implementation. In addition, the 1984 plan gave new environmental protection priority to the coal, energy, and chemical industries and to certain industrial centers. Interesting, too, was the standard first-place mention of water resources, one of the GDR's major and continuing problems.

(2) The State Budget for 1984, matching the economic plan, was resolved.[239]

(3) A "Law Regarding the Use of Atomic Energy and Protection Against Its Dangers -- Atomic Energy Law" was passed, replacing the earlier 1962 statute (see p. 38). That earlier law,[240] had declared in its preamble that peaceful use of atomic energy was "necessary for the rapid expansion of socialist development". Measures for protection of life and health of people working in nuclear research and technology were mentioned in the second section of the first article of basic principles; two later articles dealt with radiation protection and preventive health measures.

The new 1983 law, however,[241] dealt specifically with protection from the dangers of atomic energy, as its title indicated. Thus it reflected increased international awareness and experience with this form of technology and its relationship to the environment. In fact, specific reference was made in Article 4 to the "newest scientific-technological knowledge".

Repeating the GDR's reason for developing atomic energy, as stated in the earlier 1962 law, the preamble of the new statute now also said in its third sentence that

> *The use of atomic energy is permissable only if all necessary measures to guarantee the security and protection of life and human health, as well as protection of the environment, are taken.*

98

Thus the language of the new legislation addressed some of the essential criticisms of Cibulka and others, that is, that nuclear energy should serve the need and *well-being* of the socialist society and that the life and health of the people, as well as the environment per se, should be protected. Further, the article on general principles declared health and environmental protection more important than economic gain:

> *The protection of life and the health of people, as well as protection of the environment against the danger of atomic energy usage is to be guaranteed and has priority over national economic and other advantages which result from the use of atomic energy.*

In addition, and unlike the 1962 law, responsibility was assigned not only to the Council of Ministers' Scientific Council for Peaceful Use of Atomic Energy and the Office for Nuclear Research and Nuclear Technology. Now included were the Academy of Sciences, scientific and educational institutions, the local Peoples' Assemblies, and plant managers. Five articles of the new law (No. 5, 10-13) provided legal punishment for violation of the law and assigned specific control to the State Office for Atomic Safety and Radioactivity Protection.

Also of major significance in late 1983 was a big conference of a major **interest group** in the GDR, the country's social scientists representing many professional societes, scientific institution, and universities. Called by the SED Central Committee, the meeting was a kind of "stock-taking", i.e., reporting on three years of work toward the goals of the central research plan formulated for 1981-1985 (see pp. 46, 51). About 850 participants attended the mid-December conference which included presentation of 19 major papers and more than two dozen interim research reports.

Interestingly, in the SED's view one of the major achievments was that the conference "showed the vitality of Marxism/Leninism, its historical optimism", or, put another way, reaffirmed belief in the concept of progress. At the same time, the party felt that social scientists must (a) relate their research to practice more consequently than before and understand more exactly the daily life and daily consciousness of people, (b) intensify interdisciplinary cooperation between the social, natural, and technical sciences, and (c) master the dialectic-materialist method, especially the principal of contradictions; that was essential for seeing that "the effect of varying, contrasting tendencies in one and the same social phenomenon as an entirely normal process in the development of our country".[242]

Those conclusions were drawn by the party leadership from the more than two dozen interim research progress-reports representing countless disciplines within the GDR social sciences. Especially relevant were three reports which reflected the tone of the conference vis-a-vis the ecological and progress debate.

One report was by Kurt Hager, SED Secretary for Culture and Science.[243] He began his opening challenge to the conference by conceding and reminding his colleagues that socialism is not built overnight. Moreover, socialism would be inconceivable without economic growth plus the scientific-technological revolution which had experienced a "turbulent development" since the 1960s. The result, said Hager, had been a multiplicity of economic, social, and spiritual/cultural problems which needed thorough and interdisciplinary researching by the social sciences. The pessimistic premises of the West should be energetically countered, Hager insisted. At the same time, of course, "in all measures to protect the environment, the point of departure must constantly be the real, existing economic conditions and possibilities" facing the GDR.[244]

In this "agitated and conflict-rife time", Hager said, literature and the arts have a special responsibility to help people sort out motives for their personal thoughts and actions, to give them courage, strength, and the feeling that the struggle is worth the effort. In short, "Literary and artistic scholars carry great responsibility for the process of public understanding in our society about socialism's values".[245] As for the social sciences, they, too, must find answers to "the burning, vital questions of today and tomorrow" -- GDR citizens, well educated and active, want more than empty words from their social scientists. "The truth is on our side", Hager concluded, "but it must be disseminated in good time and persuasively".[246]

Hans Koch (director of the Institute for Marxist/Leninist Culture and Artistic Sciences of the SED's Academy for Social Sciences) spoke on "The Arts in the Shaping of Socialism's Values". Assuring the conference that the problem of value and evaluation in the arts was in the forefront of aesthetic research, Koch said current emphases included reconsideration of human relationships of all kinds, including those with nature. A major problem, however, was incorporation of old socialist values into current and future situations -- for instance, the traditional values of "social security" and "collectivity".[247]

Horst Paucke (leader of the ecology research group in the Central Institute for Philosophy within the Academy of Sciences) took up the subject "Ecological Problems and Their Meaning for the Present". He, too, opened his remarks with assurances -- not only the GDR, he said, but all the Warsaw Treaty states realized that the global ecological problem facing them was directly related to maintenance of peace. Solving it and environmental problems had become part of the international class confrontation by which socialism and capitalism would be judged:

*the attraction of socialism for workers in the capital-
istic and developing countries (will be) determined by
its capacity to offer solutions to environmental and
ecological problems.*[248]

Thus, Paucke reported, the GDR's Academy of Science was devoting
increased attention to the national and international dimension of
the problem. But while the socialist countries had put environmental laws on the books very early, it was becoming increasingly
important to educate public opinion, especially attitudes and behavior toward the cardinal problem of humanity/nature relationships. Although environmental protection measures were an integral part of the economic plans at all levels, implementation was
a real problem -- "this is still a wide open area".[249]

    The messages of such gatherings of social scientists, a mix-
ture of "progress reports" and "action plans", were fed into the
political culture via all the SED's political communication channels. Thus it perhaps was not surprising that by the end of 1983
observers were reporting significantly increased public awareness
of ecological problems at the local levels of the GDR society.

    In part, of course, that new consciousness had been stimu-
lated not only by literary and other public *discussions*, but also
by local church *activities* and those of the Society for Nature and
the Environment. The latter had been organized precisely to involve citizens within their own communities, and that list of
practical projects was rather impressive: expansion of a network
of hiking trails in Schwerin, landscape plantings in Leipzig,
founding of a Nature and Environment Youth Club in Rostock, protection of environmentally endangered animals is the area of Lüb-
ben, organizing a two-week series of environmental lectures during
Science Days in Lausitz, arranging a traveling exhibit on nature
and environment for the Dresden district, protection of a park
area in Riesa, etc.[250]

2. 1984

    If 1983 was a year of heightened feedback discussions regard-
ing ecological problems and the concept of progress in the GDR,
then 1984 was an energized year. Interestingly, **literature** led
off with an important review (possibly *the* "establishment" review)
of Cibulka's book version of *Swantow*, by the GDR's Deputy Minister
of Culture Klaus Höpcke.[251]

    Published in *Sinn und Form*, the journal of the Academy of
Arts, Höpcke's assessment came nearly three years after the initial *NDL* excerpts and consequent controversy, about two years
after Hermann Ley's highly critical response to the excerpt, and

slightly more than one year after *Swantow's* sell-out appearance as a book. It might be suggested, therefore, that Höpcke's views in early 1984 represented the aggregated interests of the so-called cultural establishment after a lengthy period of public discussion had clarified some of the parameters of the ecological debate.

Within this context, Höpcke still did not entirely like Hanns Cibulka's book (perhaps less a personal view than one motivated by his role as a state official). The few aspect he complimented included Cibulka's general "ecological concern", passages about how a writer creates his poetry or prose, the author's implied critique of "the lack of a sense of mutuality", and his direct call for individual responsibility regarding environmental protection. On the negative side, Höpcke found Cibulka's descriptions of nature at times inaccurate, his discussion of "death and dying" inadequate, and use of the wasp nest symbol as ambiguous.

Central to the review, however, was Höpcke's displeasure with Cibulka's "intellectual premise", i.e., the author's skepticism about scientific progress, and with the superficiality of his ecological critique. Specifically, Höpcke criticized Cibulka for generalizing blame ("the economy", "science", "power mentality"), misunderstanding problems scientifically and yet offering artist's conclusions, failing to acknowledge concrete measures being taken in the GDR as well as basic differences between socialist and capitalistic approaches to solving environmental problems, seeking ecological solutions in illusions, overlooking international political events affecting peace, rearmament, environmental protection, etc.

The fifth section of the review, in which the Deputy Minister of Culture discussed the manuscript-editing for the final book version, i.e., revision of the excerpts published in *NDL*, was especially suggestive. Höpcke not only found the changes justified but apparently would himself have made even more. He was particularly pleased with the edited version of the nuclear energy plant discussion (an interesting assessment vis-a-vis his Ministry's request for such text changes) because

> *comments about a nuclear power plant in the northern part of the GDR (was) no longer tied to passages about nuclear energy plants in literature from Western countries. The radioactivity output through radionuclides, which is lower here, no longer appears as if were as high as elsewhere.*[252]

This, however, is a somewhat strange comment, too, since in the initial version of *Swantow* "passages of literature about nuclear energy plants" were never attributed to Western sources, i.e., they were anonymous citations. And in the final book version there was no *direct* mention of any nuclear energy plants in the

102

GDR. Instead, it was implied -- in one part of the poem about a nuclear plant measuring the land "by the fathom cord of death" (see p. 74) and in the observtion about "Lubmin" (see p. 69) which GDR readers might know was the site of the country's atomic energy plant for industrial use.

On the other hand, Höpcke still remained dissatisfied with the critique of science appearing in Cibulka's book:

It would have been worthwhile to call to readers' attention how science and technology also create conditions for improved environmental protection and guarantee them so that progress including this sector is possible.

Relating that statement to Ley's earlier critique of the excerpted version of *Swantow* is not illogical, for Höpcke clearly wrote that he agreed in principle with his colleage. However, Höpcke also reprimanded the natural scientist for an unliterary critique which ignored the fact that a literary work demands

a different approach...Above all it wants and must be judged by the validity -- as measured by contemporary life -- of the artistic answers it tries to give to the questions it has raised.[253]

Höpcke himself had, of course, already delivered just that judgment earlier in his review with the negative artistic assessment implied in his rhetorical question, "To what extent does the book *Swantow* in the future help one to live with knowledge of the danger and to actively counter it?"[254] In closing his review, Höpcke referred to Politburo resolutions and an interview with the Environment Minister to "prove" that Cibulka's artist-answers to issues lacked current validity. What is more, Höpcke wrote, other books on the environment were better, for they included more concrete possibilities for improvement.

And so a second major reaction to *Swantow* had found fault with the environmental views of its sensitive, poetic author, not because of his love for nature, but for his opinion of why nature had been and was being irreversibly polluted. Both the first critique, with Ley's natural science orientation, and the second, written from Höpcke's cultural policy view, had focused on the same basic point -- Cibulka's scientific pessimism and its implied denial of the sanctity of economic and social progress concepts. Thus the critique sector of the GDR's literary institution had spoken, reacting negatively to writing which seemed to challenge the official political culture.

Following such specifically critical assessments of *Swantow*, statements in the next months of 1984 frequently returned to various aspects of the overall discussion to reinforce optimism toward

103

science and technology or the concept of progress itself. For instance, the vice-president of Urania, the GDR's **mass organization** for adult education, took up the much-discussed subject of technology. Writing in *Einheit*, Lutz-Günter Fleischer began with the usual acknowledgement of a problem, that is, the contradictory interrelationships between certain economic and ecological interests within the society, especially regarding energy. But, like Höpcke, Fleischer then asserted that the problem arose not from "too much" science or "overemphasized" technology, but rather from currently inadequate developments exactly in those fields."[255] And in *Deutsche Zeitschrift für Philosophie*, Günter Hoell, professor at the University for Economics in Berlin, took up the global dimension to ecological problems which had been called for, in an article about nutrition.[256]

Werner Jehser (professor for culture and the arts at the Central Committees's Academy of Social Sciences), in an *Einheit* article, returned to some of the SED concerns with literature Höpcke had mentioned or implied in his review of *Swantow*. Jehser's primary concern was what is truth in the arts and "how is the truth-quotient of artistic images to be determined?", possibly relating to Höpcke's criticism of Cibulka's unscientific approach to scientific problems.

Jehser's answer was that "truth" and "reality" in the arts are to be assessed vis-a-vis their mirroring of existing society but also by "what *new* information they present about discovered possibilities for people and society, with which they enrich and deepen our knowledge about people".[257] For Marxists/Leninists, Jehser said, the concept of "truth" constantly relates to accurate reflection of "an *historically determined relationship of humankind to reality* at any given time". That, in turn, meant that an author was expected to know what was objectively significant in a social sense, i.e., what was significant at a certain level of social development for human progress. (This again seemed to affirm Ley and Höpcke's criticism of Cibulka for writing superficially about current scientific questions.) According to Jehser, GDR readers at their present level of development were dissatisfied with a narrow view of described events and are

> against indecisiveness in evaluation, against pure des-
> cription of individual facts, against incomprehensible
> limitation of content considered worthy of sharing to
> the purely subjective experiences of the author.[258]

Such critique by Jehser, Höpcke, Ley, and other SED spokespersons focused on authors who allegedly did not know what they were talking about and readers who wanted more and better information.

This view was reinforced by the SED through a small book published in 1984 by the Party University's department for cultural

policy. In *Arbeiterklasse und Künstler im Bündnis*, Kurt Rauschek
wrote quite bluntly that "expertise and understanding", prerequi-
sites for participating in current controversies over issues such
as environment and the role of science, apparently were not always
present among artists. Thus, practical steps were being taken, he
wrote. For instance, various intellectual groups were encouraged
to deepen their knowledge and broaden their insights through intensified dialogues with each other, for instance, writers with
natural and social scientists. In addition, according to Raus-
check, the need for better informed writers had led to seminars,
excursions into industrial plants, etc., to enlarge writers' knowledge of Marxism/Leninism and economic practice.[259]

During the spring months of 1984 the vigor of the ecological
debate and its feedback interrelations were seen, too, at another
level, that of the **church**. At a conference on environmental pollution held in spring, the regional Evangelical Academy proposed a
nationwide Environment Decade (similar to the Peace Decade announced in the early 1980s). Speakers pointed out that the longer
one waited, the worse the ecological problems would become. A major problem for the 250 participants at the conference was the
continuing lack of public information about the GDR's environmental problems.[260]

Observers reported that the conference discussions strongly
emphasized the possibility of working in local residential areas
or through state environmental groups. That was seen as a middle
course between individual "little steps", on the one hand, and resignation about the possibility of environmental protection improvement, on the other hand. One of those "little steps" the
churches continued to recommend was the annual "Mobil Without
Auto" action, traditionally held the first weekend in June. Thus,
in 1984 religious leaders called particularly on church workers to
set an example by bicycling or walking, rather than using their
office or private passenger cars. Frugal use of water was another
of the "small steps" called for, this time at an early June nationwide environmental conference "Concern About Creation" held at
the Church Research Center in Wittenberg, known for its ecological
engagement.[261]

And in mid-June, some 1,000 GDR citizens, attending an Environment Worship Service (*Umweltgottesdienst*) in Mölbis, near
Leipzig, were again asked by clergymen to follow a less consumer-
oriented lifestyle. According to reporters, the regional bishop
assured listeners that "the engagement of church environmental
groups has also contributed to the fact that the GDR leadership is
increasingly willing to take into account the problem of the environment". The bishop reminded his audience, too, that the cause
for ecological problems was found in humankind's own egoism,[262]
seemingly echoing Cibulka's urgent call for individual responsibility.

Not only religious, but materialist philosophers, too, as voices of their discipline and intellectual **interest group**, began to enter the ecological dialogue with criticisms. In spring 1984, for instance, GDR citizens could read in the *Deutsche Zeitschrift für Philosophie* that in the biotechnical field it no longer sufficed to arrive at decisions based on natural science and technical knowledge, plus economic statistics. Instead, new syntheses were needed which related scientific-technological tasks to a whole net of *social* factors.[263] Engineers, too, were chastized in another article which asserted that they needed to take their ecological responsibility more seriously. That they did not, the author claimed, was seen in the results of opinion polls among 2,000 technical students preparing to be engineers.[264]

At the **literature** level, Deputy Culture Minister Höpcke again entered the progress debate, in mid-June with an article in the official SED newspaper, *Neues Deutschland*.[265] This time his theme was that in the present troubled times readers needed "heroes whose actions achieve progress". To many readers this may have been an old topic, but Höpcke used the context to reemphasize superficiality and inactivity, for which he had criticized *Swantow*. In his *ND* article, Höpcke said the problem was the absence both of "a capacity for overall political thought and behavior" and of "social and political activity for the progress of society". Similarly, he repeated his call for scientific optimism: "The basis and the optimistic spirit of the Marxist/Leninist scientific world view is appropriate for encouragement by literature".

In his appeal for thinking, active "heroes" who promoted progress, Höpcke did not, however, appear to be asking writers to again create one-sidely positive figures common to the "construction" (*Aufbau*) phase of GDR literature. Instead, he seemed to agree with literary scholars calling for balance. For instance, in a 1983 study, Christel Berger, at the SED's Academy of Social Sciences, had returned to the old theme of "heroes" (defined as the "important figure" or "the main character"), but maintained that they could be used to express everything "which appears humanely important to the author...and that is not only that which is positive".[266]

Berger, like Höpcke, had also made a strong case for active involvement by writers, characterizing young GDR authors of the 1970s as "observers" rather than "activists". Berger found that these "chroniclers of reality" had offered central figures whose 'that's just the way I am' lifestyle was presented as a "rather suitable daily existence, incorporating positive and negative aspects equally." Creators of such "heroes" had then left value judgments about them entirely up to the readers. The impression frequently created, according to Berger, was a "helpless and synthetic" one, with the author appearing less competent and more helpless than the reader.

Instead, in Berger's view, literature should show that the author is "a competent partner in society...who also makes suggestions, shares dreams, and in challenges to the reader makes his own standpoint clear".[267] In another article, Höpcke articulated this common thesis again. He wrote that focusing primarily on social criticism as the purpose of literature would lead to "a grave dimunition of literature's possibilities in socialism". Instead, to contribute to progress, literature also had to be positive.[268]

Thus, the message from the GDR's decision-makers and literary establishment to Cibulka and other ecological critics seemed to be that the sanctity of progress remained intact. Based on that premise, loyal opposition, offering critique *plus* specific suggestions for environmental improvement, apparently was acceptable and welcome. In other words, because of the special role literature traditionally had been accorded in the socialist system, it also had been assigned this particular and continuing responsibility-- to be "art for the improvement of socialism". Apparently literature could be otherwise, but then it and its authors probably would be criticized, as Cibulka and others surely had been.

Meanwhile, on the **state** output side of the GDR's socio-political system, there were some actions suggesting possibilities for environmental improvement. Environmental Minister Reichelt met with FRG representatives in June to discuss mutual pollution problems and in the same month attended the international environmental conference on air pollution in Munich (and reported on it in *Neues Deutschland*). In September, Reichelt was again on the road, to Denmark, and again greeted FRG guests, this time Jo Leinen, the environmental activist. (Honecker also met with Leinen and reportedly told him the environmental engagement of the GDR churches was a good thing.[269])

Nevertheless, a **church** environmental meeting in mid-July complained anew about the lack of information relating to the GDR's ecology.[270] Other misgivings were heard at autumn meetings. In September, the 4th Synod of the Federation of Evangelical Churches in the GDR met in Greifswald, bringing together 60 members representing the eight regional churches of the country. "Environment" had been placed prominently on the discussion agenda. In that context, despite what Honecker reportedly had told Leinen, complaints were heard from church leaders about the "suspicion and mistrust" of state offices toward projects of church environmental groups. Nonetheless, the conference encouraged such groups to increase their activity because it was believed this would be "recognized" by the state.[271] Specifically, the Synod repeated its recommendation that such involvement be channeled through non-church, that is, through state channels -- "that congregation members also utilize the social possibilities, for example, in local commissions, work groups, and the Society for Nature and Environment".[272]

107

A month later, at the Saxony regional synodical meeting, church leaders repeated their old appeal to GDR decision-makers--"to include the citizenry in the solution of problems through 'information and disclosure of interrelationships'". At the same time, the church decided to hold a special conference in early 1985 under the motto, "Peace, Justice and Preservation of Creation", thus reflecting the relationship between peace and ecology called for by SED leaders.[273]

Moreover, church observers reported that during the church's "Peace Decade" numerous readings by poets and writers had been part of the discussions, exhibits, meetings, etc., which emphasized especially "the connection between environmental destruction and maintenanance of peace".[274] In fact, as a church newspaper wrote, "The environmental circles thus were on the way to relegating the disarmament question, hotly debated a year ago, to a No. 2 place".[275]

In the context of such public concern expressed through the churches, it was interesting that at about the same time a philosophy professor used the pages of the *Deutsche Zeitschrift für Philosophy* to make the case for "mass consciousness" as an active force for realizing social progress. Rather pointedly he wrote that "precisely in the present situation" it was necessary to recall the effectiveness of the traditional slogan "teach the masses, learn from the masses".[276]

Further concerns of the professional **interest group** of philosophers about environmental and ecological problems was a focus of their important Philosophy Congress held in mid-October 1984. For instance, following Erich Hahn's wide-ranging opening comment, the ten major lectures which followed included one on "Atomic Energy - a Challenge to Mankind, another on "Vital Demands and Values on the Threshold of the 21st Century", and one about "The Socialist State - Power of Humaneness". In the latter, Heinrich Opitz contended that it was exactly current experiences which underlined the need to develop socialist democracy more resolutely -- after all, since one learns to govern "primarily through the exercise of power", the effect on citizens of personal political experience could hardly be overestimated.[277]

It was in the ten workshops (*Arbeitskreise*) of the conference, however, that really substantive "differences of opinion" and "vigorous constructive discussion" were reported. For example, in a response to Opitz, Uwe-Jens Heuer, earlier cited as an advocate of developing socialist democracy, reminded his colleagues that democracy was not a question of form or method, but rather of content, that is, whether the interests of the masses were being realized. The response to Heuer's comments were recorded as "a lively debate about the standards and criteria of socialistic democratic determination and development".[278]

According to the Congress report, this same study group showed lively interest in a paper discussing the theoretical problem of social and political stability in socialism. Here the trenchent question posed was whether socio-economic performance (progress) or public consciousness was more important to stability, or both together.[279]

In still another workshop, on "Scientific-Technological Revolution - Creativity - Responsibility", Hermann Ley again made the case for his natural science colleagues. Asserting that engineers and natural scientists could be made insecure through the current criticism of them, he suggested defensively that they might consequently "renege, at least partially, on making their creative potential available". To this not very subtle challenge, another conferee responded that while natural scientists surely had the right to emphasize their "existing expertise", at the same they also had to take seriously "authors' criticism about underestimation of humaneness, emotionality, and individuality".[280]

Of unusually intensive interest apparently was the study group on "Socialism and Humanistic Shaping of the Future - Society and Nature", led by Alfred Kosing and Hans Kulow.[281] Here the following points, relevant to the sharpening ecological/environmental discussion, were made:

-- The relationship between nature and society had become important in public discussion.

-- The systemic character of nature/society "interrelationships", thus, required more attention.

-- Economic growth was not the enemy of ecological demands, but environmental protection had to be achieved primarily through resource-saving procedures.

-- Much had been achieved in environmental protection, without fanfare, including the fact that air pollution was no longer increasing.

-- Economic laws had been extended so that they now included aspects of the nature/society relationship.

-- Changed priorities, including environmental protection, surely would play a significant role in the utilization of economic growth results.

-- In the "mass consciousness", i.e., the political culture, the new relationship of socialist society and individual responsibility for the natural environment had become "an important ingredient of the socialist consciousness...As one could speak of work morale, so now one also could speak of an environmental morale" among the people.[282]

Possibly responding to such evocative feedback challenges from church and literature, along with signalled demands for social change from within its own ranks, the GDR's ruling SED party leadership undertook a major communications response. It made environmental policy a special discussion subject in *Einheit*, devoting about a third of the journal's November, 1984 issue to the theme "Environmental Policy in Our Society".

Divided into nine separate articles, the discussion represented the broadened spectrum from which the decision-making center now viewed the keen debate over the ecological problems facing its socio-political system.. Included were views representing overall environmental concerns, philosophy, social organizations, technology, agriculture, water management, sociology/social policy, etc. Together these articles reflected developments of the 1970s and early 1980s in the GDR — heightened controversy and concern about ecology and the environment, reaffirmation of relevant Marxist/Leninist principles, new urgency and insights, and strengthened practical measures to deal with the problems.

Understandably the journal's discussion began with an article by Environment Minister Reichelt, reaffirming and repeating basic premises: Environmental policy was related to security and peace; Marxism/Leninism was capable of analyzing the interrelationship between "humankind, society, and nature", the GDR was legally committed by its constitution to serve that interrelationship; the concern was translated into specific economic plans and regional tasks; progress was based on economic growth. While protection of nature was emphasized, Reichelt reported, so, too, were other environmental aspects including reduction of noise levels and occupational accidents and improvement of the attractiveness of recreational areas.

Particularly important, Reichelt wrote, were local citizen initiatives. These were seen in the activities of the League of Culture, Chamber of Technology, National Front, Urania, and societies for fishermen, small gardners, hikers, etc. At the other end of the spectrum, Reichelt reminded, environmental policy called for *international* cooperation, as in the 160 scientific-technological projects making up the program for "Protection of Nature" adopted by Eastern Europe's Council for Mututal Economic Cooperation, or RGW.[283]

Representing the views of philosophy, Alfred Kosing (of the Institute for Marxist/Leninist Philosophy at the SED's Academy for Social Sciences) acknowledged in his *Einheit* contribution that the increased public attention to the relationship between human society and its natural environment had brought deeply philosophical issues to the surface. For instance, increased questioning about

110

how technological possibilities were used and whom nature should serve involved basic philosophical concepts of the nature of humankind, society, and social change. Clearly, Kosing said, the philosophy of socialism and its belief in progress meant that "the further progress of humankind" would be served. But, he added, objectively that would not happen overnight; it was a matter of long-range plans and goals and step-by-step implementation to reduce and eventually solve environmental problems.[284]

Writing on behalf of the League of Culture, Manfred Fiedler used facts and figures to document Reichelt's reference to increased involvement of GDR citizens in solving their country's environmental problems. Obviously Fiedler's emphasis was on the newly-founded Society for Nature and Environment (GNU), with its 50,000 members. Moreover, he reported to *Einheit* readers, some 40,000 of those members were experts working through "specialist groups" to contribute their professional knowledge. But Fiedler also especially noted the *general* public by referring to "inclusion of social forces in decision-making", the public nature of the current ecological discussion, and the organized public information work of the League of Culture and its GNU. Perhaps responding to the church's charge about lack of information, Fiedler made a special point of spelling out how such programs reached from

debate of basic interrelationships between maintenence of peace and environmental protection, to colloquia on problems and strategies in various environmental areas, forums with experts, club discussions, lecture series, special science and national culture days, excursions, exhibits, establishment of national culture displays in recreation areas, publications, and much more.[285]

Turning to the field of technology, Manfred Schubert, president of the influential interest group KDT and professor at Dresden's Technical University, reported a significant environmental achievment to *Einheit* readers:

for the first time in the history of our Republic, the growth in national income was achieved in 1982 with an absolute reduction in usage of energy sources, raw materials, and other materials as compared to the previous year.[286]

That saving of resources, Schubert wrote, promoted environmental protection as well as economic growth. Also important in the GDR's approach to environmental progress was reduction of waste and recycling of waste products, as called for in the five-year economic plans. This goal involved many activities, from the well-known recycling of paper to 72 investments "to reprocess and reuse secondary raw materials".

111

In addition, Schubert explained how the KDT itself played a significant role both on the input and output side of the ecological issue. As input, the KDT's Environment Commission proposed new technological procedures for decision-maker consideration, held competitions for new ideas, supported exchanges of ideas among the GDR's professional societies and its industrial sectors; on the output side, the KDT trained specialists and was a channel for cooperative work within the RGW context.

From agriculture, too, *Einheit* readers received progress reports of close cooperation between the collective farms (LPGs) and their local state units ("local councils", "Department of Environmental Protection of the District Council", "Community Councils"). Moreover, specific examples of forestry and water conservation suggested real achievments in these areas.[287]

In addition, an *Einheit* editorial report on the *legal* basis of the GDR's environmental protection measures made clear that while laws had been on the books a long time, environmental pollution would be more severely punished in the future. Under the 1977 Criminal Law Code (*Strafgesetzbuch*) and the 1979 and 1984 measures against illegalities (*Ordnungswidrigkeiten*), "legal stipulations concerning offenses against environmental protection are sharpened; causing an environmental danger is threatened with imprisonment".[288]

Saving perhaps the most provocative until last, *Einheit* closed out its unusually broad discussion of the GDR's environmental policies with an article about the thorny problem of environmental information. Chosen to author it was the leader of the ecological research group in the Institute for Sociology and Social Policy at the Academy of Sciences, Horst Paucke. Surveying this key issue in the national debate, Paucke chose to examine the output of information via *scientific journalism (wissenschaftlichen Publizistik)*, especially books. Paucke began with Marx and Engels' writings about nature and next cited GDR books about environmental protection published since the 1960s. The most comprehensive GDR book on environmental problems, in Paucke's view, was the 1975 volume *Im Mittelpunkt der Mensch* (edited by Lohs/Döring for Berlin's Akademie Verlag). In conclusion, Paucke believe that his small bibliographic survey documented

> how science in cooperation with practice translated the strategic orientation of the party and state leadership into goal-oriented actions and helps to realize the social policy of the SED which integrates the component of environmental policy.[289]

Clearly missing in Paucke's comments, however, was any response to the widespread public complaint about the lack of environmental information in the *mass media*.

Also missing in this special section of *Einheit* was any contribution from the field of literature. However, the journal had placed an article by Kurt Hager, on the unity of science, education, and culture, just preceding its section on environmental policy. In it Hager had made a strong case for culture's relationship to environmental awareness. It is culture, he wrote, which deepens

> *our knowledge of reality, our understanding of the meaning of life, of values on which life depends, and thereby creates impulses for creative thought and behavior which are especially important for scientific work.*[290]

About the same time that *Einheit* published this collection of thoughts about progress and the environment from the current point of view of the decision-making center, **literature** spoke out, too. Several significant discussions within the institution of literature suggested that there were new trends in the debate about humanity/nature/society.

For instance, in *Weimarer Beiträge* in October, science fiction specialist Olaf R. Spittel reviewed the Steinmüller's novel *Andymon* (see p. 95). He found it "one of the most remarkable books of recent GDR science fiction", an unusual contribution to the new dialogue about the old problem of humankind's relationship to nature. Instead of showing humans ruling nature, the Steinmüllers emphasis was on humanity as part of a nature which it could seek to form but could not rule. The book's uniqueness, Spittel found, was that it took dreams and ideals existing in the GDR and made them the goals of Andymon's development toward social harmony. Everyday dreams as goals —- a "conceptual literary experiment having model quality for the present".[291]

In another major discussion article in that same issue of *Weimarer Beiträge*, prominent literature specialists tried to sort out what GDR literature was and where it was going.[292] There was general agreement that GDR literature (a) was different ("GDR literature not only asks different questions but also poses the questions differently than bourgeoise literature can"[293]) and (b) was asking new questions in the 1980s (about the meaning of life, the truth in life, the values in daily life[294]). In addition to the new emphasis on values, Schlenstedt (as noted on p. 20) thought a new context for literature also was emerging, what he called "critical socialist realism"; since it was "self-critical", he found that progressive.[295]

Literary concepts such as these did not necessarily suggest that Cibulka and others had been on the wrong track with their value questions and ecological criticisms. But an article in the next issue of *Weimarer Beiträge* suggested that perhaps the questions had not always been put correctly, that the ecology critics

113

had ignored a central and essential standard of GDR writers--
that is, their political role. In an insightful interview by Silvia Schlenstedt, Stephan Hermlin dealt with this issue which repeatedly had come up in "outsider" (natural scientists, technicians, etc.) discussions about the role literature was/should be
playing in the debate about ecology and progress. In this context, Hermlin said about the non-political interests of writers,

> I believe in every talented artist there is a desire to
> say something more, to be involved with things other
> than daily political trifles. That cannot be the task
> of art and never has been. In its entire development,
> art has sought to answer great existential questions.[296]

Taken alone, that statement, too, seemed to clear authors such as
Cibulka, who currently were concerned with humankind's survival
vis a-vis radioactive fallout. Going on, Hermlin, nevertheless,
saw an especial *socialist* responsibility for GDR authors which
seemed to agree with what Höpcke, for instance, had written about
Cibulka's book. Hermlin said,

> socia*l*ist authors have a socialist ethos which says,
> 'Whether you wish it or not, in everything you write the
> question arises whether you have helped people to move a
> step forward with what you have created'. Therefore,
> one is one's own task-master; that is uncomfortable, but
> it cannot be otherwise.[297]

Precisely what was meant to write *politically*, even if not always
about politics, remained open to debate. Were the socialist writers to be "representatives of society", or, as a Western observer
phrased the dilemma its "advocates for truth", that is "attorneys
for real socialism vis-a-vis the officially spoiled interpretation"?[298]

Another level of literature's institutional life soon illustrated author Hermlin's points about literary responsibility to
people and concern with current issues. At a November meeting in
Karl-Marx-Stadt, 600 GDR readers met with 24 of their authors (see
p. 17). As reported by *Sonntag*, the conclusion of the meeting
confirmed what Höpcke had maintained -- GDR readers wanted prob-
lem-oriented literature which gave them possibilities for self-
identification and problem-solving: "The concepts of life represented by the literary heroes were repeatedly compared with one's
own values...Identification was generally sought". In addition,
the readers wanted "more books which brought out contentious socialist value concepts".[299]

These, and other wishes, were also expressed in letters from
readers which continued to reach Hanns Cibulka's desk, especially
after 12,000 copies of *Swantow* had been reprinted in a second

edition. A 45-year-old agricultural scientist, for instance, wrote,

> *I was simply struck and deeply impressed by the judicious choice of words through which you openly and honestly addressed facts about endangered peace, threatened nature, and human cooperation.*

An Erfurt reader, after finishing *Swantow*, wrote that he was "deeply impressed" by the book's

> *openness toward problems of our times, which, as you write, should be an important aspect of contemporary art. Surely in earlier books you already have subjected yourself to critical self-questioning, but in none is it as concrete, almost relentless, as in this one. What is significant is that the solutions always remain transparent.*
>
> *It occurred to me while reading your book that the problems which you treated have a general validity and are hardly limited to our state. Could one not say humanism -- measure of society, science, and, or precisely, art. But `is the standpoint, the partisanship of an artist, not always determined more by society and science, stronger than ever before, and do not the borders between these categories gradually blur without at the same time achieving a repeal?*

Meanwhile the cultural/literary community also participated in another round of the natural scientist vs writer debate. In a late 1984 issue of *Sinn und Form*, Erhard Geissler -- under the provocative title "Brother Frankenstein or - Foster Cases Through Retort?" -- criticized writers such as Heinar Kipphardt, Ernst Schumacher, Jurij Brězan, and Christa Wolf for brusquely and consciously ignoring modern biology and instead defaming geneticists "as Eichmanns".[300]

Spirited literary responses came very soon.[301] Defending the attacked writers, Werner Creutziger asked Prof. Geissler why it was so difficult to understand that people were frightened and that writers, in expressing such feelings, were "for once really almost exactly vox populi". In addition, Jürgen Hauschke criticized molecular biologist Geissler for his treatment of the writer Brezan, saying the author had offered his novel as a stimulus to public discussion about the discrepancy between human knowledge and moral maturity and not as a text book. Art is *one* organ of social understanding, Hauschke insisted, science another. Manfred Wolter added pointedly that the more natural scientists expressed scientific certainty, such as Geissler had done, the more persistent become the second thoughts of writers.

115

GDR literature's deep and deepening concern about its specific role in the ongoing societal dialogue was also mirrored in a Leipzig University conference. Literary specialists had precedentially asked colleagues from the field of philosophy to join them in an interdisciplinary discussion of the changing presentation of conflict in GDR literature. The literary scientists emphasized that moral conflict was the "metier" of literature, but social conflicts were increasingly being presented; the philosophers insisted that a sharp distinction could not be drawn between the two. Both disciplines agreed, however, that conflict presentation, indeed, had changed. It no longer was confrontation between characters with contradictory attitudes to ethical positions but rather contradictions growing out of humanity's general, existential condition. Interestingly, too, while interdisciplinary discussion was seen as essential, the philosophers pointedly called on their literary colleagues to make it more effective by doing their philosophical "homework"; the literature specialists, in turn, challenged the philosophers to understand more clearly the objects and methods of literary science.[302]

In autumn 1984, after months of such animated conceptual tug-of-war in 'the political culture between new and old interpretations of progress, the decision-making center once again acted, or reacted. A new **state** regulation further legally guaranteeing nuclear safety and protection from radioactivity was passed, on October 11.[303]

And, as the year drew to a close, it was time again for the system's leaders to take stock of that year's economic performance and to formulate a new plan for 1985. As noted earlier, the 1984 economic plan had called for measures curbing water and air pollution noise levels and waste disposal especially in the coal, energy, and chemical industries. In the assessment of progress toward those goals at the end of 1984, it was found that the measures had been implemented and emphasis on evironmental protection in certain urban industrial areas had begun. But, the assessment added, measures for environmental protection making use of new scientific-technological knowledge had to be related more closely to "the recovery of valuable materials from waste products and waste water".[304]

Based on the 1984 achievments and long-range goals, the economic plan for 1985, then, included some new ecological aspects: (1) Instead of just referring to "environmental protection", the new plan also used a broader term, "environmental structuring" (Umweltgestaltung). (2) The 1985 concept first asserted the importance of general "measures for rational utilization and protection of natural resources" and within that broad context then specifically called for the water, air, and other measurs of previous plans but without special references to the coal, energy, and chemical industrie, (3) The city of Cottbus was added to the

116

previous industrial centers which were to reeceive special environmental protection attention, and it was said such emphases
should improve "environmental conditions", a broader spectrum than
earlier plans suggested. (4) And finally, the 1985 plan incorporated the recycling efforts which the year-end assessment said
were missing.[305]

In addition to such rule-making actions, probably in response
to input demands from within the system, there also was evidence
by late 1984 that other output functions,too, were dealing with
some of the demands flowing into the decision-making center. For
instance, local state units, especially Peoples' Assemblies, were
encouraged to become more active in implementing national policies, that is, applying rules on the books. While they had made
progress, apparently the intensified environmental protection measures had brought new problems, as well. Ecological activities
required elected representatives with specialized, often scientific knowledge and skills at the same time that the SED was calling
for more worker-representation on the Assemblies.[306] The two developments had not always meshed. In addition, local input into
rule-application was likely to increase since the Council of Ministers had issued new guidelines easing the petition process. GDR
citizens now could register their complaints verbally, as well as
in writing.[307]

Also in the adjudicative, or conflict-resolution, function of
the system's output there were changes suggesting increased concern for environmental problems. After years of relative judicial
laxity toward ecological violations, a new strictness was being
reported, especially toward responsible authorities. Stiffer
sanctions, for instance, had been made available for punishment in
water pollution cases -- fines up to 10,000 Marks. This, it was
felt, would help create an atmosphere of greater alertness and im-
patience with environmental violations and a general lack of discipline in this area.

For instance, *Der Schöffe* reported a 1984 case of water pollution which had come before "District Court W". The charge was
illegal disposal of paper mill waste into a nearby river. The de-
fendents, the plant manager and technician of the mill, were
charged with "economic damage" and "causing an environmental danger". Found guilty, both were put on two-year probation and fined
a month's salary. If probation conditions were not met, it was
said each one could receive a one-year prison sentence.[308]

Clearly, too, as frequently illustrated, the political communication output concerning ecological and environmental issues,
flowing from the decision-making center to the population, had
been accelerated. At the same time, so had the vigorous communication flow from the political culture to the center, via the institutions of church and literature plus party units and other

117

interest groups. In short, the GDR's feedback process appeared alive and astonishingly vital in 1984.

3. 1985

Relative to all the evidenced energy in the GDR dialogue about environment in the early 1980s, the deca-midyear of 1985 might in review be seen as calm. And yet the case could be made that it was a period of "settling in" rather than "settling down". Many new issues introduced into the discussion in earlier years were repeatedly taken up and deepened; initiated actions and programs were expanded. In short, the parameters earlier determined were being filled in.

For instance, at the **church** level of the dialogue the head of the institution in Saxony, Bishop Hempel, in February met with SED leader Erich Honecker to confirm the church/state cooperation agreed to earlier. The Bishop's comments were fully reported on the first page of *Neues Deutschland*.[309] Thus the way was clear for continued cooperation in the questions of environment and ecology that so troubled the GDR's church leaders and members.

In March, **literature**'s running debate with natural scientists about the validity of progress, took a new turn. The scope of the controversy was unusually broadened when the Academy of Arts' *Sinn und Form* opened its pages to a *West German* natural scientist. Köln University's geneticist Benno Müller-Hill was given space to respond to the ideas of Erhard Geissler publicized in late 1984 (see p. 115). Writing under the title "Colleague Mengele - Not Brother Eichmann", Müller-Hill said that the second-thoughts, in a *form*, among disciplinary colleagues went back to World War II. The fact that geneticists and physicists then misused their knowledge to murder Gypsies and Jews was a problem which had never really been discussed. This, too, should be considered, the West German scientist suggested, vis-a-vis current genetic experimentation. To stop experiments would be absurd; it was realistic, however, to insist that a scientist carry out his research according to his conscience.[310] In the following issue of *Sinn und Form* other natural scientists, from within the GDR, continued the discussion with Geissler. While one, for instance, defended his charge of science-defamation by writers, a second believed that scientists simply had to accept the writers' fears as "real" and continue to discuss their causes.[311]

The conceptual tug-of-war within intellectual **interest groups** was further suggested by key ideas in two articles appearing in the *Deutsche Zeitschrift für Philosophie* in March. Horst Paucke, Academy of Sciences sociologist, again defended, as often before, the GDR's ecology concepts against bourgeoise charges that Marxism had nothing constructive to offer in the current environmental

debate.[312] On the other hand, in the next issue of the philosophical journal, Wolfgang Luutz asserted that the contradictions in
socialism must be researched more thoroughly. The University of
Leipzig professor for Marxism/Leninism wrote that it was necessary
to examine the formation of socialist consciousness in a more differentiated way. Specifically, Luutz felt it was essential to
know which "*daily experiences*" are produced by socialism[313], in
short, what and how personal experiences effect the political culture. The implication of Luutz's research challenge for the continuing environmental debate was clear. GDR citizens' *personal*
encounters with environmental problems might be having exactly
that modifying effect which political socialization theory hypothesized -- that is, personal experiences frequently change earlier
values and attitudes officially socialized through schools and the
media.

Sociologists, too, participated actively in discussions of
how individual GDR citizens perceived their present situation. At
the Congress of Sociology, held in late March, it was reported
that "spontaneous scientific dispute was possible" among the 900
conferees. Moreover, "one could discuss controversially" and
"open questions could remain open".[314] Some of those questions
concerned the nature of work in the context of the scientific-
technological revolution's 'progress', as well as creativity and
democratic activity.[315] In short, according to initial reports,
the GDR's sociologists were increasingly concerned with what people *wanted*, rather than with what they should do.[316] After the
years of dialogue, it apparently now was accepted that the public,
indeed, had *wants*, as in the area of environmental policy, and
research's new task was to determine exactly what they were.

In March the **state** took an important step, perhaps in response to the demands from many levels within the system for more
attention to citizens' needs. That State Council recommended,
i.e., put pressure on, agencies to process petitions from citizens more quickly and seriously. If implementation of the State
Council's new recommendation would meaningfully strengthen the
feedback process in the GDR, as intended[317], the discrepancy which
citizens perceived between words and deeds -- made more visible
through the continuing dialogue -- might be diminished. In SED
General Secretary Erich Honecker's view, the effective processing
of petitions was a top political assignment for all state organs
and was a measure for the "further deepening of socialist democracy".[318]

Pressure for more such deeds, or corrective feedback, from
the decision-makers continued to come from the **church**. For instance, at a synodical meeting in Mecklenburg in late March, the
head of the Church Research Institute in Wittenberg lectured on
the continuing restrictive reporting by GDR media of environmental
problems in the country.[319] Then at an April meeting of the

119

representatives of 25 environmental groups at the Wittenberg Research Center delegates reported that environmental activists were willing to work with the GNU of the League of Culture while maintaining their own independence as church groups. Indeed, in spring members of the County Council for the Magdeburg area had met with church leaders and emphasized their willingness to include church members in regional environmental protection work. For its part, the church and its leaders hoped through such cooperation to gain, among other things, more information about the real environmental situation in the GDR.[320]

Thus, it seemed that by 1985 the church had evolved its approach -- within religious activities there was more emphasis on environment and within the society more cooperation with state agencies to achieve improvements. For instance, the June environmental church service (Umweltgottesdienst) in Pötzschau focused on the problems of brown coal strip mining which threatened the area.[321] In addition, the GDR churches had intensified the international dimension of their concern and dialogue. By mid-1985 three interrelated crises usually were discussed and considered together: world armaments, environmental destruction, and international economic repression and exploitation. Within this context, the GDR churches were planning to participate actively in the international World Council of Churches conference on "Peace, Justice, and the Preservation of Creation" which had been called for 1990.[322]

In May it was the turn of legal scholars and political scientists to be heard on issues relating to progress in the GDR's socio-political system. In anticipation of a big **interest group** conference of these disciplines, preparatory "think pieces" were offered in the journals Neue Justiz and Staat und Recht. Eberhard Poppe, for instance, published his concerns about the development of socialist democracy as a social force. Although political and legal scholars (Staats- und Rechtswissenschaftler) had done a lot of work in this area, Poppe felt that there was a need to make democratic processes much clearer to citizens. Moreover, the specialists should also examine existing mechanisms to see whether they were really adequate to influence the kinds of behavior and consciousness essential to socialist democracy. In Poppe's view, the needs of the people, including those in the ecological and environmental fields, demanded more attention and recognition. As for years, he criticized individual employees in the bureaucracy for their lack of concern.[323] Uwe-Jens Heuer also again called for more participation by workers in the decision-making of the system.[324] These ideas were among those discussed at the late June conference on "State and Law in the Further Development of the Advantages and Dynamic of the Socialist System."

While the GDR's legal and political science scholars thus concentrated on the system of socialism, a colleague in the field of economics went into print with a much less frequently heard idea. Concerned about the roots of problems arising from the development of science and technology, Rolf Espenhayn contended that many problems and risks were "system neutral". Writing in the leading economic journal *Wirtschaftswissenschaft*, Espenhayn said that some problems are "present to the same degree and with the same sharpness in socialism" as in capitalism.[325]

By the end of summer 1985 the **church** again reviewed its efforts to promote improved environmental conditions in the GDR. In an interview with the weekly church newspaper *Glaube und Heimat*, a church official in the county of Gera summarized state/church discussions about environmental questions. In those discussions it was clear that practical projects, such as caring for forest areas or a park, won more approval from state officials that did the church groups' general criticism about environmental deficits. In fact, a summer meeting of church environmental groups had reported that state officials seemed pleased with three forms of environmental cooperation by Christians: (1) increasingly exercising their environmental concerns on the job, i.e., living by laws on the books, (2) carrying out practical projects, such as park care, and (3) participating in the official GNU organization.[326]

By autumn there again were several significant **state** output actions, or responsive reactions, relevant to the environmental dialogue and the issues at its center. For instance, the Ministry of Higher Education announced a new program of environmental instruction for the 1985/86 school year. The program of courses would be part of the basic technical and economic education at schools of engineering and other technical schools in the GDR. Planned were two-hour introductory presentations. Attention would also be focused on specific aspects of environmental protection and environmental structure which the GDR had set as priorities, such as the increased utilization of waste products and energy-conserving technologies. Environmental specialists in the engineering schools were to be given additional special training for meeting the new goals.[327]

The sharp thrust of demands about individual participation being fed into the system's center may after a time also have contributed to other outputs. For example, on September 1, a new law went into effect to strengthen the role of mayors and to allocate responsibility to the *local* level for policy planning and guidance, including measures to improve environmental conditions. Specifically, the new law, replacing earlier 1963 legislation, concerned the local Peoples' Assemblies, giving them environmental responsibility at the county level, along with the County Council.[328]

Seen as a step in developing socialist democracy, the Assemblies were given the right to make their recommendation to Council members, leaders of firms, as well as chairpersons of collectives and to be informed of the result within two weeks. In addition, citizens could serve on commissions, etc., more than they previously had. Throughout the law, the principle of openness in the work of state agencies was emphasized repeatedly. In the context of the constitutional right of citizens to participate in their socio-political system, the new measure elevated that premise to law, that is, it required officials

> to deal consciously with the information, concerns and complaints of the citizen, to constantly be and remain in close touch with the citizens, to decide promptly on citizens' concerns, with humane understanding and expertise based on the laws, and to answer persuasively, always dealing with the citizen politely and attentively.[329]

In a radio interview, a GDR spokesperson added that the protection of nature was among the needs of citizens represented with great involvement at the local level.[330]

Potentially very significant was the new state unit for environmental inspection (*Umweltinspektion*) which also went into effect on September 1. Specifically, it was to carry out more unified control over environmental conditions by working closely with other state agencies, factories, and social organizations.[331] Operating within the Environment Ministry and at the County Council level, the new State Environmental Inspection Agency was given comprehensive competence to control implementation of laws.

Another output from the state in September 1985 took a quite different form -- a booklet. Entitled *Environmental Protection-Goals and Results*, the publication was prepared by Panorama, the GDR's press agency for feature material, distributed primarily abroad.[332] As an official overview of GDR priorities and achievements in the environmental area after years of discussion and actions, it provided an interesting and comprehensive stocktaking.

The 72-page illustrated booklet opened, for instance, with acknowledgment of the wide discussion about environmental questions in the 1980s, plus the assertion that the SED had long been on record regarding their importance. A second initial point made was that the GDR's environmental protection depended on *how* economic growth was reached, for ecological priorities were not automatic. Therefore, the GDR not only emphasized "cleaning up" existing pollution, but also more efficient use of raw materials, absolute reduction of energy and water usage, improved secondary use of raw materials, recycling of waste products, and improved developments in production procedures. In other words, by going to the base of the economy to make better use of materials, both pollution would be reduced and resources saved.

This point was especially important, the authors made clear, for a country not blessed with many raw materials, except for brown, or lignite, coal. Its water supply, for instance, barely equalled needs. Thus, the GDR emphasized saving what it had. For instance, about 12% of needed raw materials came from secondary products (or, put another way, 42% of all waste products were re-used), and that use of waste products had doubled in the past ten years. The numerous laws regulating collection and reuse of mate-rials covered metal, paper, oil, glass, textiles, tires, plastics, garbage, construction waste, ashes, etc.[333]

Another point the booklet stressed was the GDR's active par-ticipation in international projects, since environmental problems were seldom soley of national origin. Within the RGW, the GDR took part in more than 600 research projects. Governmental struc-tures, too, must be adequate for carrying out environmental poli-cies, and the GDR booklet suggested that these were amply avail-able to the system -- the Environmental Ministry, Peoples' Assem-blies to coordinate measures, the State Environmental Inspection Agency, Chamber of Technology, GNU, League of Culture activities, the FDJ youth organization's reforestation projects, etc.

Public education, too, was part of a serious national program of environmental protection. For instance, the booklet reported, GDR kindergarten teachers were trained to use children's books for teaching basic ideas about ecology and environmental protection. Polytechnical high schools included environmental protection in their natural science instruction, and classes carried out speci-fic practical projects. At the trade school level, instruction was offered in environmental law and protection, and engineering schools taught basic environmental policy, especially procedures such as recycling. Finally, the universities and other schools of higher education had Commissions for Environmental Protection and for Environmental Planning, including special teaching chairs for those fields of instruction.

Finally, the publication emphasized special tasks which the state and its citizens carried out, from waste product collection to air pollution reduction. In the area of soil conservation, the Panorama booklet reported, 1% of the small country's territory was in nature preserves (numbering 733 by mid-1986) and another 18% in protected national culture areas (totaling 403 in 1986).[334]

In fall a new and heated debate broke out within the institu-tion of **literature** about the alleged "pessimism" of writers. This time Volker Braun's new novel *Hinze-Kunze-Roman* was the center of the controversy. Deputy Minister of Culture Höpcke reviewed the book *before* publication,[335] and when it appeared in print in September it had an extraordinary explanatory "prologue" at the end. Written by Germanist Dieter Schlenstedt, the elaborate "footnote" to Braun's novel was perceived as a publishing house justification for printing the novel.[336]

About the same time, Braun published an essay in *Sinn und Form* which defended young writers[337], and at a September meeting of the Writers' Union, SED Secretary for Culture Kurt Hager criticized them. Young authors, Hager said, were pessimistic and resigned vis-a-vis the nuclear threat and/or negative personal experiences.[338] The renewal of this debate about the role of young writers was reminiscent of what Karin Hirdina had written several years earlier in her spirited defense of so-called "problem literature". Relativizing criticism of writers who concentrated on descriptions of daily life, Hirdina had written that for many readers "orientation" (such as Cibulka and others provided) was an essential role of literature -- "to put into words experiences, behaviors which are widely present in everyday life but are not the object of public discussion". Thus, "the investigation of life's real actualities and possibilities - both together - constitute the decisive function and potential of literature".[339]

In October a harsh critique of Braun's novel appeared in the SED's newspaper *Neues Deutschland*. The political critique of the author was that Braun's readers know "what he opposes, but not with whom and for what he struggles".[340] At the same time, however, the author appparently was not to be ostracized, for on 27 November he publically read from his works and answered questions at an Academy of Arts meeting.[341]

Also in November, the genre of science fiction and its relationship to progress, environment, science, and technology was again brought to the attention of the GDR reading public. The newspaper *Sonntag*, published by the League of Culture, featured a page-long interview with science fiction novelists Angela and Karlheinz Steinmüller who had offered provocative new insights into 'progress' in 1982 (see pp. 95ff). Especial attention was given to apects which made their novels, such as *Andymon*, different. For instance, Ms. Steinmüller was quoted as saying that science fiction could serve a warning function, but sometimes a specific tendency was emphasized to the exclusion of other facts. Elaborating on this, Mr. Steinmüller commented that

> *exactly this has become fashion in the West since the 1960s. There the anti-Utopia was only an excuse for exotic adventures and playing with fear. We hope it becomes clear in our books that the much-described ambivalence of technology is not only a matter of use and misuse, but that technology also has, among other things, unforeseen and undesirable secondary effects on nature and society...When we take up problems which are meaningful and reality-oriented, if we conjur up a play*

124

*world which is also in tune, in the social sense, then
interesting and action-loaded conflicts result. These
are not only exciting, but also give the reader insight
into our reality. Especially the latter is what we call
realism in fantsy.*342

As 1985 drew to a close, Hanns Cibulka, too, was heard again.
He had published another diary, this one called *Seedorn*, which
also intended to mediate between humankind, nature, and society.
Erhard Weinholz, reviewing the new publication for *Sonntag*, found
positive the author's concern that dynamic expansion would lead to
problems if people did not learn to be more saving with the treasures of nature. That, said the reviewer, was in agreement with
the society's economic goals of using less materials in production. On the other hand, Weinholz was less impressed with Cibulka's contention that people sought success on the wrong frequency;
that ignored the fact that growth in consumption was essential to
communism but was not a goal in itself. Perhaps this diary,
though apparently less concerned with ecology per se than *Swantow*
had been, would also become part of the GDR's general dialogue
about progress. Clearly Cibulka was still being heard in the dialogue -- as in a Berliner Rundfunk broadcast in late September.
Entitled "Authors Speak Out", the broadcast was an opportunity for
Cibulka to discuss his newest work and insights.343

As the year's end neared, there apparently was satisfaction
at the **SED** level with its output. Not only had important measures
been offered to meet domestic demands, but internationally, too,
the priority of cooperation had made good progress, especially
with neighboring states. Throughout the year there had been
constant discussions, almost monthly, with officials of the West
German government or other FRG public leaders.344 Environmental
agreements signed had included those with West Berlin (waste water disposal), Poland (water management), Denmark, Hungary, and
Austria.345 In addition, Environmental Minister Reichelt often
participated in international conferences and consultations which,
in turn, were reported in the GDR.346

Thus, though relatively quiet, 1985 in many ways had been a
year of movement forward in the pursuit of acceptable social
change. With hindsight, one later would say it had been 'the lull
before the fallout' of Chernobyl.

4. 1986

As the GDR moved into the second half of the 1980s, signals
of changing socio-political values and demands seemed evident at
various points within the political culture. That the signals for
social change would peak dramatically in spring was, of course,
not foreseen.

125

At the beginning of 1986, for instance, the **church** summed up its role, its participation in public dialogue. Former chairperson of the Church Federation, Albrecht Schönherr, strongly felt that the church in the GDR had come to a point where it must not permit itself to be drawn into undifferentiated opposition to the state and, at the same time, must not simply confirm existing opinions. Instead, the church accepted the fact that public opinion was guided with the power and information-monopoly of the state and party, but nevertheless "claimed for itself the right to interfere in public affairs and, indeed, to articulate them".

Schönherr also believed that exactly that role of the church in the GDR was unique and difficult because of its importance in Western media. "The church here lives in two publics which are antagonistically opposed to each other", he said. "Unfortunately, it is a fact that the Western media are considered very important by GDR representatives and often are used as an argument against the church". Nevertheless, Schönherr believed the church had done well in carrying out its mission of representing the weak within the society:

> Our commission, which has become clearer to us in recent years, focuses on the preservation of God's creation, our environment. I am pleased that the broader discussion about environmental questions has come to the public essentially through us Christians.[347]

Heinz Wagner, veteran radio journalist for religious affairs in the GDR, also felt the church had come a long way in its public work. In addition to the fact that the Bible could again be used in secondary instruction,[348] the church also had been granted the possibility of a monthly Saturday evening informational radio broadcast, as well as a television program. The latter, called "Moutling (Begegnung), was used by the church since 1978 to, in a sense, introduce itself and what it did in society. In addition, Sunday morning church radio broadcasts, begun immediately after World War II, had never been interrupted. Thus, Wagner concluded, "The church has a public. And it must realize that task".[349]

To Erhart Neubert, in the Theology Studies Department of the Church Federation, the church had another special task in the GDR because of the country's rapid urbanization -- to help citizens reorient themselves to social change. Groups within the church, for example the peace and environmental groups, were significant to the socialization of GDR citizens. As Neubert wrote,

> Suddenly and without previous concepts, a large number of groups grew out of the society. They were all interested in social problems. And these groups turned to the church...They had arisen out of the deficits of urban change.

One of their concerns was environment and ecology and the challenges of social change. In Neubert's view, that meant that

> The church must not constantly interpret theologically
> how the church remains church, but rather accept the
> task of changing reality, in the name of peace, jus-
> tice, and preservation of nature. In that way, urban
> change also will be digested and mastered.[350]

And so as 1986 got underway, the church set about planning
hopefully for the coming summer months. For example, the GDR
section of "Action Reconciliation" (*Aktion Sühnezeichen*) would
participate in restoration of Jewish cemetaries (Dessau, Berlin,
Oranienburg), and the ecological study group (*Arbeitskreis*) in the
Dresden church district would continue its summer project "Clean
Air for Vacationing Children". For three years host families had
provided holidays along the Baltic, in the Mecklenburg interior,
or in mountain areas for children from air-polluted areas such as
Leipzig, Halle, Bitterfeld, etc.[351]

Within the institution of **literature**, too, a kind of inven-
tory seemed to be underway. One concern was the evidence of
trends in readers' interests (*Leserverhalten*) -- while GDR citizens were not necessarily reading less, they were reading differently. That, in turn, might mean changes in literature's socializing influences on values of the political culture.

For instance, literature specialists were considering the
findings of the second emperical study by literature sociologists
at Halle University.[352] Their earlier survey data of 1970, collected primarily among pupils, apprentices, pensioners, house-
wives, and self-employed, had found that completion of the tenth
class of education was significant in influencing reading habits.
The newer data, collected in 1978 from industrial and agricultural enterprises, concentrated on workers and collective farmers. It
confirmed that age, gender, education, and activity (work, social
involvement, etc.), indeed, were important influences, and that
the education and activity levels were especially significant vis-
a-vis sophisticated, or exacting, reading.[353]

Also interesting was the finding that book reading was "dis-
continuous", not routinized, in contrast, for instance, to the
daily press.[354] In addition, unlike the earlier study, contemporary literature was not preferred by the industrial workers and
farmers surveyed, but rather travel literature and adventure and
historical novels. This preference, the Halle scholars suggested,
might reflect the fact that contemporary literature was not as
interesting or exciting as adventure literature, for example. Or,
as a reviewer said, contemporary GDR literature failed to meet the
reading needs of such large population groups because it was not
"broadly effective".[355]

The journal of the GDR book trade, in assessing the Halle data, found that such research did not always concentrate on the same groups of readers and so made comparisons and trends problematic. Nevertheless, it was clear that

> on the one hand, in keeping with our cultural policy goals, a great mass basis for effectuation of the specific potential of our literature has been achieved; but, on the other hand, the intensity of book usage within that large group of readers shows significant reserves...above all, workers, apprentices, unskilled employees, farmers.[356]

The consequences seemed clear to book specialists -- since reading time for books correlated with physical stress on the job, libraries, too, must take that into account. Within a context of attractive, entertaining audio-visual media, for instance, the book trade generally could encourage book-reading by emphasizing the special potential of books as storehouses of human knowledge and experience.[357]

New facts about the reading habits specifically of youth also were available. Here, too, the evidence showed that youngsters were not reading less (despite the availability of television, radio, records, or cassettes), but rather were reading differently. That is, they preferred daily newspapers, illustrated magazines, popular science literature -- in short, exciting, entertaining reading. In addition, while the number of youth who read a great deal was increasing, so was the number of non-readers.

The conclusion of this study, then, was that teachers needed to do more to cultivate an interest in literature among their pupils, and their instruction should include more emphasis on contemporary literature.[358] Such observations apparently had been reflected in the reformed study plans for literature instruction in the ten-year polytechnical high schools (POS), beginning with the school year 1986/87 -- to fit literary readings more closely to the reading interests of the pupils was the goal of the reform.[359]

In this discussions about literature and reading habits, the public interest in television and film obviously was a central issue. The electronic media, however, were not usually seen as competitors to books and mass print media. Instead, audio-visual offerings were considered supplementary, meeting different needs. For instance, television-watching was found to be popular because, among other things, it was an at-home-activity, shared within family and friendship circles; the popularity of movie-going was often combined with the pleasure of social relationships furthered by the "Kinocafes" or "Kinobars". Moreover, movies could be enjoyed in afternoons and early evenings, a time for leisure which fit into the time schedules of GDR citizens working night shifts.

Then, too, since GDR television included many literary adaptations in its programming, the specialists said it could not be said that TV was necessarily "winning out" over literature.[360]

Nevertheless, the so-called "entertainment arts" had become part of the GDR cultural scene and so were central to the discussion among scholars concerned with the socialization process. There was general agreement that it was essential to improve this art genre which reached a mass public. A key concern was "to take the popular arts seriously and to create public awareness about socialism's cultural possibilities also in this area", rather than just taking over what the West had to offer.[361] The magazine *Entertainment Arts* (*Unterhaltungskunst*), of course, had been around for a long time (by 1986 it was in its 17th volume), but a special school of higher education was necessary to provide training for this field.[362]

In the context of this discussion, statistics from the world of books for the first half of the 1980s were interesting. The book stores reported that 59% of all their visitors were citizens between the ages of 18 and 35. Of all the books bought, about 35% was belletristic, 21% children and youth books, about the same percent popular science, 12% natural science/technology, and less than 10% each for social science, travel, and art books. A serious problem, of course, continued to be the availability of books -- only 38% of the customers could find on the shelves the book they had come to the store to purchase. According to that book store survey, favorite genre included detective stories, adventures, and utopias.[363]

Despite the shortages, the GDR's book efforts were sizable and growing. Where there had been 680 book stores in 1980, the total by 1985 was 700; in the same period, books available at libraries had increased from 91 to 112 million titles (of which 30% was belletristic, 30% scientific and technical literature, and 40% children's literature); library loans had increased from 105 to 115 million and library users from 5.1 to 5.7 million.

Book production showed equally interesting results. In 1980, the GDR had produced 6,109 titles; it 1985 it was 6,400 titles and 142 million copies. For the years up to 1990, the publishing plan called for the same 6,400 titles but with 150 million copies. The exchange of foreign titles was uneven --- from 1975 to 1984 the GDR had taken 5,469 titles from non-socialist countries, and they, in turn, had taken only 4,347 (the United States, for instance, exactly 3). The total of all foreign titles published in 1985 had been 1,200, or roughly one-third of the reported production of 6,400.[364]

Meanwhile, science fiction was continuing to develop its own trends. In addition to the Steinmüller's *Andymon*, another novel

had taken up anew the relationship between the individual, society, and environment from an innovative point of view. Heiner Hüfner's utopian novel *Sonnenfünf* had as its theme the question of
gaining energy from the sun.[365] When the author read from his
novel at a Karl Marx Stadt book store, his public was primarily
youth,[366] perhaps including some who had their doubts about nuclear energy.

In the view of a science fiction editor at the publishing
house Das Neue Berlin, such literature, which formerly had been
called "futuristic novels", was more aptly described as "contemporary literature". Authors were making contemporary statements,
projected as far into the future as possible, without sketching in
detail a situation they could not adequately conceptualize. After
all, the editor said, science fiction "is a literature which
should convey philosophical thoughts and stimulate them...The utopian is a forward-looking historian".[367]

Meanwhile, within literature the substantive debate over
Volker Braun's *Hinze-Kunze-Roman* continued. Reviews and pro/can
assessments appeared in leading literary and cultural publications.[368] The related issue of GDR writers' concentration on
their search for personal identity, the tension for them between
the ideal of equality and the reality of inequality, again was a
subject of discussion.[369]

Within the **interest group** of natural scientists, the beginning of 1986 brought a final summing-up from Erhard Geissler, who
had set off the prolonged round of dialogue between natural scientists and writers with his 1984 article "Brother Frankenstein"
(see p. 115). Writing again in *Sinn und Form*, Geissler now entitled his article "Frankenstein's Death - Comments on a Discussion".[370] From his natural science point of view, that discussion
within the writers' Union had been one of "objective reactions".
There had been both acceptance and rejection of his theses, among
natural scientists as well as literary specialists. Throughout,
Geissler concluded, the basic theme had been that science and
technology must serve humankind by preserving life and freedom,
and that scientific-technological progress dare not leave humankind behind. Geissler still felt that while artists must pose
questions, for them to give absolute answers without expert knowledge was irresponsible.

Concerning the dialogue contribution from the Köln geneticist
Müller-Hill, Geissler wrote that this was an especially significant point, but one should remember that "Auschwitz was not the
product of geneticists", but rather of Social Darwinists. It was,
therefore, upsetting to Geissler that the West Berlin radio station RIAS had broadcast a half-hour program, "Genetic Research and
Biotechnology in the GDR", based on the discussion in *Sinn und
Form*, which had "misinformed" listeners. Overall positive,

however, was the fact that the desired broad discussion "got going and apparently will continue and hopefully clean away remaining misunderstandings".

Other interest groups also reviewed achievments and plans in the early months of 1986. The Chamber of Technology, for instance, representing 280,000 engineers and other scientific-technological specialists organized in 17 societies, work groups, and commissions, met in Berlin for its annual conference. Priorities for the new year were said to include more progress in the areas of micro-electronics, robot technology, and other automated construction and production.[371] Another intensified goal was providing continuing education through KDT for the country's scientific-technological specialists; through training courses and correspondence courses, KDT made it possible for about 75,000 specialists each year to update their knowledge.[372]

The importance of environmental and ecological concerns to such interest groups was reflected with especial clarity on January 21 -- the Academy of Sciences founded a "Council for the Basics of Environmental Structuring and Environmental Protection" within the presidium of the Academy. This body would coordinate basic research relevant to environmental questions and so make a significant contribution to implementation of long-range environmental policy as part of the GDR's social strategies.[373] The Academy itself was reported by 1986 to include 20,000 members, organized in a dozen natural and social science associations, which held about 700 annual meetings attracting some 41,000 participants. (In addition, there was the Agricultural Society with 2,800 firms and groups as members, holding some 200 annual meetings which drew in around 14,000 participants.)[374]

The **state and party** output side of the GDR's socio-political system was active, too, in early 1986. On March 25, for example, a new regulation was passed regarding medical observation and care of persons who might be exposed to radioactivity.[375] Replacing a 1970 measure, the new regulation provided for repeated examinations of exposed workers every 1 to 4 years. In unusual cases, the examinations would take place at other times, as well. The new regulation also stipulated the levels of accumulated exposure which constituted 'special' cases. In addition, protective medical care was to be carried out by specialized physicians, controlled by and responsible to the State Office for Atomic Safety and Radioactivity.

In preparation for the 11th SED Party Congress scheduled for spring, legal and political scientists again gave special attention to the issue of citizens' petitions. At the previous Congress, General Secretary Honecker had emphasized that deepening the relationship of confidence between the party and the people was a matter of great importance, that is, it was an essential step forward in development of the advanced socialist society in the GDR.

In the first issue of *Staat und Recht* published in 1986, Horst Lehmann and Heidrun Pohl thus took up the subject of "Citizens' Petitions and Further Development of Socialist Democracy". Tracing the historical background of the petition right in socialism, the authors pointed out that the right had become constitutional law in the GDR through the country's 1974 revised constitution. In addition, the 1985 law concerning Peoples' Assemblies had strengthened the petition right and specifically located its implementation at the local level. At the national level, a special committee of the People's Chamber, concerned with petitions, reported problems, questions and suggestions to the Council of Ministers or other concerned state agencies. The leaders of central state agencies and chairpersons of local councils who bore responsibility for implementation of the petition law also reported to the Council of Ministers. The State Council, as well, received local reports and made recommendations.

Using the city of Stralsund as an example, authors Lehmann and Pohl cited numerous instances of citizens' concern, but without any emphasis on environmental/ecological petitions which might have reached the responsible agencies.[376] Yet the significance of this discussion for environmental questions would soon be seen-- in GDR citizens' reactions to Chernobyl.

Another reflection of the SED's interest in strengthening ties between the party leadership and the people was found in its continuing political communication output about development of democratic socialism. For instance, the Institute for Scientific Communism in the Central Committee's Academy for Social Sciences devoted its first information bulletin of the year to the issue of "The Socialist Way of Life and Democratic Activity".[377] First announcing establishment of a study group (*Problemrates*), the *Bulletin* explained that the interdisciplinary group, after years of practical experience, felt the theme of democratic activities in socialism had to become a key reserch concern. The central question would be "How do we achieve higher quality and effective democratic activity?" Throughout the 79 pages of the publication, aspects of democratizing the socialist way of life were discussed, including activities among workers and within the trade union, within the medical care profession and physical education, etc.

As a form of followup, Karl A. Mollnau in *Einheit* in February, explained the interrelationship between democratic societal structures and personality development.[378] In the GDR, the author argued, "the individual does not have to achieve his own personal development contra the state". Instead it was the state which created increasingly advantageous material as well as non-material conditions for such achievement. Individual development along with that of all citizens in the society, Mollnau wrote, were both achieved in proportion to active and conscious realization by every citizen of his/her rights and duties.

In addition to reinforcement of decision-maker views about the importance of the petition right and the need to develop socialist democracy generally, the beginning of 1986 also saw renewed political communication about Peoples' Assemblies as a channel for direct citizen input. Returning to the law passed some months earlier to increase the authority of those bodies, three Halle University professors used the January pages of *Staat und Recht* to discuss again the importance of effective local representation.[379]

Throughout Eastern Europe, the authors said, there was a trend for Assemblies to use the elements of democracy more directly than before. Specifically, Assembly meetings should be more substantive, discussions more lively, and options broader, with social organizations increasingly included. The strengthened authority and responsibility of Assembly delegates also was important; the law had devoted a whole chapter to their rights and duties. Young cadre and workers were especially sought for nomination by the parties and mass organizations.

Against this background of political communication, then, Secretary Honecker's major report to the 11th Party Congress in April tied petitions, local Peoples' Assemblies, and socialist democracy together into a recommendation regarding the "further development and improvement of socialist democracy" in the GDR. (In fact, as later reported in the *Western* press, before the Congress opened Secretary Honecker had personally received a 10-page petition from 21 young GDR citizens asking for a "widespread dialogue" between citizens and leaders concerned about the social policy, the role of the party, freedoms, etc.[380]) Under our conditions, Erich Honecker, told the Party Congress,

> local politics is, in the best sense of the word, politics for and with the community. Every citizen can directly influence decisions of local concern...In order to further develop socialist democracy, the cooperation of local state organs, the citizens, and their Peoples' Assemblies is of great importance...To respect the rights of the citizens, their suggestions and critical instructions, to preserve their justified interest, is an obligatory commandment for everyone who carries responsibility in our state. Thus it is said with all clarity that whoever behaves indifferently vis-a-vis the peoples' concerns, behaves politically irresponsibly. Many petitions to central party and state organs could already have been taken care of on the spot, quickly and unbureaucratically through careful investigation and responsible clarification.[381]

133

Secretary Honecker also had words for environmental/ecological concerns in his report to the party:

> Related inseparably to everything is the further protection of the natural environment. We expend significant resources to expand or to establish appropriate new capacities in industry and agriculture. We increasingly introduce new technologies which make possible the regaining of productive substances and their reintroduction into economic circulation. The frugal use of resources offers an additional guarantee to improving air and water quality, as well as forest protection.[382]

The Central Committee's directive for the next five-year economic plan, adopted by the Party Congress, reported a major achievement in this area: "increased production and labor productivity with an increased reduction of energy and material usage and improved utilization of basic resources".[383] This trend was to be continued, since the new plan for the years 1986 to 1990 included these goals:

-- absolute reduction in the use of raw materials and substances (average annual reduction of 4%)

-- decreased energy consumption (equivalent to 80 million tons of raw brown coal)

-- development of technologies and procedures in industrial and agricultural production which produce less waste products, along with maximum economic utilization of waste products, to reduce pollution of air, forest, earth, and water

-- reduction of overall energy intensity of the economy (average 4% -3% annually)[384]

Specifically in Section 8 the Directive dealt with "Development of Environmental and Water Management". It made clear the GDR's two-fold strategy of less and better use of productive materials:

> In the interests of an effective domestic economy, as well as the constant improvement of working and living conditions for the people, the protection of the natural environment and its management through utilization of new scientific-technological knowledge is to be related closely with the task of extracting and returning waste products to the reproduction process.
> Especially in the energy, metallurgy, chemical, cellulose, and paper industries, along with agriculture and the food stuffs industry, essential capacities are to be created for regaining valuable materials to reuse in

*production and for rationalizing and expanding the cur-
tailment of emissions, waste water, and solid waste products.*

*For air purity and forest protection, all essential
measures are to be implemented to reextract valuable
materials and to increase energy utilization through
desulphuration of emissions.*[385]

5. Chernobyl

Four days after the SED's Party Congress ended, in the morning hours of April 26, Western Europe learned of a nuclear accident at Chernobyl in the Ukraine. The next day Prof. Georg Sitzlack, head of the GDR's State Office for Atomic Safety and Radioactivity Protection, traveled to Denmark with a delegation of experts. He was there when confirmation of the accident in the Soviet Union came via a Tass news agency report on April 28.

On April 29, in Copenhagen, Sitzlack gave a statement to the
press. This first official reaction, in the view of Werner Gruhn,
"was a clear criticism of improprieties in Soviet nuclear plant
construction where defective products were used and safety regulations violated in order to meet plan norms". In later announce-
ments from within the GDR, Gruhn found that such distancing from
athe Soviet position was avoided. According to Gruhn's study,
special steps had been taken on the 28th to measure radioactive
fallout in the GDR.[386] And during the same time, April 28-30, GDR
environmental specialists were confering with their counterparts
from the FRG.

From April 30 on, the GDR's State Office for Atomic Safety
issued reassuring notices to the public. For instance, on May 2
Prof. Lanius and Prof. Flach, of the Academy of Sciences, wrote in
Neues Deutschland that the GDR reactors were different from those
in the USSR and that panic was being cultivated in the West. The
professors also generally approved of nuclear plants but called
for "constantly building into existing systems additional safety
measures, reflecting the newest developments, to further reduce
the risk of accidents."[387] The next day *Neues Deutschland* published radioactivity measurements in the GDR, but not those of the
accident area itself.[388]

On May 14, Dr. Sitzlack and a GDR delegation were in Bonn to
carry on routine discussions about effectiveness of nuclear environmental protection and how best to protect citizens from radioactivity.[389] How "routine" the post-Chernobyl discussions were
was not immediately clear. Similarly, it seemed logical to assume that Chernobyl was a theme at the May 21 meeting of the
League of Culture presidium which reportedly discussed the "multitude of initiatives for further improvement of environmental

protection and water management".[390] Meanwhile, the West German press reported on May 23 that the GDR had urged increased exchange of information with the Federal Republic about nuclear reactor safety.[391]

Some of the public's first critical reactions apparently came from within the church. According to a later Western report, a church peace and environmental group in Berlin-Lichtenberg on May 1 wrote to the GDR government, demanding a stop to nuclear energy production.[392] At a synodical meeting in Potsdam on May 23-25, the USSR reportedly was severely criticized for delaying information about the accident. GDR officials, too, were reprimanded for not making measurements of radioactivity fully public. Demands for open, public discussion about the risks of nuclear energy, as well as alternative energy sources, were loud.[393] Demands and resolutions to phase out nuclear energy were also heard within other church circles.

In addition, it was reported that "shocking timliness" was a common church reaction to a study released only a few days before Chernobyl by the GDR Federation of Churches. Entitled "Physicians Against Nuclear Danger", it alleged that the dangers to the GDR of nuclear attacks or catastrophes had been played down and that only selected GDR doctors had been permitted to join the committee of physicians.[394] Apparently, too, in early June a seven-page "Appeal from the Independent Peace and Ecology Movement and Other Concerned Citizens to the Government and People of the GDR" was circulating throughout the country.[395]

Calming environmental reports continued to be heard over the GDR's electronic media. On May 30, for instance, listeners were assured that progress in environmental protection had been made especially through increased recycling of waste products, and that the Ministers Council and its Advisory Council for Environmental Protection were strictly controlling plant emissions, etc.[396]

Interestingly, in light of actions GDR citizens would take in the next weeks, the June issue of *Neue Justiz* appeared in print with an article by the GDR's Deputy State Attorney General, Harri Harrland. In it, he made a strong case for the petition right. Harrland called specifically on state attorneys to assure strict observation of socialist legality in this area; citizens' petitions relating to the work of the attorneys were to be given special attention, as well as those concerning investigative agencies. The television series, "The Attorney Has the Word", Harrland wrote, had stimulated citizens to ask questions, express opinions, and demand information. In Harrland's view, four weeks would be adequate to process a petition or to respond.[397]

International Environment Day was observed on June 5. Environment Minister Reichelt issued a press statement,[398] and at observances at Tharandt, Deputy Minister Thoms reported that the GDR's contribution to the UN's environmental work was especially important for countries in the developing world.[399] The GDR public, however, had a different message.

On International Environment Day, GDR citizens, taking seriously previous statements by Honecker, Harrland, and many other party and state officials, dramatically exercised their petition right -- underwritten with 141 signatures, a citizens' petition was handed in to the Peoples' Chamber and to the Council of Ministers. It demanded a construction stop to the nuclear power plant being built at Stendal and withdrawal from nuclear energy use. Entitled, "Appeal 'Chernobyl is Everywhere'", the petition was signed by representatives of peace and ecology groups in the GDR.

The appeal, as published in a West German newspaper, said Chernobyl had caused feelings of insecurity and danger among the people, not only because of the accident itself but also the information policy concerning it in East and West. Furthermore, the dangers of reactor plants were underestimated in socialist countries and not discussed, especially in the GDR. Critical voices, the petition said, had scarcely been able to articulate their ideas about atomic power; it had been almost impossible for citizens to inform themselves. Therefore, it was necessary to rethink and restructure previous energy, economic, and information policies. The plans to expand the GDR's nuclear energy capacity with a plant at Stendal and expansion at Lubmin should be stopped and alternative sources developed, instead.[400] Other groups and citizens, independent of each other, were said to also have submitted petitions to the Council of Ministers.[401]

A second act of "socialist democracy" -- perhaps even more dramatic and historic than the petition - was undertaken. A week or so after the "Appeal", four young members of the peace movement submitted a petition to the Peoples' Chamber for a public referendum -- the first time such a request was ever made in the GDR. Under the GDR Constitution, Article 21 guarantees citizens participation in forming the socialist society, and Article 53 empowers the Chamber, if it wishes, to resolve to hold such a referendum. Therefore, the petition said the question of nuclear energy's future should be decided by the people, reminded that citizen participation was possible under the Constitution, and requested to be informed about how the citizenry might prepare a plebiscite.[402]

GDR leaders, too began to react publically. At a meeting of the SED Central Committee on June 13, Erich Honecker mentioned Chernobyl.[403] The newspaper *Horizont* appeared with an article taking the West to task for its current criticism of Chernobyl vis-a-vis its own past record with environmental accidents-- "Agent Orange", Seveso, Bophol, etc.[404] And speaking at the June

137

16-17 meeting of the new Peoples' Chamber (elected June 8), the GDR's distinguished physicist and Chamber member, Manfred von Ardenne, said the country's withdrawl from nuclear energy was unthinkable, but since Chernobyl it was clear that the safety of hi-tech was limited.[405]

But meanwhile it seemed that SED Secretary Honecker might also have had other second thoughts. In a late June interview with a Swedish newspaper,[406] the General Secretary had been asked, "What is your view about the benefits of nuclear energy after Chernobyl?" In his answer, Honecker said that nucler energy "played a certain role", but lignite coal remained the GDR's major source;[407] although the environmental problems of the latter were more serious, the GDR was nevertheless glad that it had decided in its favor and not for nuclear energy. The safety technology of the GDR nuclear power plants was at a high level, Honecker said, and the GDR intended to expand nuclear energy further. But for the present, the GDR awaited a comprehenoive report about Chernobyl, Honecker said, and added,"In my opinion, nuclear energy is not the last word."[408]

Next to be prominently heard from in the post-Chernobyl dialogue was literature. At the 49th International Pen Congress, meeting in Hamburg in late June, GDR author Stefan Heym called on writer colleagues throughout the world to demand an end to nuclear energy. "After the events of Chernobyl", Heym said, it was time to rethink, especially in the socialist countries where a change in energy policy might yet be possible. "We should begin to talk about it, loudly and openly", Heym said, departing from his prepared text.[409]

Interest groups probably also discussed Chernobyl, although at the time of this writing such evidence in the professional literature of the GDR was not yet available. For instance, at the June 26 annual meeting of the GDR's adult education organization Urania, Chernobyl would have been a logical subject within the discussion of how "the authority of science could involve itself to prevent a nuclear inferno".[410] Similarly, it probably was included in the four-day meeting in Dresden with West German citizens invited by the Chamber of Technology and the League of Culture to participate in a German-German symposium on "Environment '86".[411]

Clear statements of concern about Chernobyl were reported from church meetings held about the same time. Magdeburg's traditional "Peace Sunday" on June 28-29 was preoccupied with the atomic energy theme. And the 5th annual "Peace Workshop" held on June 29 at the Church of the Redemption in Berlin this time had 1,500 visitors -- the topic was the "Appeal, 'Chernobyl is Everywhere'". In the Mecklenburg area a group conducted an unprecedented *public* protest against a special waste depot at the town of Schönberg near the West German border. The church ecology group presented a petition to local officials demanding an immediate stop to the import of West European waste for deposit there.[412]

In July, too, the church continued its post-Chernobyl dialogue. On the 8th, the Conference of Evangelical Church Leadership said it was urgent for churches to rethink the social accountability of nuclear energy production. While it was possible that the GDR would have to live for a while with the risk of nuclear energy production, after the catastrophe of Chernobyl there no longer was reason to think that an optimistic assessment of this technology was possible. Thus, the church welcomed and encouraged all activities directed toward a more effective and conserving use of energy, as well as development of alternative, less dangerous energies. It was also announced at the conference that the permanent Church and Society Committee of the Church Federation would be concerned long-range with the problem of "Energy and the Future".[413]

In the following months, reactions to Chernobyl undoubtedly would also be reflected by other interest groups. Nevertheless, it was significant that it was the institutions of church and literature which once again had quickly and openly addressed this most dramatic incident thus far in the GDR's environmental dialogue. And if that dialogue of the 1980s had had any influence at all, perhaps it was seen most clearly in the citizen petitions, a direct input into the system, concerning environment and ecology.

6. Summary

This chapter's survey of selected actions and reactions during the years immediately following publication of *Swantow* -- at the levels of literature, church, interest groups, and party/state decision-makers -- illustrated some of the processes of feedback within the GDR's socio-political system. At the center of the continuing dialogue were environmental/ecological policy inputs and outputs reflecting differing interpretations of social and economic 'progress'. The conflict between a priority for economic growth or for environmental protection frequently was reminiscent of profit-first vs protection-first arguments in Western industrial societies.

As **1983** began, there were, for example, the Theses for the Karl Marx Year underlining progress within socialism, and, on the other hand, the writer Christa Wolf's very skeptical reflections about the role of science. Philosopher Jürgen Kuczynski reprimanded social scientists for not criticizing "the dull spots on the surface" of the GDR socio-political system, and the superconference of economic scientists assessed progress made in their ambitious five-year research plan. The Society for Nature and

Environment, operating on the output side of the system, was active in applying environmental rules on the books and sensitizing GDR citizens to their individual responsibilities for ecology. The church, too, worked to increase public awareness by putting environmental issues on the discussion agendas of regional church conferences and organizing public actions. Meanwhile, Cibulka collected letters from readers, and a science fiction writer-team, the Steinmüllers, were being positively reviewed for their evocative new presentation of 'progress'. Ethics specialists added to the dialogue their calls for worker-oriented standards of judgment, and philosophers their reminders of Marxism/Leninism's basic optimism.

Major interest group journals in the GDR also took the ecology debate to their publics. The SED, for instance, used its monthly *Einheit* to present a broad reexamination of the "meaning of life and work" in a Marxist/Leninist socio-political system. The same month the cultural journal *Weimarer Beiträge* published an aesthetic answer to the "meaning of life" question which openly and directly confronted the ecology issue. Frequently in such writings a reader sensed reprimands addressed to unnamed authors, such as Hanns Cibulka.

At the system's rule-making level, ecology and environmental protection priorities were given more attention in the annual economic plan, and a new atomic energy law was passed with extensive protective provisions. The SED's big conference for the social sciences at the end of 1983 included many reports suggesting not only theoretical belief in social progress but also objective achievements and growing concern.

Continuing into **1984**, the energized debate interestingly included a January review of Cibulka's *Swantow*, by Klaus Höpcke, Deputy Minister of Culture. Writing about a year after the book's publication, Höpcke still objected to what he thought was scientific pessimism, superficiality, and over-generalization. Approving of the revisions which had been undertaken before book publication, Höpcke suggested that he would have made even more. In short, he simply did not think that a book such as *Swantow* would be of much practical help to readers who recognized ecological dangers but wanted actively to do something about them. Thus both major initial 'establishment' reactions to *Swantow* -- the first from the natural science point of view, the second from the literary/cultural -- objected to the author's skepticism about progress.

As a spokesperson for literature, Höpcke thereafter published several additional major articles which called for what he had missed in writings such as *Swantow*, that is, positive central characters facing tough and real current problems but working toward solutions. Literature, is this view, was to be created not just for the sake of social criticism but to make a positive contribution to progress, as well.

Many other GDR leaders, representing various disciplines and often responding to Western criticisms, also put onto paper and fed into the dialogue their perspectives of technology, "truth in the arts", and "expertise" in the ecological discussion. Philosophers, for instance, called for new syntheses which would relate scientific-technological tasks to a whole set of social factors, for engineers who would take their ecological responsibilities more seriously, and for more attention to "global" dimensions of current problems. The big Philosophy Congress at the end of 1984 reflected an astonishingly candid discussion of various aspects of the ecology debate, including the concessions that the scientific-technological revolution had produced some partially negative results, economic priorities must increasingly include environmental protection, and, indeed, environmental protection had become an important value in the GDR's political culture. On the other end of the philosophy spectrum, church leaders were particularly adamant in their demand for more information for the public and consistent in the advocacy of not only "little steps" of individual actions but also involvement in state environmental groups (such as the GNU).

The SED, too, accelerated its output of political communication. Toward the end of 1984, for example, it devoted a third of its theoretical journal *Einheit* to the specific theme of environmental policy. Traditional Marxist/Leninist principles were reaffirmed, new urgency and insights conceded, practical measures to be taken discussed. Social progress as a concept was still sanctified, perhaps more than ever, in the party's view. It, however, needed more realistic redefinition and articulation in this time of doubt.

Literary voices agreed that new value questions were being asked, that a kind of "critical socialist realism" had begun to evolve. And the old problem of humankind's relationship to nature was being presented in a new way in science fiction -- humans, as a part of nature, were trying to form not rule it. In the present context, some literature specialists said GDR writers had particular *socialist* responsibilities, that is, to *help* people. "The people", too, apparently fed the same idea of wanting orientation from literature back to their authors, for instance at a unique and big meeting which brought 600 readers together with two dozen authors. While *Swantow* continued to harvest reviews, literary scholars together with philosophers tried to sort out concepts of conflict-presentation in contemporary writing. At the same time, some natural scientists, believing authors were doing a wretched job of discussing socio-scientific issues, took their case onto the pages of *Sinn und Form*. The result was a months-long debate between the two disciplines.

Perhaps most significant among the party/state output actions was the GDR's new economic plan for 1985. It broadened
significantly the scope of environmental activity, now referred to
as "environmental structuring" rather than just "environmental
protection". In addition, the possibility of citizens to input
protest locally via *petitions* was strengthened, at the same time
that fines for violating environmental laws were increased.

Thus, the GDR's dialogue and feedback processes appeared
alive and astonishingly vital -- a process in which Cibulka's
writing, and the conceptual discussions it helped to stimulate,
apparently had played a role. That it would continue to do so
seemed assured with a third edition of 20,000 copies scheduled for
reprinting in 1985.

In **1985** the GDR's dialogue about environment and ecology
seemed to reflect a certain "settling in". The church, for example, after renewing its agreement of cooperation with the state,
continued throughout the year to demand more information from the
decision-makers about environmental conditions in the country. If
that were not directly forthcoming, the church resolved to carry
on its cooperation with state agencies in order to, among other
things, perhaps in that way obtain the information the people
wanted.

On the output side, the state urgently recommended that governmental agencies take seriously the petition process available
to citizens, a step essential to the East Europe-wide move to develop socialist democracy. Following up on this challenge (and
mandate), political science and legal scholars, in articles and
conferences, debated the *procedures* of socialist democracy, as
well as its *substance*. Philosophers and sociologists, too, communicated broadly within their interest groups and to opinion leaders about the need to focus more attention on the citizens as individuals -- scrutinize their "daily personal experiences", examine their "wants" and not only their "shoulds", and understand the
impact of their direct participation on the development of a more
democratic system facing serious problems arising out of the sci-
entific-technologicl revolution and its impact, e.g. on ecology.

Another round of significant official output followed. The
party/state decision-making center upgraded the program of higher
education for environmental studies, passed a new law strengthening the role of Peoples' Assemblies, established a State Environmental Inspection Agency for improved implementation of ecological
measures, and signed international environmental agreements, especially with neighboring states.

At the level of literature, 1985 saw, among other developments, a cease-fire in the verbal battle between natural scientists and writers, another diary publication by Hanns Cibulka, and

a new science fiction presentation of 'progress' within the context of the scientific-technological revolution.

The first year of the second half of the 1980s, that is **1986**, seemed to begin with "stock-taking" at various levels of the system. The overviews presented were contexts for further discussion and development of priorities related to socio-political progress.

The church, for example, feeling it had played a crucial role in making environmental and ecological issues more "public", resolved a continued "claim for itself" to exactly that right of articulation. Literature, concerned with new evidence of not less but different kinds of reading, sought to make books more attractive and to positively incorporate the so-called "entertainment arts" into the system's socialization processes. In addition, "orientation", or "problem literature", such as Cibulka's environmental challenge, was advocated, and science fiction reflecting contemporary problems was applauded.

On the output side, the Academy of Sciences established a new council for coordinating basic environmental research, and the state passed new regulations for medical observation and care for workers exposed to radioactivity. In addition, the new five-year economic plan strengthened the GDR's answer to its environmental problems -- "more and better for less", i.e., increased economic growth with less use of raw materials.

At the same time, the decision-making center's urging to substantively and procedurally develop democratic socialism continued, to deal with, among other things, demands such as those arising from the political culture about environment and ecology. The thrust was underlined through official political communication output, especially about citizens' participation in their Peoples' Assemblies and their right to petition.

All of this dialogue throughout the 1980s in the GDR was catalyzed by the nuclear reactor accident at **Chernobyl** in the Ukraine on April 26, 1986.

The institutions of church and parts of literature, for instance, responded quickly and openly, as they had over the past half-decade. In addition, organized and independent groups petitioned their government and demanded a national plebescite from it.

This "completely new democratic feeling" a Western publication saw in the events,[414] was not exactly what struck other observers. While, indeed, the *form* of democratic expression was a precedent in the GDR it was, nevertheless, logical -- the decision-making center had for years communicated very precisely its encouragement of the petition right. Moreover, the *substance*, the

143

'feeling' behind the action was more "completely natural" than "completely new" to those who had watched the environmental dialogue develop in the GDR during the 1980s. The signals of changing political culture values, of stimuli to social change, had been there for the reading and hearing.

In this context, a final development in the state's feedback response to all that had gone before was suggestive. Later in autumn the Committee for Citizens' Petitions of the Peoples' Chamber reported that in the *first half* of 1986 (Emphasis - AM) some 140,000 citizens had turned to local state organs with petitions of suggestion, instructions, and criticism.[415] How many concerned environmental and ecological problems, and whether those petitions had been processed and responded to, remained to be seen and researched.

Nevertheless, after Chernobyl, it seemed clear that the GDR's environmental dilogue would continue, newly reinvigorated. The dialogue about dialogue would intensify, as well. After all, within all the new direct communications from the bottom up after Chernobyl, i.e., the petitions, there had been resolute public demands for more communications from the top down.

Chapter V

SUMMARY AND CONCLUSIONS

The preceding chapters have presented a political communication case study of the GDR in the 1980s. The examination concentrated on the public dialogue -- two-way communication -- about
environmental and ecological issues and its related challenges to
the concept of "progress".

Goals

The study was undertaken with both literary and political
science in mind. Relevant to the former, the research sought new
insights into literature's institutional role within the GDR's
socio-political system and its interrelationship with other parts
of that system. For political science, the search concentrated on
literary reflections of and influences on the continuous tug-of-
war between old and new values and norms in the GDR political culture. It also collected evidence of corresponding demands for en-
vironmental/ecological change emerging from the political culture
and of possible interconnections between those demands (*input*)
conveyed through the system and party/state *output* (decisions/ac-
tions). Overall, the study focused on understanding social change
as a complex and constant process of action and reaction.

Approach

These goals were pursued first through a case study of Hanns
Cibulka's ecologically challenging diary *Swantow*. Its context,
content, and reception not only illustrated literature's role in
stimulating debate and feedback within the GDR's political culture, but also reflected intensifying public doubt about "progress", as well as official defense of it.

Second, an analysis was undertaken of other selected highlights in the public dialogue from 1983 through mid-1986, i.e.,
post-Chernobyl. Frequent responses to *Swantow*'s conceptual challenges were found at many points throughout the GDR's socio-political system -- especially within the institutions of literature
and church and in mass organizations, interest groups, and SED
party units. Involved in the discussions about progress was an
interrelated constellation of political culture values, such as
nature, science, technology, performance, accomplishments, "the
good life", role of the arts, etc. In addition, surveying the
potentially influential, though not causative, dialogue *chronolog-
ically*, suggested dynamic interactions between official responses
and accelerating public feedback, or demands, in the GDR.

This study, therefore, seems to have been fruitful, despite some misgivings about attempting a new research approach, that is, initiating a **political sociology of literature** with the help of systems/functional analysis. The conceptual framework, used not as a set model or prescription but rather as an aid for collecting information otherwise not generally available, helped to order a multitude of developments in the GDR. It also suggested inter-dependencies in an industrial society grappling with the enormity of ecological and environmental problems.

For instance, by focusing on the *channels of socialization* available to literature as an institution within the political culture, it was found that change-oriented concepts were a central theme in books, reviews, readings, discussions, and analytical essays. Especially the GDR's literary/cultural journals seemed to function as "agenda-setters" for opinion leaders throughout the system, offering them a forum for candid, substantive discussion about various aspects of the so-called progress-debate.

By focusing on such communicators within the political cul-ture, the research found that the church as an institution had a significant impact, too, on changing values and norms. Its envi-ronment-related communication, along with public actions, contri-buted importantly to heightening awareness and motivating demands. For example, on the one hand, the church repeatedly called on the government for more information about environmental conditions and, on the other hand, tried to make such information available itself. In this effort, the church reflected a need felt far be-yond its own interest group members, as reactions to Chernobyl illustrated. In short, church feedback -- that is, reactions to existing conditions and suggestions for improvement -- were loud and clear manifestations of a trend toward change underway in the GDR's political culture.

Similarly, the research approach suggested that within the GDR's political culture the mass organizations also played a role in socialization. At this level, the analysis of dialogue high-lights showed that the League of Kulture (*KB*) and its Society for Nature and Environment (*GNU*) were, in fact, particularly active in the environmental/ecological discussion, and that both, in turn, interacted with the institutions of literature and church.

The research approach also signaled the importance of *inter-est groups* as sources of *input* relating to the environmental dia-logue. The examination of that function, then, found the GDR's professions and academic disciplines especially vigorous in artic-ulating feedback through articles in their interest group journals but also crossing disciplinary publishing lines to appear in print in literary/cultural publications. Conference papers, but more so conference workshop discussions, evidenced new concerns being discussed within professions or professional societies, as did institutional research plans or the activities of organizations such as the Chamber of Technology (*KDT*). Philosophers, economists, engineers, sociologists, natural scientists, technicians, and others contributing specialized viewpoints to the debate about progress, seemed increasingly to emphasize interdisciplinary dialogue, including with literary scholars.

On the *output* side, then, the research approach indicated that the political functions to be examined included party/state decisions expressed in the *making, applying, and adjudication of rules*, along with the flow of *political communication* from the party elite (including some of the discipline representatives noted above) to party members and on to the public in general.[416] In the 1980s, as the study showed, these were especially productive areas of analysis vis-a-vis the environmental/ecological policy-making context. Indeed, that output of official words and deeds frequently suggested what might be seen as "corrective" or "responsive" political behavior, i.e., apparent readjustment of goals based on more information and public feedback, or reactions. Sometimes, in fact, the wording of the output seemed to echo specific demands heard earlier in the public dialogue, although, of course, a direct causal relationship could not be inferred.

Substance

Thus, sufficient evidence was found in the GDR's environmental/ecological dialogue to confirm the study's initial hypothesis (see p. 10) and to specify and expand it to this conclusion:

> *Literature has a political function through its influence on the political culture, that is, its participation in the interrelationships of the political socialization process of values and norms. In this context, in the 1980s the GDR's institutions of literature and church were especially significant vis-a-vis the political issue of "the nature of progress" and the political problem of environmental and ecological protection. Other interest groups, such as mass organizations, professional societies, and units of the SED, also interacted and participated actively in the dialogue through their feedback reactions. The party/state leadership consistently responded with political communication and frequently with concrete action.*

The evidence out of which these conclusions grew was presented in the previous chapters and summarized at the end of each. Clearly, however, specific in-depth analyses of the various communicators in the GDR's environmental dialogue (for example, KDT, the church, the Academies, etc.) would produce more refined and expanded conclusions. That, however, was outside the scope of this study and awaits additional research, as do continuing developments in the GDR's dialogue after the nuclear reactor accident at Chernobyl in April, 1986.

Theses

This study, then, suggests the following concluding theses and, at the same time, offers them as areas for further research:

1. Literature has a political context.

In all societies literature reflects its political context, reaffirming some aspects and challenging others. Socialized into their system's political culture, authors, on the one hand, naturally proceed from many of its basic orientations. On the other hand, gifted with sensitivity and articulation, writers challenge concepts and situations they perceive as "out of tune" with the times, needs of society, and human development. Thus, they hold up a unique mirror in which others may see life more clearly.

In the GDR, the political context of literature is more obvious than in most societies. In fact, because of the integral position of the arts in the socio-political system, opinion-leaders in the GDR often see literary/cultural policy as signalling general developments. Western observers, too, frequently tend to concentrate on the political context of GDR literature without, however, at the same time understanding the complexities of its interrelationships within its system.

Central to literature's political context is the prestigious role socialism accords its writers, that of active and creative co-builders of a new society. Much is given to literature; much is expected of it. Writers are constantly reminded, as this study has shown, of their socio-political responsibilities. The exact parameters of those responsibilities, as seen by political leaders, often vary with objective conditions, including Western reactions. As seen by writers, the parameters are the subject of unending debate and public attention. This study's findings suggest that ecologically-critical authors, such as Hanns Cibulka, in the early 1980s could choose to define their responsibilities in ways other than the GDR leaders did -- their writings probably would not be entirely banned, but they also could anticipate severe official critique.

Clearly the political context of GDR literature played a predominant role in the reception of Cibulka's *Swantow*:

(1) Hanns Cibulka's message was political. He criticized ecological/environmental conditions resulting from political and economic decision-making, just as church leaders had.

(2) Accordingly, public comments plus official reviews and revisions applied political standards. Initial comments emphasized the differences between *official* political culture values and some of the *mass* values and norms reflected by the author. Moreover, when compared with the initial excerpt, the revisions for the final book version strikingly paralleled ecological/environmental concepts being communicated into the society by the GDR's leaders. In fact, they seemed for some time to be responding indirectly to Cibulka, albeit in monologues, repeatedly reprimanding intellectual neglect of politics, e.g., East/West differences.

(3) As a political message, eliciting a political response, Cibulka's writing, in turn, could possibly have a limited, indirect political influence. By contributing to the public dialogue going on at various levels of the system, Cibulka's writing was one of many influences affecting new ecological/environmental demands developing both within official and mass values and norms. In this context, it is interesting to note, without inferring a cause/effect relationship, that some of Cibulka's criticism soon seemed to be reflected in the system's output -- a new atomic energy law, for instance, was passed which included protective provisions against dangers the author had articulated; new research programs, courses of study, and economic plans seemed to mirror his appeal for more urgent responses to ecological/environmental problems in the GDR.

2. Literature in the GDR is significantly influenced by its institutional role.

Although adequate delineation of literature as an institution in the GDR is not yet available, it has been suggested that such an analysis would include the functions of teaching, publishing, reviewing, writing, distributing, etc., in their *political*, as well as social, context.

Of especial importance to these functions -- and possibly literature's institutional uniqueness in socialism -- is its "people-ties", i.e., that which the GDR says is the "alliance" (*Bündnis*) between artists and the people, the non-elitist approach to the arts. This function includes the whole range of activities involved in "taking literature to the people", and, in turn, actively involving them with its creators and creations. It is an aspect of literature's "mediator" (*Vermittler*) function.

In that role, literature is part of the *political socialization* process which orients citizens to their system. Literature transmits images about the political system per se, specific political roles/structures within it, individual groups fulfilling those functions, and specific principles and problems. For instance, in the case of ecological/environmental protection,

149

literature's socializing messages included images about socialism
as a system capable of dealing with the consequences of industrialization, the adequacy of governmental management of the environment and ecology, the ability of specifically scientists and economists to contribute to environmental problem-solving, and the
reality of "progress" as a basic social and economic principle
vis-a-vis the ecology issue.

The values, expectations, and aspirations thus conveyed by
literature both reflect and challenge the psychological base of
the socio-political system, the *political culture*. Literature
touches the "mass consciousness", or general attitudinal orientations, to which GDR citizens have been socialized through education, family and friends, information, and experiences.

In short, in carrying out its part of the socializing function, literature as an institution affects and is effected by
structures and processes and a system of complex interdependent
relationships which are *political* (that is, concerned with authoritative allocation of values for society, or deciding "who gets
what and why"). Through a *literary political sociology* approach,
that political context of GDR literature and its role and function
within the socio-political system become clearer.

A past example of how literature functions was suggested by
the "institutional" treatment of Plenzdorf's *Die neue Leiden des
jungen W*, as analyzed by David Bathrick.[417] He found that the
Academy of Arts first excerpted the story in its journal *Sinn und
Form*; 14 stages of the country presented the dramatic performance;
the Academy of Arts sponsored a public discussion and reported on
it in *Sinn und Form*; it was reviewed in literary/cultural publications. Additional research probably would show that the work also
was discussed in factory and office units that in, at the people" level, as well as analyzed and taught in university courses.

As that and other examples show, the GDR's cultural journals,
such as *Sinn und Form, Neue deutsche Literatur*, and *Weimarer Beiträge*, have an especially vital function within the institution of
literature. While they frequently are criticized in the GDR for
catering to literary reviews that are too intellectualized and too
cautious, the journals, on the other hand, open their pages to
relatively uninhibited give-and-take debate. In this way, journals, free of pre-publication review, may be said to set the agenda
for public discussion. In fct, they at times seem to be launch-
ers of socio-political "trial balloons", publishing discussions of
topics generally regarded as "non-topics". That can be quite a
venturesome role, as this study suggests, especially when the
journals publish excerpts of works which later earn official dis-
favor (Gabriel Eckart's *So sehe ick die Sache*, concerning agricultural problems) or essays by writers under severe criticism (Volker Braun in 1986).

The 1981-1982 case of Hanns Cibulka and his diary *Swantow* clearly illustrate this and other institutional aspects of literature in the GDR:

An author, stimulated in part by Western media reports of environmental pollution, wrote a book manuscript containing ecological protest. It was recommended to and accepted by a county SED publishing house for printing. Editors at the Writers' Union journal *Neue deutsche Literatur* selected, for excerpted publication, portions of the manuscript which included the largely taboo subject matter of atomic energy plants. Western media reacted to the excerpts in the journal, assessing some of them as system-challenging to the GDR. Economic leaders within the GDR system, reacting, in turn, to the Western reaction, protested the author's criticism of the atomic energy industry. The Ministry of Culture, responding to the economic protest, asked the publishing house to modify the book text. Public comment and "Establishment" reviews accepted the author's right to publish criticism but made clear the disagreements with him. The first pressrun of 20,000 copies of the modified book version sold out in several days. Subsequently, the author was invited to readings and discussions throughout the country, with church, state, party, scientific, and worker groups. A cross-section of about 300 GDR readers wrote the author about his book. Its interest and institutional acceptance was confirmed with a second printing of 12,000 copies, followed by a third of 20,000.

It is the controversial nature of such GDR literature and public reaction to it that has led some Western scholars, as noted earlier, to suggest that part of literature's institutional role in the GDR is to fill in for absence of "real" public discussion, for instance through newspapers. This function has been called "substitute publicness" (*Ersatzöffentlichkeit*). That contention, however, requires careful analysis.

To begin, there is the question of what is "controversial"? Among other things, it obviously includes significant challenges to official GDR political culture values, such as those Cibulka presented. But the old question remains -- to what extent is "significant" and "challenging" defined primarily according to GDR domestic considerations, and to what degree does it include real or presumed external influences, such as Western media reactions fed into the GDR's mass political culture? In short, it remains unclear to what extent it is *Western* reactions which define and determine "dissident" and "controversial". What is clear, however, as this study and others show, is a serious concern among some GDR intellectuals and institutions about restrictions on

their maneuverability which result from defensive official GDR reactions to Western influences; such responses, it is said, suggest
a continuing lack of self-confidence among some leaders.

That question of real or presumed literary challenges would
be irrelevant, some Western scholars counter, if public discussion
in the GDR were adequate and thus did not draw Western media attention. In addition, such criticism suggests, if GDR mass media
were "better" and public debate more "open", literature would be
different, that is, less socio-politically oriented and discussed.

Other scholars, however, believe that the critical orientation of GDR literature probably would go on precisely because of
its own overall, institutional, orientation -- socialist writers
would still choose to write about, as Stephan Hermlin said, "the
big existential questions", that is, to signal social change. The
broad public discussion of literature would continue because of
its institutionalized "people-contacts" and socialization function. On the other hand, if GDR newspapers, for instance, were
"better", a change might, indeed, occur in the style of GDR literature, if not in its thrust; GDR literature would perhaps contain less factual information than it now does (for example, Cibulka's inclusion in his revised book of a list of radioactive
substances and their half-life rates).

In addition, the point is made that there are levels and
forms of discussion and feedback in socialist countries other than
the prevailing Western image of "public debate" equalling opposing
ideological editorial columns in newspapers and free-for-all radio
and television "talk shows" and "phone-ins". Western scholars
looking for dialogue in unaccustomed places often find it, for example, in workplace, housing, and study collectives, as well as at
meetings of basic SED party units and surely also cultural/lit-
erary gatherings. Until the many and various forms of GDR discussion and dialogue have been adequately studied, and literary feedback looked at *institutionally*, the idea that literature provides
a "substitute publicness" remains an interesting hypothesis.

3. Critical writing is not necessarily "anti-political-sys-tem" writing.

The findings of this study do not suggest that Hanns Cibulka,
as the author of *Swantow*, was a "political subculture" or an
"anti-systemic" writer, but rather one of many "socially critical"
authors. For at least a decade before he published his diary,
protest against prevailing environmental conditions and ecological
concepts had been heard in the GDR. While warnings of pending
problems communicated through official channels were subdued, in
the *mass* political culture the related concepts of performance
(*Leistung*) and of progress (*Fortschritt*) had been vigorously

challenged in the 1970s by both literary and church messages.
Thus, in the 1980s Cibulka's *Swantow* joined existent interest-
group challenges to *official* political culture values. The criticism was "loyal opposition", since Cibulka's challenge to socialism was for it to live up to its *own* promise that science would
serve humanity.

Furthermore, first publication of *Swantow*'s "loyal opposition" criticism in the official journal of the Writers' Union,
Neue deutsche Literatur, gave it considerable credibility, as well
as exposure. In this context, it could be seen as "normal" input
into a society's never-ending intellectual dialogue about social
change. But at the same time, the unusually intensive "Establishment" responses to *Swantow*'s concepts seem to underline (a) the
significance of literature's role in the interrelationships of the
GDR system (in this case, especilly with science and economics),
but just as importantly (b) the significance of Western media influences on reactions. What might have been acceptable loyal opposition within the GDR's political context for literature, became questionable when Western media elevated it to system-
threatening critique and fed that message back into the GDR.

Finally, in assessing the systemic nature of Cibulka's challenge, it is relevant to note that at the time he wrote and published, there apparently was considerable support within the institution of literature for socio-critical questioning. On the
other hand, disagreements about the particular manner of questioning were also widely discussed. As noted, encouragement of so-
sically critical literature included Dieter Schlenstedt's positive
acknowledgement of the GDR's emerging "socialist (self-) critical
realism". In short, viewing Cibulka's *Swantow* within the political culture context of GDR literature as an institution, the
author did not seem with this work at that time to earn the label
of either a "subgroup" or "anti-system" writer.

4. Stimuli for socio-political change from numerous sources are reflected in the political culture.

In all societies, the political culture reflects a constant
tug-of-war between old and new orientations. The tussle often is
especially intense in relatively new political systems, such as
the GDR; for the time being, traditional political culture may
remain the primary orientation of the *masses*, while political
leaders intensively communicate new values and norms central to an
official political culture of socialism. Moreover, the competition between the old and the new is probably moe acute in the
GDR than in some other new socialist countries, since reaffirma-
tions of traditional orientations are continuously fed into the
GDR by the mass media and citizens of "the other German state",
the Federal Republic.

In any case, because orientations of the popuotion cannot be broadly and systematically measured, Western scholars lack definitive evidence that either the traditional or the new political culture is *dominant* at the masslevel in the GDR. In this context, it is clear, however, that the mass political culture does not always reflect primarily "old" values and the official political culture the "new".

For instance, in the case of ecological/environmental issues in the GDR, impulses for "new" change originated with political subgroups at the base of the system. As the dialogue progressed, the demands gradually found more support within the mass political culture and its legitimized interest groups and institutions. From there, inputs for change apparently were transmitted to the decision-making center and may have contributed to output responses which reflected some of the "new" values.

In other words, this jousting between the old and new, going on in all socio-political systems, is the stuff of which social change is made. Such currents of change often can be sensed through analysis of competing messages originated and transmitted back and forth by the decision-making center and groups reflecting various interests within the system. Without such focus on the political culture tug-of-war between differing feedback reactions, current change in the GDR might be less understandable.

For instance, among the signals of changing ecological/environmental concepts showing up in the mass political culture were these:

(a) The church as an institution insisted that there were moral value questions related to the use of science, economic productivity was not the Alpha and Omega of a humane socialist society, consumerism should be braked, progress was at best an "ambivalent" concept, the nature of Nature needed redefinition, nuclear energy was not a taboo topic, and incessant "pressure to perform" (*Leistungsdruck*) affected the cultural niveau negatively.

(b) Literature portrayed nature as something to be formed but not ruled, youth as resentful of regimentation of pressure to perform, evolution of a new "socialist personality" as a long historical process, science as having lost sight of humankind's needs, citizens as disillusioned by discrepancies between words and deeds, and the concerns of social life less immediate than those of personal, daily life.

(c) Intellectual and disciplinary reexaminations of basic concepts transmitted compelling new calls for fundamental philosophical reconsideration of old shibboleths, appeals to both military and natural science to admit their new responsibility for preventing battles rather than planning to win them, challenges to natural science to avoid philosophical dilettantism by conceding science's limitations,[418] and contentions (energetically disputed) from social scientists that the discrepancy between environmental law and practice was grave and that environmental protection should be given priority in strategic economic planning.[419]

In the field of aesthetics, too, efforts were underway to redefine the value of nature in an *industrial* society, thus moving away from idyllic, simplistic, sentimental concepts of nature (ofen found in the arts, it was charged). It was essential, a professor wrote, to bridge the contradictions between existing "feelings for nature" (*Naturgefühl*) and "knowledge of nature" (*Naturwissen*).[420] In short, a one official spokesperson summarized the intensified stimuli for socio-political change in the GDR, "The concern about the protection of the natural environment *from* people has changed to a multifaceted system of measures to care for the environment *for* the people".[421]

In addition, there were some indications that such impulses for change conveyed to the mass political culture (via literature, church, foreign media, international experience, etc.) and then transmitted by interest groups to the decision-makers, may, in turn, have influenced their official political culture concepts and communication. For instance, after initially defensive reactions, party/state spokespersons gradually conceded and emphasized that environmental protection, indeed, was an extremely complex problem, acceptance of setbacks was part of the process, interdisciplinary and sophisticated research was essential, individual initiatives were crucial, specific optimistic and active literary visions for the future were desired, better implementation of the system's rules was critical, and environmental protection had become part of the political culture.

An interrelationship, although obviously not "provable", between such modifications in official communication and expressed demands for socio-political change coming from the political culture base, seems logically deducible. There clearly was movement forward, even if radical problem-solving and dramatic change were not evidenced.

5.   There are multiple influences on policy-making in the GDR, including literature's primarily indirect political impact.

Despite systemic limitations on groups, institutions, and so-called "movement" which might fundamentally challenge existing policies, all is not static in the GDR. On the contrary, the influences on policy-making are multiple and appear to be intensifying. This is especially seen in the expression of interests and in the feedback within the system. The role of social organizations, for example, seems particularly promising in a stage of

155

development where GDR officials repeatedly call for more active public input to develop socialist democracy.

Thus, based on the survey evidence gathered for this study, it seems justified to *suggest* influences which may have played a role vis-a-vis key ecological/environmental issues:

-- ***Danger of nuclear power plants and radioactivity***

Inputs: International developments and discussions; church discussion and criticism; literary criticisms (including Cibulka's); precedential church discussions with atomic scientists; post-Chernobyl citizen petitions and church resolutions calling for a stop to nuclear energy expansion and phase-out of existing operations.

Outputs: New 1983 atomic energy law with extensive provisions for radioactivity protection; additional 1984 guarantees of nuclear safety and radioactivity protection; 1985 establishment of the State Environmental Inspection Agency; 1986 regulations regarding medical care for workers exposed to radioactivity; Erich Honecker's doubts after Chernobyl about the ultimate essentiality of nuclear energy.

-- **Need for more public information about environmental problems**

Inputs: Repeated church demands for information, self-generated information, use of natural scientists' information; literary demands for information and self-generated background material; natural science critiques of inaccurate information from non scientific (for example, literary) sources; post-Chernobyl church resolutions and citizen petitions demanding information.

Outputs: Classification of *specific* environmental data as secret vs somewhat broadened *general* information from the decision-making center, e.g., extensive *Einheit* discussions of environmental policy, numerous interviews with Environment Minister, Urania specialist-information, GNU public information campaigns, increased popular science publishing

-- **Demand for increased environmental protection**

Inputs: Church resolutions and activities; literary discussions (Kunert, Cibulka, etc.); citizen group

156

initiatives; interest group views (scientists, technicians, social scientists, etc.).

Outputs: Concessions of needs; strengthened environmental protection priorities in national economic plans; increased research and educational priorities for structuring and protection of the environment; increased fines for violation of environmental laws; estblishment of Environmental Inspeçtion Agency to coordinate environmenal protection efforts; numerous international agreements, especially with neighboring states.

-- **Demand for more citizen participation/feedback possibilities**

Inputs: Literary demands; church initiatives; citizen petition prior to 11th SED Congress for public discussion; post-Chernobyl petition for national plebiscite on nuclear energy.

Outputs: Establishment of Society for Nature and Environment (*GNU*) as an organization for citizen feedback; encouragement of church-group participation through GNU and other state organizations; legal strengthening in 1984 and 1985 of petition right of citizens and authority of local Peoples' Assemblies; extensive theoretical discussion and political communication about developing "socialist democracy".

The study's information, as summarized above, suggests that change-oriented reactions, or feedback, to existing policies and conditions flowed from various points in the GDR's political base through interest groups to the decision-making heart of the system. The center, in turn, reacted. Sometimes its action was positive, sometimes negative toward the demand; sometimes there were many words, and frequently there were deeds. So that the demands would not overload the system -- i.e., call for more action than leaders believed they could or wanted to take -- the center generated a great deal of persuasive political communication to convince citizens that their needs were being met. In other cases, however, inhibitive measures were used to discourage demands at the source, e.g., sanctions against environmental protesters.

This emphasis on the interrelated functions of public reaction and demand, on the one hand, and official output, on the other, enables researchers to focus on a system's responsiveness to social change. Seen this way, it is clear that there is sociopolitical change in the GDR, despite firm systemic limitations on unplanned, radical actions. Decision-makers have allowed the church, for instance, wider parameters of operation, organized

157

more responsive/relevant organizations and procedures for citizen participation in ameliorating ecological/environmental problems, differentiated their own "messages" on these issues, and have not ostracized editors, publishing houses, or writers conveying different messages.

In turn, church environmental activity has remained vital, touching the political culture orientations of many; interest group demands (especially from scientists, technicians, and humanists) have reflected dissatisfaction with existing traditional values and norms of the system; literary discussions have tended to show increasing recognition for the complexity of the ecology debate. In short, the influences for change revealed in the feedback from the political culture, indeed, are numerous and active, especially so since the nuclear accident at Chernobyl.

6. "Progress" remains sanctified, but elucidated.

With increasing international polarization of environmental issues and positions, the GDR's leaders remain very sensitive to suggestions and charges that socialism's approach to ecology is not different from that of the West. An equally touchy area is that of optimism regarding scientific progress. Both are cardinal tenets of Marxism/Leninism. At the same time, decision-makers and opinion leaders seem to recognize the necessity to discuss those tenets anew, that is, within the specific context of public anxiety about environmental dangers. They have moved from dogmatic positions of "That is how it is, period" to "That is how it is because..."

Thus, "progress" as the motor of historic development has not at all been given up. But dialogue has elucidated the concept:

-- The "price for progress" need not continue to be "too high". New research plans, courses of study, and environmental priorities are seeking to come to grips with an unusually complex phenomenon. Involved is not just "environmental protection", but also "environmental structuring".

-- One need not be so pessimistic. Socialism has workable concepts of ecological/environmental protection; Western charges and claims must be put into systemic perspective.

-- Environmental protection remains dependent on availability of economic resources. That entails progress in economic production, science, and technology. To argue otherwise is to deny logic. But that logic needs to be clarified.

-- It is true that social progress is not linear. Moreover, it requires specific activity for realization. There are

contradictions in the GDR's development which must be understood. GDR writers are inadequately schooled in Marxist/Len-
inist concepts, especially such dialectic analysis.

-- While the general concept of social progress is sanctified, the invitation is out to discuss its meaning. New definitions are possible, including those of "effectiveness".

-- The aesthetics of scientific/technological progress in an
industrial society need reconsideration. "Garden dwarfs"
(*Gartenzwerge*) are not entirely outdated, but they must be
supplemented.

-- Basic to the whole challenge to progress is public education.

-- After Chernobyl, one may think that nuclear energy is
"not the last word".

It is fascinating to speculate where all of this reconsideration will take the GDR in the coming years. It surely cannot be
easy for the leaders and population of a change-oriented socio-
politicl system to concede, after four decades of significant
achievement, that perhaps their greatest error was the original
belief that even more could be accomplished.

The ecology/environmental issue and the widespread doubt
which it generated about social and economic progress has brought
many to difficult reexamination of premises and others to resignation. Literature, as part of that flow of communication, of the
GDR's dialogue, will continue to send signals about where the GDR
goes from here. Especially the dialogue about dialogue is far
from concluded.

Appendix A

Hanns Cibulka's *Swantow*, initially excerpted in *Neue deutsche Literatur*, contained four major statements concerning environmental issues:

3. August

. . . .
Ein Gedanke, der mich seit Tagen beschäftigt: der Kuppelbau bei den Atomkraftwerken. Es gibt für die Kuppel keine technische Notwendigkeit. Vielleicht ist es eine Erinnerung an die Kohlenmeiler des Waldes, an die alten Kuppelgräber. Solche Zeichen kommen von weit, reichen tief, sind immer das Ergebnis einer umfassenderen Anschauung. In solchen Formen können sich aber auch uralte Tabus andeuten. Daten und Namen kann man löschen, Formen tauchen immer wieder auf, geben dem Menschen zu denken. Es scheint, als umschließe auch heute noch der Rundbau, die Kuppel aus meterdickem Beton, ein Geheimnis, ein bedenkliches Geheimnis.

„...Im Normalbetrieb gibt ein Atomkraftwerk ständig Radionuklide an die Umwelt ab. Bei einem mittleren Atomkraftwerk werden jährlich 80 000 Ci über den Kamin in die Umgebung abgeblasen. Ein großer Anteil dieser Radionuklide ist das Krypton-89 mit einer hohen Halbwertzeit. Wenn jedes Jahr die gleiche Menge Krypton-89 in die Umwelt gelangt, steigt die Strahlenbelastung ständig an, denn das Krypton vom Vorjahr ist immer noch vorhanden und nur zu einem winzigen Teil zerfallen.
Über das Abwasser wird ebenfalls eine Vielzahl radioaktiver Substanzen abgelassen. Von einigen Nukliden weiß man bereits heute, wie gefährlich sie sind.
Im Normalbetrieb eines Atomkraftwerkes wird die Bevölkerung vor allen Dingen mit Strahlen im niedrigen Dosisbereich belastet. Diese Strahlung führt zu einer unspezifischen Störung der Normalordnung des Chemismus und in den Strukturen der betroffenen Zellen. Strahlengeschädigte Zellen, die sich weiter vermehren, zeigen erst nach vielen Zellgenerationen einen sichtbaren Schaden. Der zeitliche Abstand zwischen der Bestrahlung und dem sichtbaren Schaden kann viele Jahre betragen. Bei Erbschäden beträgt die Latenzzeit oft mehrere Generationen.
Inkorporierte Alpha- und Beta-Strahlen können meßtechnisch nicht erfaßt werden, da ihre Strahlung wegen der geringen Durchdringungsfähigkeit im biologischen Gewebe nicht bis zur Oberfläche des Körpers durchdringt. Zum Beispiel kann Strontium völlig unbemerkt vom Organismus aufgenommen und gespeichert werden. Es gibt praktisch keine Möglichkeit, seine Existenz im lebenden Körper festzustellen und nachzuweisen. Die Verseuchung erfolgt im meßtechnischen Dunkel. Falsch ist der Schluß: Was ich nicht messen kann, ist ungefährlich."
. . . . .

161

. . . .

Weiter in der Lektüre „Kernkraftwerke". Die Verfasserin spricht von einer vollkommenen Gefahrlosigkeit der in Betrieb befindlichen Kernkraftwerke für ihre Umgebung.

Sie schreibt: „Die völlige Ausschaltung des schädlichen Einflusses auf die Umgebung erfordert bei der Projektierung, beim Bau und Betrieb Maßnahmen, die schwere Havarien, bei denen Spaltprodukte nach außen gelangen, sicher ausschließen, bzw. Maßnahmen, die eine radioaktive Verseuchung der Umgebung verhindern. Der Mangel an Betriebserfahrungen führte u. a. dazu, daß ein Mindestabstand der Kernkraftwerke zu großen Ortschaften festgelegt wurde. Daher gibt es in den Projektierungsvorschriften aller Länder Normen für die Mindestentfernung der Kernkraftwerke von großen Ortschaften. In der UdSSR war dies anfangs auf minimal 35 km festgelegt worden. Das hat insbesondere auch die Entwicklung der Kernkraftwerke als reine Kondensationskraftwerke und nicht als Heizkraftwerke bestimmt.

Eine lange und gründliche Kontrolle des Luftraumes in der Umgebung von Kraftwerken auf schädliche Auswürfe hat einerseits die vollkommene Gefahrlosigkeit der in Betrieb befindlichen Kernkraftwerke für ihre Umgebung sowie die Wirksamkeit der oben erwähnten Maßnahmen gezeigt und andererseits für die Gesundheit bedeutend schädlichere Auswirkungen durch Wärmekraftwerke mit fossilen Brennstoffen nachgewiesen, insbesondere bei aschereichen festen Brennstoffen und – in noch höherem Maße – bei Kohle und Erdöl mit hohem Schwefelgehalt."

11. August

. . . .

MIT der Klafter des Todes
vermessen
die Schnellen Brüter
das Land.

Im Wasserbett
Kernstäbe,
Primärkreislauf,
abgeblasen
über den Kamin
die Radionuklide.
Der Mensch
im Strahlengeviert.
In den Abwässern
staut sich die
Schuld.

Sind wir nicht auf dem besten Weg, die grundlegenden Gesetze der Natur und das Zusammenwirken aller Dinge zu mißachten?

Unsere Krankheiten wachsen in dem Maße, in dem die Chemisierung des Lebens zunimmt. Wir zahlen bereits heute einen viel zu hohen Preis für unser zweifelhaftes Wohlleben. Aus den bescheidenen Anfängen der Chemie ist ein hydraköpfiges Ungeheuer geworden; künstliche Düngemittel, Herbizide, Vergiftungen der Luft und der Gewässer, radioaktiver Niederschlag, und das alles soll sich auf die Gesundheit eines Menschen nicht auswirken? Die Wartezimmer in den Polikliniken sind überfüllt, die Legion der Ärzte wird immer größer, der Mensch immer anfälliger, bald werden wir nur noch einer Armee von Spezialisten gegenüberstehen, der Hausarzt, wie ich ihn aus meiner Kindheit noch kenne, ist zur Legende geworden.

Die Massenmedien wollen uns glauben machen, wir hätten ein wissenschaftliches Zeitalter; wir haben es nicht. Was uns bis heute fehlt, ist die Wissenschaft vom Menschen, die endlich einmal danach fragt, wie der Mensch leben und arbeiten soll, was zu einem menschenwürdigen Dasein überhaupt notwendig ist. Wie wäre es sonst möglich, daß ein Drittel der Menschheit krank ist, nicht nur physisch. Wir leben wie die Blinden unter den Blinden, gehen ins Krankenhaus, um uns heilen zu lassen, hoffen auf Heilung, sehen aber nicht, daß auch die Medizin bereits am Stock geht. Der Fortschritt der Medizin führt heute vorwiegend über den Operationstisch, über das Messer. Wir leben in einem unsichtbaren Schützengraben, von allen Seiten liegen wir unter Beschuß: Wasser, Luft, Ernährung, Strahlungsfelder.

Bei unserem gestrigen Spaziergang sagte mir der Doktor: Wir brauchen keine neuen Operationssäle, keine neuen radiologischen Kliniken, was uns not tut, ist eine gesunde Lebensführung nach innen und nach außen. Die Mehrzahl der Krankheiten, an denen wir heute leiden, sind das Ergebnis unserer Lebensweise, unserer Umwelt. Bereits hier müßte der Kampf der Mediziner beginnen und nicht erst am Operationstisch. Eine Vielzahl von Krankheiten haben wir uns in den letzten Jahrzehnten selbst in die Welt gesetzt, sie sind das Ergebnis unserer Lebenssucht. Der Mensch hat sich selbst versklavt.

„Du mußt dein Leben ändern" – heißt das nicht auch, sein Bewußtsein ändern, den Kampf gegen sich selber aufnehmen, unnachgiebig sein, ohne Konzession? Warum haben wir nicht den Mut, uns gegen die eigenen Lebensgewohnheiten zu stellen? Die Natur hat gar nicht mehr die Kraft, all das zu erneuern, was wir täglich in uns und in unserer Umwelt zerstören. Der Mensch mordet sich selbst, allerdings ist es ein Mord auf Zeit.

Wie oft schon hat man uns gesagt, daß sich das Wissen in den letzten dreißig Jahren nicht nur verdoppelt, daß es sich auf verschiedenen Gebieten verzehnfacht habe. Was aber haben wir mit diesem Wissen angefangen? An unserer inneren Front haben wir Waffenstillstand geschlossen, verstopfen uns die Ohren, machen kleine schlaue Umwege vor uns selbst, doch die Wahrheit können wir auf die Dauer nicht vor uns her schieben.

Es ist und bleibt die Aufgabe des Menschen, dem Wunder Leben gerecht zu werden, dafür zu sorgen, daß es ein Wunder bleibt und nicht dahinsiecht. Was haben wir durch unsere egoistische Lebensweise nicht alles schon zugeschüttet?

Die schwierigste aller Revolutionen steht uns immer noch bevor: die Revolution gegenüber uns selbst, gegen unsere eigene Trägheit, den Egoismus, den Machtinstinkt, eine Revolution, die uns lehrt, ganz anders über den Menschen zu denken als bisher.

Die Wahrheit ist den Menschen nicht nur zumutbar, sie ist bereits heute Voraussetzung für seine weitere Existenz.

Welcher Politiker spricht heute noch über die Kraft, die im Verzicht liegt?

27. August

Das archaische Landschaftsbild ist auch auf Rügen im Verblassen. Metallene Riesenvögel ziehen durch die Luft, Kampfhubschrauber fliegen in Kirchturmhöhe über das Land, vor der Küste liegen die Zerstörer. Die Spannung, die eine solche Umwelt auslöst, geht an keinem Menschen spurlos vorbei, sie überträgt sich auf sein Denken, Fühlen, Handeln, schon im Unterbewußtsein der Kinder setzen sich diese Spannungselemente fest, schlagen um in Aggressivität.

Auch in dieser Nacht steht über Swantow ein Sternenhimmel, der seit vielen tausend Jahren zu unseren Weisheiten, aber auch zu unseren Verbrechen gleichmäßig schweigt.

VATERLAND,
wer kann heute noch sagen:
Ich,
Pilatus,
wasche meine Hände in Unschuld.
Zahllos sind die Äpfel
der Versuchung.
Aber dies
ist auch mein Land,
kein Theorem,
das nur dem Staat
in seine Hand gegeben.
Die anderen
reden vom Fortgehen,
ich bleibe,
ich weiß,
der Docht ist verrußt,
nur langsam
wächst im Menschen
das Licht.
Solange noch ein Wort
an deinen Augen sich entzündet,
Leben,
bleibt das immer zu Nennende:
Erde, Wasser, Luft.

164

Appendix B

Bonner General-Anzeiger

Ein Lyriker aus Swantow

HANNS CIBULKA LÖSTE DISKUSSIONEN AUS
Von Reinhard Losik

Der DDR-Schriftsteller Hanns Cibulka hat mit literarischen Tagebuchaufzeichnungen der Kritik in und an der Deutschen Demokratischen Republik eine neue Dimension gegeben. Um das Erscheinen des 30seitigen Beitrags in der jüngsten Ausgabe der Monatszeitshrift des Schriftstellerverbandes „Neue deutsche Literatur' gab es dann auch, wie aus Ostberlin zu hören ist, eine heftige Auseinandersetzung.

Cibulka, Lyriker aus Swantow auf der Ostsee-Insel Rügen, setzt seine Kritik nicht am politisch-ideologischen System der DDR an, sondern überträgt die europäische Zivilisationskritik direkt und korrekt auf den „ersten deutschen Arbeiter- und Bauernstaat'.

„Die Massenmedien wollen uns glauben machen, wir hätten ein wissenschaftliches Zeitalter. Wir haben es nicht. Was uns bis heute fehlt, ist die Wissenschaft vom Menschen, die endlich einmal danach fragt, wie der Mensch leben und arbeiten soll, was zu einem menschenwürdigen Dasein überhaupt notwendig ist", schreibt Cibulka. Für den wissenschaftlichen Sozialismus, der in der DDR die Ausbeutung des Menschen durch den Menschen beseitigt haben soll, ist das so etwas wie ein Todesurteil. Cibulka ist der erste Alternative, der erste Grüne der DDR.

An anderer Stelle hört sich der Zorn aus Swantow so an:
„Von den drei Söhnen stand nur ein einziger am Sterbebett. Bei dem Ältesten, der in Hamburg lebt, verzögerte sich die Einreise. Man hörte den Schimmel der Bürokratie bis an das Sterbebett wiehern. Der Mittlere war auf Montage in Vietnam. So blieb der Mutter nur noch der Jüngste. Sterbehilfe gebon, wer kann das heute noch in unseren Kliniken? Es wird eine Zeit kommen, da werden sie den Sterbenden am Fußende noch einen Farbfernseher hinstellen, damit er von seinem eigenen Streben abgelenkt wird, damit er sich bis zum letzten Atemzug mit den oberflächlichen Dingen des Lebens beschäftigen kann."

Erstmals wird damit in der DDR, wo der Mensch offiziell im Mittelpunkt steht, hart nach dem Menschlichen gefragt. Ideologischer Anspruch und die Realitäten der politischen Propaganda werden nicht nur wie Luft behandelt. Cibulka verurteilt ihre Belastung durch das „hydraköpfige Ungeheuer" die volkseigene Chemie.

„Unsere Krankheiten wachsen in dem Maße, in dem die Chemisierung des Lebens zunimmt. Wir zahlen bereits heute einen viel zu hohen Preis für unser zweifelhaftes Wohlleben." Gleich danach wird er noch deutlicher: „Künstliche Düngemittel, Herbizide vergiften Luft, unsere Gewässer, radioaktiver Niederschlag und das alles soll sich auf die Gesundheit nicht auswirken?"

Der jetzt in Westberlin lebende ehemalige DDR-Schriftsteller Thomas Brasch rea-

gierte verblüfft auf Töne dieser Art „ausgerechnet in einem offiziellen Organ des Schritstellerverbandes". Doch Cibulka geht in seinen Tagebuchaufzeichnungen noch einen Schritt weiter.

Er verbindet Militär mit Aggression. Im August vorigen Janres rand im Ostseeraum das Manöver des Warschauer Pakts „Waffenbrüderschaft 80" statt. Unter dem 27. des Monats notierte er: „Das archaische Landschaftsbild ist auch auf Rügen im Verblassen. Metallene Riesenvögel ziehen durch die Luft. Kampfhubschraube fliegen in Kirchturmhöhe über das Land, vor der Küste liegen die Zerstörer. Die Spannung die eine solche Umwelt auslost, geht an keinem Menschen spurlos vorbei."

Die Spannung übertrage sic auf das Denken, Fühlen und Handeln, warnt der Mann, auf Rügen. „Schon im Unterbewußtsein der Kinder setzen sich diese Spannungselemente fest, schlagen um in Aggressivität." Und weiter: „Auch in dieser Nacht steht über Swantow ein Sternenhimmel, der seit vielen tausend Jahren zu unseren Weisheiten aber auch zu unseren Verbrechen gleichmäßig schweigt. Vaterland, wer kann heute noch sagen: ich, Pilatus, wasche meine Hände in Unschuld?"

Wie aus informierten Kreisen Ostberlins verlautet, hat es nicht nur vor dem Erschei-

nen der literarischen Tagebuchaufzeichnungen Auseinandersetzungen gegeben. Die Kontroverse um den brisanten Text gehe weiter.

Hanns Cibulka schrieb darin auch: „Zahllos wie die Apfel der Versuchung. Aber dies ist mein Land, kein Theorem, das nur dem Staat in seine Hände gegeben. Die anderen reden vom Fortgehen, ich bleibe. Ich weiß ... Leben, bleibst das immer zu Nennende — Erde, Wasser, Luft."

Die Situation der DDR und die der Menschen, die in ihr leben, wird damit auf einer Ebene angegriffen, die selbst nur sehr schwer angreifbar ist. Cibulka überspringt die Forderung nach mehr Menschenrechten und mehr politischen Freiheiten. Dennoch sieht sich die DDR-Führung plötzlich einer politischen Kritik ausgesetzt, die an die Wurzeln geht.

Wie schwierig es für sie ist, die Alternative „Grün" als antisozialistisch zu verdächtigen, um ihr von vornherein jeden Zulauf zu nehmen, zeigt, daß die literarischen Tagebuchaufzeichnungen in einem offiziellen DDR-Organ erscheinen konnten.

REFERENCE NOTES

1. Maureen Whitebrook, "Politics and Literature", *News for Teachers of Political Science* (Washington, DC: American Political Science Association), 39 (Fall) 1983, pp. 12ff.

2. Heinrich Mohr, "DDR-Literatur als Provokation der Literaturwissenschaft in der Bundesrepublik Deutschland", *Deutschland Archiv*, 8/1986, pp. 844-849.

3. Patricia Herminghouse, "Studying GDR Literature in the U.S.-- A Survey", in *Research and Study of the German Democratic Republic*. Washington, DC: American Institute for Contemporary German Studies, German Issues 3, 1986, pp. 28-29.

4. Peter U. Hohendahl, "Beyond Reception Aesthetics", *New German Critique*, Winter 1983, p. 146.

5. Dietrich Sommer, Dietrich Löffler, Achim Walter, und Eva Maria Scherf, hrsg. *Funktion und Wirkung* (1978), *Leseerfahrung. Lebenserfahrung* (1982). Berlin/Weimar: Aufbau Verlag.

6. *Funktion und Wirkung, ibid.*, p. 396.

7. Eberhard Günther, "Aus verlegerischer Sicht -- Einige Gedanken zur Entwicklung der Zeitgenössischen DDR-Literatur", in *Position 1. Wortmeldungen zur DDR-Literatur.* Halle/Leipzig: Mitteldeutscher Verlag, 1984.

8. *Funktion und Wirkung, op. cit.* (fn. 5), p. 398.

9. *Ibid.*

10. *Ibid.*, p. 399.

11. *Ibid.*

12. *Ibid.*, pp. 438-440.

13. *Ibid.*, p. 412.

14. *Ibid.*, p. 192.

15. *Ibid.*, p. 202.

16. Anita M. Mallinckrodt, "WANTED: Theoretical Framework for GDR Studies. FOR SALE: A Systems/Functional Approach", *GDR Monitor*, Winter 1983/84, pp. 12-27.

17. See, for example, *Comparative Public Policy. The Politics of Social Choice in Europe and America*, 2nd ed., by Heidenheimer/Heclo/Adams (New York: St. Martin's Press, 1983), pp. 1-8.

18. Patricia McGee Crotty, "Introducing American Government Students to Data Analysis", in *News for Teachers of Political Science* (Washington, DC: The American Political Science Association), No. 48, 1986, p. 14.

19. Gabriel A. Almond/G. Bingham Powell Jr., eds., *Comparative Politics Today. A World View*, 3rd ed. Boston: Little, Brown and Company, 1984.

20. The "corporatism" and "pluralism" approaches are insightfully discussed in *Pluralism in the Soviet Union* (ed. Susan Gross Soloman. New York: St. Martin's Press, 1983), a volume of essays honoring H. Gordon Skilling who pioneered the "pluralism" approach to Soviet studies.

21. See, for example, *Die gesellschaftlichen Organisationen im politischen System des Sozialismus*. Aktuelle Beiträge der Staats- und Rechtswissenschaft, Heft 271. Potsdam-Babelsberg: Akademie für Staats- und Rechtswissenschaft der DDR, 1982, p. 7.

22. *Pluralism in the Soviet Union*, op. cit. (fn. 20), p. 52.

23. *Ibid.*, p. 67.

24. Donald E. Schulz, "Political Participation in Communist Systems: The Conceptual Frontier", in *Political Participation in Communist Systems*, eds. Donald Schulz/Jan Adams. New York: Pergamon Press, 1981, pp. 1-2.

25. *Pluralism in the Soviet Union*, op. cit. (fn. 20), p. 52.

26. *Ibid.*, p. 54.

27. Antonia Grunenberg, "Die gespaltene Identität. Gesellschaftliches Doppelleben in der DDR", Band 200 die Schriftenreihe *Die Identität der Deutschen*. Bonn: Bundeszentrale für politische Bildung, 1983.

28. "Einheit von Politik, Ökonomie und Ideologie", *Kleines Politisches Wörterbuch*. Berlin: Dietz Verlag, 1973, pp. 182-186.

29. Gabriel A. Almond/G. Bingham Powell Jr. *Comparative Politics: A Developmental Approach*. Boston: Little, Brown and Company, 1966.

30. W. Müller. "Subjektiver Faktor und Massenbewußtsein", *Deutsche Zeitschrift für Philosophie*, 8-9/1984, pp. 796ff.

31. Almond and Powell, *op. cit.* (fn. 29); Gabriel A. Almond and Sidney Verba. *The Civic Culture.* Princeton, 1963; Lucian W. Pye and Sidney Verba. *Political Culture and Political Development.* Princeton, 1965.

32. Archie Brown and Jack Gray, eds. *Political Culture and Political Change in Communist States.* New York: Holmes and Meier Publishers, Inc., 2nd ed., 1979; Stephan White. *Political Culture and Soviet Politics.* New York: St. Martin's Press, 1979. (Updated political culture concepts by Brown and White, presented at a 1980 conference, have been published in a new collection of essays (*Political Culture and Communist Studies*, ed. Archie Brown. Armonk, New York: M. E. Sharpe, Inc., 1985) which also includes chapters by John Miller, David W. Paul, and Mary McAuley.)

33. White, *ibid.*, p. 12.

34. Barbara Jancar, "Political Culture and Political Change", *Studies in Comparative Communism*, Spring/Summer 1983, pp. 69-82.

35. Lowell Dittmer, "Comparative Communist Political Culture", *Studies in Comparative Communism*, Spring/Summer 1983, pp. 9-23.

36. Jancar, *op. cit.* (fn. 34).

37. *Ibid.*

38. James Ceaser, "Alexis de Tocqueville on Political Science, Political Culture, and the Role of the Intellectual", *The American Political Science Review*, September 1985, p. 671.

39. Volker Gransow, "Fünf Kulturen und ein Trilemma. Notizen zur DDR-Kulturpolitik", *DDR Report*, 8/1984, pp. 430-433.

40. H. Haase, W. Hartinger, U. Heukenkamp, K. Jarmatz, J. Pischel, D. Schlenstedt, "DDR-Literaturentwicklung in der Diskussion", *Weimarer Beiträge*, 10/1984, p. 1590.

41. *Leseerfahrung. Lebenserfahrung*, *op. cit.* (fn. 5), pp. 179ff.

42. *Sozialismus und Frieden. Humanismus in den Kämpfen unserer Zeit. VI. Philosophiekongreß der DDR vom 17. bis 19. Oktober 1984 in Berlin.* Berlin: Dietz Verlag, 1985, p. 245.

43. Fritz Böhme, "Die Aufgaben der Grundorganisationen bei der politisch-ideologischen Leitung kultureller Prozesse in den Betrieben", *Der Parteiarbeiter.* Berlin: Dietz Verlag, 1982, p. 45.

44. *Ibid.*, pp. 41-46.

45. *Ibid.*, p. 38.

46. *Börsenblatt für den Deutschen Buchhandel*, 13 (1 April) 1986, p. 224.

47. Böhme, *op. cit.* (fn. 43), pp. 41-46.

48. Hans-Joachim Hoffmann/Werner Kühn, "Auftrag der Kunst - Kunst im Auftrag", *Einheit*, 6/1974, pp. 723-732.

49. Kurt Rauschek. *Arbeiterklasse und Künstler im Bündnis.* Berlin: Dietz Verlag, 1984, p. 76.

50. Helmut Baierl, Mitglied des Präsidiums der Schriftstellerverbandes der DDR. *Protokoll des 10. FDGB-Kongresses 1982*, pp. 102-104.

51. Hans Koch. *Grundlagen sozialistischer Kulturpolitik in der Deutschen Demokratischen Republik.* Berlin: Dietz Verlag, 1983, p. 77.

52. Radio DDR 1, 22 March 1986, 1803 GMT.

53. Hermann Kant. *Rede. IX. Schriftstellerkongreß der DDR (von 31.5. - 2.6.83).* Berlin, p. 38. (See also the Halle University studies (fn. 2) concerning who reads what and why.)

54. Klaus Walther, "Redezeit für Leser. 2. Tagung der sozialistischen Gegenwartsliteratur der DDR", *Sonntag*, 47/1984, p. 4.

55. "Geschichte, Kunst und Umwelt: Aus Aktionsprogrammen der Bezirksorganisationen des Kulturbundes", *Sonntag*, 46/1985, p. 7.

56. "Für wen sind die Bezirksliteraturzentren gedacht?", *Presse-Informationen,* 31 (14 March) 1986, p. 5.

57. Benjamin R. Barber/Michael J. Gargas McGrath, eds. *The Artist and Political Vision.* New Jersey: Transaction Books, 1982, p. x.

58. Christine Schöfer, "A Public Voice - Politics and Literature in the GDR", University of California/Berkeley PhD Dissertation, 1985.

59. Whitebrook, *op. cit.* (fn. 1), p. 12.

60. Haase, et. al., *op. cit.* (fn. 40), p. 1606.

61. Christel Berger. *Der Autor und sein Held.* Berlin: Dietz Verlag, 1983, p. 9.

62. Margy Gerber, "'Wie hoch ist eigentlich der Preis der Emanzipation?' - Social issues in recent GDR women's writing", *GDR Moni-*

tor (Loughborough, England), 16, Winter 1986/87, pp. 55-83.

63. Robert A. White, "Mass Communication and Culture: Transition to a New Paradigm", *Journal of Communication*, 3/1983, p. 296.

64. Arthur M. Hanhardt, Jr. and Gregory Swint, "Literature and Political Culture", in *The German Democratic Republic: A Developed Socialist Society*, ed. Lyman H. Legters. Boulder, Colorado: Westview Press, 1978, p. 175.

65. Schöfer, *op. cit.* (fn. 58).

66. Irma Hanke, "Anpassung, Apathie und Ritualisierung von Politik", in *Bürger im Staat*. Stuttgart: Verlag W. Kohlhammer. Taschenbücher Band 1064, 1983, pp. 146-168.

67. Eckart Förtsch, "Literatur als Wissenschaftskritik", in *Lebensbedingungen in der DDR*. Köln: Verlag Wissenschaft und Politik, Edition Deutschland Archiv, 1984, p. 157.

68. Hubertus Knabe, "Zweifel an der Industriegesellschaft. Ökologische Kritik in der erzählenden DDR-Literatur", in *Umweltprobleme und Umweltbewußtsein in der DDR*. Köln: Verlag Wissenschaft und Politik, 1985, p. 202.

69. Schöfer, *op. cit.* (fn. 58).

70. Haase, et. al., *op. cit.* (fn. 40), pp. 1604-1605.

71. *Ibid.*

72. Andreas Schrade, "Leipziger Konferenz zu dialektischem Widerspruch und literarischem Konflikt", *Weimarer Beiträge*, 9/1985, pp. 1543-1548.

73. Jürgen Kuczynski, "Brief an Hermann Kant", *Neue deutsche Literature*, 10/1980, p. 158. (See also Kuczynski's "Bedeutung der Oberfläche", *Neue deutsche Literatur*, 2/1983, pp. 81ff.)

74. Walter Rosenbaum. *Political Culture*. New York: Praeger Publishers, 1975, p. 151.

75. H. Gordon Skilling, "Opposition in Communist East Europe", in *Regimes and Oppositions*, ed. Robert A. Dahl. New Haven: Yale University Press, 1973, pp. 89ff.

76. *Ibid.*

77. "Spiegel Gespräch – 'Die Generation nach uns ist freier'", *Der Spiegel*, 36 (1 September) 1986, pp. 74-78.

171

78. Mallinckrodt, *op. cit.* (fn. 16).

79. J. B. Bury. *The Idea of Progress.* Reissued with Introduction by Charles A. Beard, 1932. New York: Dover Publications, Inc., 1955, pp. xxi-xl.

80. Marx/Engels: *Werke*, Bd. 13, p. 640.

81. *Grundlagen der marxistisch-leninistischen Philosophie.* Berlin: Dietz Verlag, 1971, pp. 543ff.

82. Frank Rupprecht. *Realer Optimismus. Kraftquelle im Kampf um Frieden und Fortschritt.* Berlin: Dietz Verlag, 1983, p. 78.

83. W. I. Lenin. "Über die Junius-Broschüre", in *Werke*, Bd. 22, p. 315.

84. Friedrich Engels/Karl Marx. *Die heilige Familie.* Marx/Engels Werke, Bd. 2, p. 98.

85. *Gesetzblatt der Deutschen Demokratischen Republik*, 8 October 1949.

86. *Programm der Sozialistischen Einheitspartei Deutschlands.* Berlin: Dietz Verlag, 1963.

87. Hartmut Zimmermann, "Power Distribution and Opportunities for Participation", in *Policymaking in the German Democratic Republic.* New York: St. Martin's Press, 1983, p. 77.

88. *The Constitution of the German Democratic Republic.* Berlin: Staatsverlag der Deutschen Demokratischen Republik and Verlag Zeit im Bild, 1968.

89. *Gesetzblatt der Deutschen Demokratischen Republik*, 7 October 1974.

90. *Programm der Sozialistischen Einheitspartei Deutschlands.* Berlin: Dietz Verlag, 1976.

91. *Bericht des Zentralkomitees der Sozialistischen Einheitspartei Deutschlands an den X. Parteitag der SED.* Berlin: Dietz Verlag, 1981, p. 49.

92. Dieter Staritz, "DDR: Herausforderungen der achtziger Jahre", in *Die DDR vor den Herausforderungen der achtziger Jahre.* Köln: Verlag Wissenschaft und Politik, Edition Deutschland Archiv, 1983, pp. 21-32.

93. Rupprecht, *op. cit.* (fn. 82), pp. 88, 100.

94. E. H. Meadows, D. L. Meadows, J. Randers, W. W. Behrens III.
*The Limits of Growth. A Report for the Club of Rome's Project on
the Predicament of Mankind.* New York: Universe Books, 1972, pp.
23-24.

95. Jan Kuhnert, "Wirtschaftswachstum und Lebensweise. Diskussion um Prioritäten in West- und Osteuropa", *Die DDR im Entspann-
ungs Prozess - Lebensweise in Realen Sozialismus.* Köln: Verlag
Wissenschaft und Politik, Edition Deutschland Archiv, 1980, p. 34.

96. J. Kuczynski, "Das Gleichgewicht der Null", *Zu den Theorien
des Nullwachstums.* Frankfurt/M (Lizenzausgabe), 1973, pp. 58, 63.

97. *"er (hat) in einem erleuchteten Augenblick für sich die Ver-
nunft erfunden. Nun kann er sich alle Verzichte, die er seiner
höheren Bestimmung wegen leisten muß, vollkommen plausibel machen
und auf jede Situation zweckmäßig reagieren".* (Christa Wolf. *Unter
den Linden. Drei unwahrscheinliche Geschichten.* Berlin/Weimar:
Aufbau Verlag, 1974, p. 82).

98. *"Dies ist eine bemerkenswerte Idee. Wie viele Kräfte, in
nutzlose Tragödien verwickelt, wären für die Produktion materi-
eller Güter frei geworden, worin die Menschheit bekanntlich ihren
eigentlichen Daseinszweck sieht (eine Tatsache übrigens, die ich
der regelmäßigen Lektüre dreier Tageszeitung entnehme). Bei der
leichten Schematisierbarkeit menschlicher Probleme hätten fast
alle leistungshemmenden Faktoren in diesem Nachschlagewerk erfaßt
und einer positiven Lösung zugeführt werden können; der tech-
nisch-wissenschaftliche Fortschritt wäre um Jahrzehnte früher aus-
gelöst worden and die Menschheit könnte schon in der Zukunft leb-
en. Wie wohlige Zufriedenheit, nach der es jedes Geschöpf ver-
lang, hätte sich längst ausgebreitet...* (Christa Wolf, ibid., p.
84).

99. David Bathrick, "Kultur und Öffentlichkeit in der DDR", in
Literature der DDR in den siebziger Jahren. Hrsg. P. U. Hohendahl
und P. Herminghouse. Frankfurt: Suhrkamp, 1983, p. 71.

100. "Produktivkraft Poesie. Gespräch zwischen Erwin Strittmatter
und Heinz Plavius", *Neue deutsche Literatur,* 5/1973, p. 6.

101. *VII. Schriftstellerkongreß der Deutschen Demokratischen
Republik. Protokoll* (Arbeitsgruppen). Berlin, 1973, p. 252.

102. Joseph Pischel, "Das Verhältnis Mensch-Natur in der Selbstverständigung von Schriftstellern der DDR", *Weimarer Beiträge,*
1/1976, pp. 74-99.

103. Although no new church membership statistics have been
available since the 1964 census, official estimates of 1977 reported 7.9 million members of the Evangelical Church, 1.2 million

Catholics, 0.1 million free church members (Methodist, Baptist, etc.), and 0.15 million other religious communities, including Jewish. (See "Kirchen" in *DDR-Handbuch*, Band 1, 3rd rev. ed. Köln: Verlag Wissenschaft und Politik, 1985, pp. 715ff.)

104. Hubertus Knabe, "Gesellschaftlicher Dissens im Wandel. Ökologische Discussionen und Umweltengagement in der DDR", in *Umweltprobleme und Umweltbewußtsein in der DDR*. Köln: Verlag Wissenschaft und Politik, 1985, pp. 170-171.

105. Heino Falcke, "Gerechtigkeit, ökologische Lebensfähigkeit und Partizipation. Kriterien für das Handeln", in *Beton ist Beton. Zivilisationskritik aus der DDR*. Hrsg. Peter Wensierski/Wolfgang Büscher. Hattigen: Scandica Verlag, Edition Transit, 1981, pp. 205-215.

106. Kuhnert, *op. cit.* (fn. 95), pp. 38ff.

107. *Der IX. Parteitag der SED und die Gesellschaftswissenschaften. Materialien der Konferenz der Gesellschaftswissenschaftler der DDR am 25. und 26. November 1976 in Berlin.* Berlin: Dietz Verlag, 1977, pp. 64-65.

108. *Ibid.*, p. 97.

109. *Ibid.*, p. 211.

110. Knabe, *op. cit.* (fn. 104), pp. 176, 180.

111. *Glaube und Heimat*, 1 October 1978.

112. Günter Kunert, "Antäus", *Sinn und Form*, 2/1979, pp. 403-408.

113. "Um ein Wort. Ein Briefwechsel zwischen Günter Kunert und Wilhelm Girnus", *Sinn und Form*, 2/1979, pp. 409-411.

114. "Anlässlich Ritsos. Ein Briefwechsel zwischen Günter Kunert und Wilhelm Girnus", *Sinn und Form*, 4/1979, pp. 850-864.

115. *Gesetzblatt der Deutschen Demokratischen Republik*, Teil 1/1962, pp. 47-49.

116. *Gesetzblatt der Deutschen Demokratischen Republik*, Teil 2/1973, pp. 451ff.

117. *Neues Deutschland*, 16 June, 1971.

118. *Neues Deutschland*, 14 January, 1976.

119. Horst Paucke/Adolf Bauer. *Umweltprobleme - Herausforderung der Menschheit.* Berlin: Dietz Verlag, 1979.

120. Helmut Hanke, "Kulturelle Traditionen des Sozialismus", *Zeitschrift für Geschichtswissenschaft*, 7/1985, pp. 589-604.

121. Zimmermann, *op. cit.* (fn. 87), pp. 14-15, 32.

122. Kristina Protsch/Volker Ronge, "Arbeit finden sie leichter als Freunde", *Deutschland Archiv*, 7/1985, pp. 716-725.

123. Ralf Rytlewski, "The Attended Citizen - The Change of Values in the GDR and Eastern Europe", at the Friederich Naumann Foundation conference "Change or Continuity in Value Systems in North America and Western Europe Since World War II", Seabrook Island, South Carolina, May 7-11, 1986.

124. Protsch/Ronge, *op. cit.* (fn. 122).

125. Theo Sommer, "Am Staat mäkeln, doch ihn tragen", the first of nine articles by *Die Zeit* editors appearing in No. 26-34 (June 20-August 15), 1986, and later published as a book, *Reise ins andere Deutschland* (Rowohlt Verlag, 1986).

126. *Ibid.*

127. Typical is the new West German quarterly *Kontra: Zensur in der Bundesrepublik.* For example, in an article entitled "The Invisible Muzzle", Hanno Kühnert writes that "Gentle censorship (*sanfte Zensur*) is no more or less than the dependence of journalists. Whoever strives, consciously or unconsciouly, for careerism, to be seen in print, or for power vis-a-vis an editorial office, accommodates desired opinions and for that purpose develops ominous senses and many skills" (p. 25). Further, the socially-critical graphic artist and lawyer, Klaus Staeck, probably best known in West Germany for his posters, writes that "Almost every fool meanwhile knows that self-censorship is the real problem of censorship" (p. 30). In Staeck's view, and that of many others, self-censorship makes external censorship unnecessary. An individual's fear of being censored motivates a cleaned-up text that could not possibly concern a censor. But internal censorship frequently is difficult to prove and most often is indirect. In an often not understood feedback process, fear reduces risk-taking, reduced risk-taking means less cases of visible/reported censorship, fewer reported cases strengthens the view that censorship does not exist. (*Kontra*, Vol. 1, *Zensur in der Bundesrepublik.* Köln: Förtner und Kraemer Verlag, 1985.)

128. Robert Weimann, "Kunst und Öffentlichkeit", *Sinn und Form*, 2/1979, p. 221.

129. "Dokumentation", *Frankfurter Rundschau*, 3 June, 1986.

130. Theo Sommer, "Deutschland: nichts Halbes und nichts Ganzes", *Die Zeit*, 15 August, 1986.

131. Kazimerz Wasiak, "Gesellschaftliche Auswirkung wachsender Teilnahme der DDR am internationalen Leben", *Deutschland Archiv*, 7/1985, pp. 727-739.

132. Hartmut Laube, "Kultur ohne Frieden gibt es nicht. Zum Stand der kulturell-wissenschaftlichen Beziehungen der DDR mit dem Ausland", *Horizont*, 6/1985, p. 5.

133. Knabe, *op. cit.* (fn. 104), p. 197.

134. "Entschließung der Synode". *EPD-Dokumentation*, 46-47/1980, p. 110.

135. *Kirche in Sozialismus*, 2/1984, pp. 25-30.

136. Knabe, *op. cit.* (fn. 104), p. 195.

137. In addition to the studies cited above, see also Hubertus Knabe, "'Der Mensch mordert sich selbst'. Ökologiekritik in der DDR-Literatur", *Deutschland Archiv*, 9/1983, pp. 954-973, and Werner Gruhn, "Umweltschutz als ökonomischer Faktor" in *Umweltprobleme und Umweltbewußtsein in der DDR* (Köln: Verlag Wissenschaft und Politik, 1985), pp. 97-116.

138. *Nutzung und Schutz der Umwelt*. Berlin: Volk und Wissen Volkseigener Verlag, 1980, pp. 21ff.

139. "Gesellschaftswissenschaften Bilanz und Aufgaben", *Einheit*, 12/1980. pp. 1231ff.

140. *Studienplan für das postgraduate Studium Umweltschutz (ausgewählte Probleme)*. Berlin: Ministerrat der Deutschen Demokratischen Republik, Ministerium für Hoch- und Fachschulwesen, Januar 1980, pp. 1-4.

141. Helmar Hegewald, "Moralische Triebkräfte bei der rationellen Nutzung der Naturresourcen in Sozialismus", *Deutsche Zeitschrift für Philosophie*, 12/1982, pp. 1457-1466.

142. *Direktiv des X. Parteitag der SED zum Fünfjahrplan für die Entwicklung der Volkswirtschaft der DDR in den Jahren 1981 bis 1985*. Berlin: X. Parteitag der Sozialistischen Einheitspartei Deutschlands, 11. bis 16. April, 1981, p. 61.

143. Georg Ebert/Uwe Möller, "Rationalität für oder gegen den Menschen", *Einheit*, 7-8/1980, p. 723.

144. "Politisches, klassenmäßiges Herangehen", *Probleme des Friedens und des Sozialismus*, March 1981, pp. 379–385; "Ökologischer Protest der Massen in Klassenkampf", *Probleme des Friedens und des Sozialismus*, May 1981, pp. 669–681.

145. Peter Wensierksi, "Wir haben Angst um unsere Kinder", *Spiegel*, 28 (8 July) 1985, p. 64.

146. "Beirat Umweltschutz beim Ministerrat", in *Landeskultur-Recht Lexikon*, hrsg. Akademie für Staats- und Rechtswissenschaft der DDR. Berlin: Staatsverlag, 1983.

147. Status des Ministeriums für Umweltschutz und Wasserwirtschaft. Beschluß des Ministerrates vom 23. Oktober 1975, *Gesetzblatt*, Teil I, 43 (20 November) 1975.

148. Staritz, *op. cit.* (fn. 92), p. 27.

149. "Die Massenorganizationen in der DDR - aktive Mitgestalter des Sozialismus", *Neuer Weg*, 18/1986, pp. 704–705. (See also *Handbuch gesellschaftlicher Organisationen in der DDR*. Berlin: Staatsverlag, 1985, p. 180.)

150. *Ibid.*

151. *Ibid.*

152. *Handbuch (op. cit.*, fn. 149, p. 193) reports 288,000; *Neuer Weg* (*op. cit.*, fn. 149) cites 275,236.

153. Radio DDR 1, 17 July 1985, 1000 GMT.

154. *Informationen*. Bonn: Gesamtdeutsches Institut, 14/1986, p. 9.

155. Various scientific societies are associated with the Academy of Science. These include, for instance, the societies for biologists, chemists, geographers, geologists, physicists, mathematicians, air and space specialists, meterologists, etc. (*Handbuch gesellschaftlicher Organizationen in der DDR, op. cit.* (fn. 149), p. 197.)

156. Gruhn, *op. cit.* (fn. 137), pp. 105–106.

157. Knabe, *op. cit.* (fn. 104), p. 194.

158. Gert-Joachim Glaeßner, "Wissenschaftlich-technische Revolution - Intelligenz/Politik in der DDR", in *Tradition und Fortschritt in der DDR. XIX. Tagung zum Stand der DDR-Forschung in der Bundesrepublik Deutschland. 20. bis 23. Mai 1986.* Köln: Verlag Wissenschaft und Politik, Edition Deutschland Archiv, 1986, pp. 11–28.

159. Katharina Belwe/Fred Klinger, "Der Wert der Arbeit - Aspekte des sozialen Wandels in der industriellen Arbeitswelt der DDR", in *Tradition und Fortschritt in der DDR. XIX. Tagung zum Stand der DDR-Forschung in der Bundesrepublik Deutschland, 20. bis 23. Mai 1986.* Köln: Verlag Wissenschaft und Politik, Edition Deutschland Archiv, 1986, pp. 61-86.

160. *Nutzung und Schutz der Umwelt, op. cit.* (fn. 138), p. 23.

161. "Gesellschaftswissenschaften. Bilanz und Aufgaben", *op. cit.* (fn. 139), pp. 1231, 1233.

162. *Neuer Weg, op. cit.* (fn. 149).

163. Peter Wensierski, "Die Gesellschaft für Nature und Umwelt: Kleine Innovation in der politischen Kultur der DDR", in *Umweltprobleme und Umweltbewußtsein in der DDR.* Köln: Verlag Wissenschaft und Politik, 1985, pp. 151-168.

164. Manfred Fiedler, "Initiativen für Natur und Umwelt", *Einheit,* 11/1984, pp. 1024ff.

165. Wensierski, *op. cit.* (fn. 163), p. 165.

166. "Geschichte, Kunst und Umwelt: Aus Aktionsprogrammen der Bezirksorganisationen des Kulturbunds", *Sonntag,* 46/1985, p. 7.

167. Zimmermann, *op. cit.* (fn. 87), p. 21.

168. Knabe, *op. cit.* (fn. 68, 104, 120).

169. Förtsch, *op. cit.* (fn. 67).

170. Rauschek, *op. cit.* (fn. 49), pp. 58-59.

171. Wensierski, *op. cit.* (fn. 163), p. 166.

172. Heino Falcke, cited in *Schwerter zu Pflugscharen. Friedensbewegung in der DDR.* Reinbeck, 1982, pp. 60ff.

173. Knabe, *op. cit.* (fn. 104), p. 191. (SED leaders emphasize that evidence of the GDR's "openness" is found in the fact that 12% to 14% of all publications appearing in print in the GDR are from church publishers or publishers with church interests; this point was made in the Günter Gaus/Otto Reinhold interview cited in fn. 129.)

174. Rudolf Dau, "Hanns Cibulka", in *Literature der Deutschen Demokratischen Republik.* Berlin: Volk und Wissen Volkseigener Verlag, 1979, pp. 73-89, 475-478.

175. Hanns Cibulka. *Sanddornzeit. Tagebücher von Hiddensee.*
Halle/Leipzig: Mitteldeutscher Verlag, 1971.

176. *Ibid.*, p. 9.

177. *Ibid.*, p. 14.

178. *Ibid.*, p. 67.

179. *Ibid., p. 78.*

180. Ibid., p. 92.

181. *Ibid.*, pp. 96-97.

182. *Ibid.*, p. 123.

183. Hanns Cibulka, "Swantow", *Neue deutsche Literatur*, 4/1981,
pp. 23-52.

184. *"Raketen/treiben Risse/in die Schutzhülle der Erde,/kometen-
haft/zieht über den Himmel/das Wort:/Fortschritt./Erlaubt ist
alles,/was den Denken Freude macht,/doch in der Tat,/da liegen Tod
und Leben/hautnah/beieinander." (Ibid.*, pp. 32-33).

185. *Ibid.*, pp. 39-40.

186. *Ibid.*, p. 46.

187. *Ibid.*, pp. 47-50.

188. *Ibid.*, p. 50.

189. Richard Losik, "Ein Lyriker aus Swantow", *Bonner General-
Anzeiger*, 5 June, 1981.

190. Reportedly the broadcast was from the Deutschlandfunk, but
the station could not provide a transcript/tape of such an outdated program.

191. Hermann Ley, "Über die Schwierigkeit der Wirklichkeits-
bewältigung", *Deutsche Zeitschrift für Philosophie*, 2/1982, pp.
234-247.

192. When critiquing Cibulka's discussion of medicine, Ley was unusually harsh and some said "unfair". Suggesting that Cibulka's
attack on medicine might be explained by experiences the author
had after a serious automobile accident, Ley then added the gratu-
itous assignation of guilt for the accident to Cibulka himself—
"One should not fall asleep, either at the steering wheel or in
social life".

193. Klaus Höpcke, "Phantasie für das Wirkliche", *Einheit*, 2/1982, pp. 173-179.

194. *Ibid.*, pp. 177-179.

195. Rudolf Woderich, "Prinzipien und Probleme industrielle Kultur im Sozialismus", *Weimarer Beiträge*, 6/1982, pp. 103-125.

196. Christa Wolf, "Diskussionsbeitrag", in *Es geht, es geht. Zeitgenössische Schriftsteller und ihr Beitrag zum Frieden*. B. Englemann, hrsg. München, 1982, p. 53.

197. *Kirche im Sozialismus*, 1-2/1983, p. 32.

198. *Ibid.*

199. Hanns Cibulka. *Swantow*. Halle/Leipzig: Mitteldeutscher Verlag, 1982.

200. Goethe: *"Alles was geschieht ist Symbol,/und indem es vollkommen sich darstellt/deutet es auf das Übrige."* Hugo von Hofmannsthal: *"Situationen sind symbolisch;/es ist die Schwäche der jetzigen Menschen,/daß sie sie analytisch behandeln/und dadurch das Zauberische auflösen."*

201. *Ibid.*, p. 16.

202. *Ibid.*, p. 16.

203. *Ibid.*, pp. 36-37.

204. *Ibid.*, p. 39.

205. *Ibid.*, p. 46.

206. *Ibid.*, pp. 63-64.

207. *Ibid.*, pp. 74-75.

208. *Ibid.*, pp. 77-81.

209. *Ibid.*, pp. 107-109.

210. *Ibid.*, pp. 109-110.

211. *Ibid.*, pp. 117ff.

212. *Ibid.*, pp. 127-128.

213. Karl Deutsch. *The Nerves of Government*. New York: The Free Press, 1966, p. 88.

214. "Thesen des Zentralkomitees der SED zum Karl-Marx Jahr 1983. *Einheit*, 1/1983, pp. 10-27.

215. *Speech by Erich Honecker, General Secretary of the SED Central Committee and Chairman of the GDR Council of State, at the International Theoretical Conference of the SED Central Committee on 'Karl Marx and our Time: The Struggle for Peace and Social Progress', Berlin, 11-16 April, 1983.* Dresden: Verlag Zeit im Bild, 1983, pp. 24-25.

216. Christa Wolf, "Aus den 'Frankfurter Vorlesungen'", *Sinn und Form*, 1/1983, pp. 46-47.

217. Jürgen Kuczynski, "Bedeutung der Oberfläche", *Neue deutsche Literatur*, 2/1983, pp. 77-82..

218. "Umweltschutz und rationelle Nutzung der Naturreichtümer dienen Wohl des Volkes und effektiver Volkswirtschaft", Interview mit Dr. Hans Reichelt, Stellvertreter des Vorsitzenden des Ministerrates und Minister für Umweltschutz und Wasserwirtschaft". *Neues Deutschland*, 5-6 February 1983, p. 9.

219. Wensierski, *op. cit.* (fn. 163). pp. 164-165.

220. Wolfgang Eichhorn I, "Ethik und Zukunft des Menschen", *Deutsche Zeitschrift für Philosophie*, 7/1983, pp. 842-844.

221. Rupprecht, *op. cit.* (fn. 82), p. 7.

222. See the "Chronik" section of *Kirche im Sozialismus*, 4/1983, pp. 68ff.

223. *Kirche im Sozialismus*, 4/1983, pp. 70, 72.

224. *Wirtschaftswissenschaft*, 1/1984, p. 140.

225. *Ibid.*, pp. 5-60.

226. Reinhold Miller, "Sinn des Lebens und Anspruch an sich selbst", *Einheit*, 10/1983, pp. 917-923.

227. Günther K. Lehmann, "Der wissenschaftlich-technische Fortschritt und die Ästhetik der Natur", *Weimarer Beiträge*, 10/1983, p. 1760.

228. *Ibid.*, p. 1771.

229. Monika Melchert, *Sonntag*, 34/1983.

230. Gerhard Dahne, *Neue deutsche Literatur*, 10/1983.

231. *Kritik 83. Rezensionen zur DDR-Literatur*. Hrsg. Eberhard Günther, Werner Liersch, Klaus Walter. Halle/Leipzig: Mittel-deutscher Verlag, 1983.

232. Angela und Karlheinz Steinmüller. *Andymon. Eine Weltraum-Utopie*. Stuttgart: Union Verlag, 1983 (Berlin: Verlag Neues Leben, 1982), p. 271.

233. *Ibid.*, p. 262.

234. *Ibid.*, p. 247.

235. "Realismus in der Phantastik", Die Science-fiction Autoren Angela und Karlheinz Steinmüller," *Sonntag*, 46/1985, p.4.

236. *Kirche im Sozialismus*, 6/1983, p. 63.

237. *Neues Deutschland*, 1 December 1983.

238. *Neues Deutschland*, 10-11 December 1983.

239. *Ibid.*

240. *Gesetzblatt*, *op. cit.* (fn. 115).

241. Gesetz über die Anwendung der Atomenergie und den Schutz vor ihren Gefahren. Atomenergiegesetz vom 8. Dezember 1983. *Gesetz-blatt der Deutschen Demokratischen Republik*, Teil 1 (14 Dezember) 1983, pp. 325-330. (See also Manfred Melzer, "Zum nuclearen Um-weltschutz in der DDR", in *Umweltprobleme und Umweltbewußtsein in der DDR*. Köln: Verlag Wissenschaft und Politik, 1985, pp. 83-96.)

242. Gregor Schirmer, "Zu den Ergebnissen der Gesellschaftswissen-schaften Konferenz", *Einheit*, 1/1984, pp. 19-23.

243. Kurt Hager. *Gesetzmäßigkeiten unserer Epoche - Triebkräfte und Wertes des Sozialismus. Rede auf der Gesellschaftswissen-schaftlichen Konferenz des Zentralkomitees der SED am 15. und 16. Dezember 1983 in Berlin*. Berlin: Dietz Verlag, 1984.

244. *Ibid.*, p. 46.

245. *Ibid.*, p. 60.

246. *Ibid.*, pp. 74-75.

247. *Gesetzmäßigkeiten unserer Epoche - Triebkräfte und Werte des Sozialismus. Diskussionsreden auf der Gesellschaftswissenschaft-lichen Konferenz des ZK der SED am 15. und 16. Dezember 1983 in*

Berlin. Berlin: Dietz Verlag, 1984, pp. 98-99, 103.

248. *Ibid.*, *p. 197.*

249. Ibid., p. 201.

250. Wensierski, *op. cit.* (fn. 163), pp. 158ff.

251. Klaus Höpcke, "Sicht auf Swantow - Überzeugendes und Bezweifelbares", *Sinn und Form*, 1/1984, pp. 165-177.

252. *Ibid.*, p. 175.

253. *Ibid.*

254. *Ibid.*, p. 169.

255. Lutz-Günther Fleischer, "Technologie und Gesellschaft", *Einheit*, 3/1984, pp. 217-222.

256. Günter Hoell, "Globalproblem Ernährung", *Deutsche Zeitschrift für Philosophie*, 6/1984, pp. 527-529. (See also Eichhorn, *op. cit.*, fn. 220, p. 844).

257. Werner Jehser, "Wahrheit und Parteilichkeit literarischer Wirklichkeitserkundung", *Einheit*, 4/1984, pp. 345-346.

258. *Ibid.*, p. 350.

259. Rauschek, *op. cit.* (fn. 49), pp. 59, 82-83.

260. *Kirche im Sozialismus*, 2/1984, p. 3.

261. *Ibid.*, p. 5.

262. *Ibid.*, p. 62.

263. L. Zänker, "Biologie - Technik - humanistischer Verantwortung", *Deutsche Zeitschrift für Philosophie*, 5/1984, p. 455.

264. H. Hegewald, "Berufsethos des Ingenieurs - Triebkraft humaner Gestaltung des wissenschaftlich-technischen Fortschritts im Sozialismus", *Deutsche Zeitschrift für Philosophie*, 5/1984, pp. 437ff.

265. Klaus Höpcke, "Vom Sinn unserer Literatur. Tatkräftiges Handeln für den realen Sozialismus bewirken", *Neues Deutschland*, 13 June 1984.

266. Berger, *op. cit.* (fn. 61), pp. 18-19.

267. *Ibid.*, pp. 189-190.

183

268. Klaus Höpcke, "Gründe für Streitbarkeit", *Sonntag*, 24/1984, p. 7.

269. *Kirche im Sozialism*, 4/1984, p. 5.

270. *Ibid.*, 4/1984, p. 41.

271. *Kirche im Sozialismus*, 5/1984, p. 42.

272. *epd Dokumentation*, 43/1984, p. 56.

273. *Kirche im Sozialismus*, 5/1984, p. 46.

274. *Kirche im Sozialismus*, 6/1984, p. 46.

275. *Glaube und Heimat*, 25 November 1984 (cited in *Kirche im Sozialismus* 6/1984, p. 8).

276. Müller, *op. cit.* (fn. 30), p. 800.

277. *Sozialismus und Frieden, VI. Philosophiekongreß*, *op. cit.* (fn. 42), p. 101.

278. *Ibid.*, pp. 155-156.

279. *Ibid.*, pp. 160ff.

280. *Ibid.*, p. 223.

281. *Ibid.*, pp. 166ff.

282. *Ibid.*, p. 183.

283. Hans Reichelt, "Die natürliche Umwelt rationell nutzen, gestalten, schützen", *Einheit*, 11/1984, pp. 1010-1017.

284. Alfred Kosing, "Natur und Gesellschaft", *Einheit*, 11/1984, pp. 1018-1024.

285. Manfred Fiedler, "Initiativen für Nature und Umwelt", *Einheit*, 11/1984, p. 1028.

286. Manfred Schubert, "Abproduktfreie, abproduktarme Technologien", *Einheit*, 11/1984, p. 1029.

287. Hans Brückner, "Umweltschutz im Blickfeld unserer LPG", pp. 1034-1035; Rudolf Rüthnick, "Unser Wald – Rohstoffquelle und Stätte der Erholung", pp. 1036-1038; Gerhard Voigt, "Rationelle Nutzung und Schutz des Wassers", pp. 1039-1040, *Einheit*, 11/1984.

288. "Rechtliche Grundlagen in der DDR", *Einheit*, 11/1984, pp. 1041-1042.

289. Horst Paucke, "Im Spiegel unserer wissenschaftlichen Publizistik", *Einheit*, 11/1984, p. 1046.

290. Kurt Hager, "Die Einheit von Wissenschaft, Bildung, und Kultur", *Einheit*, 11/1984, p. 982.

291. Olaf R. Spittel, "Angela und Karlheinz Steinmüller's 'Andymon. Eine Weltraum-Utopie'. Verlag Neues Leben, Berlin, 1982", *Weimarer Beiträge*, 10/1984, pp. 1715-1723.

292. Haase, et. al., *op. cit.* (fn. 40).

293. *Ibid.*, p. 1595.

294. *Ibid.*, p. 1604.

295. *Ibid.*, p. 1605.

296. Silvia Schlenstedt, "Gespräch mit Stephan Hermlin", *Weimarer Beiträge*, 11/1984, p. 1887.

297. *Ibid.*, p. 1890.

298. Annneli Hartmann, "'Wer die Sonne sucht, beginnt von dir zu lernen...' Zur Rolle der Sowjetliteratur im Prozeß der gesellschaftlichen und literarischen Selbstverständigung in der DDR", in *Jahrbuch zur Literatur in der DDR 3*, hrsg. Klussmann/Mohr. Bonn: Bouvier Verlag, 1983, pp. 99-103.

299. Klaus Walther, "Redezeit für Leser", *op. cit.* (fn. 54), p. 4.

300. Erhard Geissler, "Bruder Frankenstein oder - Pflegefälle aus der Retorte?", *Sinn und Form*, 6/1984, pp. 1289-1319.

301. Werner Creutziger, "Brief an Erhard Geissler", Jürgen Hauschke, "'Fachlektor' Kontra Brězan oder Schwierigkeiten mit Krabat", and Manfred Wolter, "Entwarnung", *Sinn und Form*, 2/1985, pp. 416-431.

302. Schrade, *op. cit.* (fn. 72).

303. *Gesetzblatt der Deutschen Demokrtischen Republik*, Teil 1 (Nr. 30) 1984.

304. *Mitteilung der Staatlichen Zentralverwaltung für Statistik der DDR über die Durchführung des Volkswirtschaftsplan 1984*. Berlin: Panorama DDR, Dokumente zur Politik der Deutschen Demokratischen Republik, 1/1985, p. 20.

305. *Gesetz über den Volkswirtschaftsplan 1985. Beschluß der Volkskammer der DDR vom 30. November 1984.* Berlin: Panorama der DDR, Dokumente zur Politik der Deutschen Demokratischen Republik, 4/1984.

306. *Staat und Recht*, 4/1984, pp. 283ff.

307. Kurt Kleinert, "Eingaben - Instrument der Mitarbeit der Bürger", *Neue Justiz*, 10/1984, pp. 393-395.

308. Heinz Duft, "Lehren und Schlußfolgerungen aus einer Gewässerverschmutzung", *Der Schöffe*, 12/1984, pp. 284-287.

309. *Neues Deutschland*, 11 February 1985.

310. Benno Müller-Hill, "Kollege Mengele - nicht Bruder Eichmann", *Sinn und Form*, 3/1985, pp. 671-676.

311. Karlheinz Lohs, Anna M. Wobus, "Zuschriften an Erhard Geissler", *Sinn und Form*, 4/1985, pp. 903-906.

312. Horst Paucke, "Marx, Engels und die Ökologie", *Deutsche Zeitschrift für Philosophie*, 3/1985, pp. 207-215.

313. Wolfgang Luutz, "Alltag und Alltagsbewußtsein", *Deutsche Zeitschrift für Philosophie*, 4/1985, pp. 348-352.

314. Hildegard Maria Nickel, "Aus der Diskussion", *Sonntag*, 14/1985, p. 8.

315. "Mitteilung über die Einberufung des 4. Soziologie-Kongress der DDR", in *Informationen zur soziologischer Forschung in der Deutschen Demokratischen Republik*, 2/1984.

316. *Neues Deutschland*, 9-10 March 1985, p. 10; 27 March 1985, pp. 1,4.

317. *Neues Deutschland*, 5 March 1985. (See also Kurt Kleinert, "Hohe Anforderungen an die Eingabenarbeit", *Organisation*, 3/1985, pp. 3-4.)

318. *Ibid.*

319. *Kirche im Sozialismus*, 2/1985, p. 85.

320. *Kirche im Sozialismus*, 3/1985, p. 89.

321. *Ibid.*, pp. 89-90.

322. *Kirche im Sozialismus*, 6/1985, p. 245.

323. Eberhard Poppe, "Dimension und Funktion sozialistischer Demokratie als gesellschaftliche Triebkraft", *Staat und Recht*, 5/1985, pp. 367-375.

324. Uwe-Jens Heuer, "Die Staatsmacht als ökonomischer Potenz", *Staat und Recht*, 5/85, ppp. 404ff.

325. Rolf Espenhayn, "Der wissenschaftlich-technische Fortschritt und das Akzeptanz Problem in der Welt des Kapitals", *Wirtschaftswissenschaft*, 5/1985, pp. 713-728.

326. *Kirche im Sozialismus*, 6/1985, p. 235.

327. Armin Martin/Heinz Weinert, "Einführung von Rahmenlehrprogrammen Umweltschutz und Umweltgestaltung im Studienjahr 1985/86 in den technischen und ökonomischen Grundstudienrichtungen an den Ingenieur- und Fachschulen der DDR", *Die Fachschule*, 8/1985, pp. 215-216.

328. "Zum neuen Gesetz über die örtlichen Volksvertretungen in der Deutschen Demokratischen Republik vom 4. Juli 1985", *Presse-Informationen*, 9 July 1985, pp. 1-14.

329. *Ibid.*

330. Stimme der DDR, 17 July 1985, 1100 GMT.

331. *Gesetzblatt der DDR*, Teil 1 (12 June) 1985, pp. 238-241.

332. *Umweltschutz - Aufgaben und Ergebnisse*, hrsg. Panorama, "Aus erster Hand" Reihe. Dresden: Verlag Zeit im Bild, 1985.

333. See also Bernd Spindler, "Die Verwertung von Sekundärrohstoffen in der DDR". Bonn: Gesamtdeutsches Institut Bundesanstalt für gesamtdeutsche Aufgaben, 1985.

334. See *Neues Deutschland*, 28 July 1986, for the mid-1986 statistics on the number of protected nature areas.

335. Klaus Höpcke, *Weltbühne*, 33/1985.

336. Volker Braun, *Hinze-Kunze-Roman*. Halle/Leipzig: Mitteldeutscher Verlag, 1985.

337. Volker Braun, *Sinn und Form*, 5/1985.

338. Kurt Hager, "Probleme der Kulturpolitik vor dem XI. Parteitag der SED", *Neue deutsche Literatur*, 1/1986, pp. 5-27.

339. Karin Hirdina, "Soziale Erkundung in der Literatur der DDR", in *Positionen 1. Wortmeldung zur DDR-Literatur.* Halle/Leipzig: Mitteldeutscher Verlag, 1984, pp. 78-105.

340. *Neues Deutschland*, 9 October 1985.

341. *Neues Deutschland*, 22 November 1985.

342. "Realismus in der Phantastik", *op. cit.* (fn. 235).

343. *Börsenblatt für den Deutschen Buchhandel*, 37 (10 September), 1985, p. 731.

344. See, for instance, *Neues Deutschland* for 11 January, 15 February, 4 April, 4 June, 3 July, 5 and 12 September, 8 October, 12 and 20 November.

345. See *Neues Deutschland*, 15 February, 23 April, 26 July, 9 August, and 24 October.

346. Especially significant was the International Environmental Protection Conference in Helsinki in September. Speaking at the meeting, Reichelt outlined the GDR's environmental program and its achievements thus far. His speech was published in *Neues Deutschland*, 9 July 1985, p. 3.

347. Albrecht Schönherr, "Öffentlichkeitsanspruch einer Minderheit", *Kirche im Sozialismus*, 4/1986, pp. 149-152.

348. *Ibid.*, p. 150.

349. Heinz Wagner, "40 Jahre Hörfunkgottesdienste", *Kirche im Sozialismus*, 4/1986, pp. 172-173.

350. Erhart Neubert, "Megapolis DDR und die Religion", *Kirche im Sozialismus*, 4/1986, pp. 155-164.

351. *Kirche im Sozialismus*, 4/1986, p. 50.

352. *Leseerfahrung. Lebenserfahrung, op. cit.* (fn. 5).

353. *Ibid.*, p. 70.

354. *Ibid.*, p. 88.

355. Dieter Kliche, "Über 'Leseerfhrung – Lebenserfahrung. Literatursoziologische Untersuchung", *Weimarer Beiträge*, 3/1986, pp. 492-503.

356. Jutta Duclaud, "Allgemeine Methoden für konkrete Leser?", *Börsenblatt für den Deutschen Buchhandel*, 37 (September 10) 1985, pp. 725-727.

357. *Ibid.*

358. Lothar Bisky, "Leseverhalten und Leseinteressen junger Menschen. Von den 24. Tagung der Kinder- und Jugendliteratur der DDR im Bezirk Neubrandenburg", *Deutsche Lehrerzeitung*, 13/1986, p. 7.

359. *Presse-Informationen*, 3 June 1986, pp. 4-5.

360. Peter Hoff, "Wettbewerbspartner oder Konkurrent?", *Rundfunk und Fernsehen* (Hamburg), 3-4/1985, pp. 437-455.

361. Helmut Hanke, "Massenkultur, populäre Künste, Unterhaltung", *Unterhaltungskunst Beilage*, 1/1986, pp. 7-12.

362. Radio DDR I, 16 July 1986, 1000 GMT.

363. Annetta Ziegs, "Käufer, Wünsche und Gespräche. Ergebnisse einer Kundenbefragung im Volksbuchhandel", Teil 1, and "Trotz vieler Titel noch manche Lücke", Schluß, *Börsenblatt für den deutschen Buchhandel*, 45/1986, pp. 855-857, and 46/1986, pp. 869-872.

364. "Dem Neuen zugewandt - Literatur im Leseland", *Börsenblatt für den deutschen Buchhandel*, 1/1986, pp. 4-5.

365. Heiner Hüfner, *Sonnenfünf*. Rudolstadt: Greifenverlag, 1985.

366. "Aus dem Buchhandel", *Börsenblatt für den Deutschen Buchhandel*, 13 (1 April) 1986, p. 224.

367. "Spektrum", Berliner Rundfunk, 30 August 1986, 1800 hours.

368. See, for example, *Neue deutsche Literatur* 2/1986, *Sinn und Form* 2/1986, and *Weimarer Beiträge*, 5/1986.

369. Rüdiger Bernhardt, "Identitätssuche als Handlungsvorgang in jüngster Prosa der DDR", *Weimarer Beiträge*, 5/1986, pp. 811-829.

370. Erhard Geissler, "Frankensteins Tod - Bemerkungen zu einer Diskussion", *Sinn und Form*, 1/1986, pp. 158-177.

371. Radio DDR I, 26 March 1986, 1200 GMT.

372. Gerhard Müller, "Diskussionsbeitrag im Plenum der Arbeitstagung", *Die Fachschule*, 12/1986, pp. 278-280.

373. *Neues Deutschland*, 21 January 1986.

374. *Presse-Informationen*, 3 August 1986, p. 6.

375. "Anordnung über die strahlenschutzmedizinische Betreung der Strahlenwerktätigen und des Bedienungspersonal - Strahlenschutzmedizinische Betreungsanordnung - vom 25. März 1986", *Gesetzblatt der DDR*, Teil 1/1986, pp. 273-276.

376. Horst Lehmann/Heidrun Pohl, "Eingaben der Bürger und weitere Vervollkommnung der sozialistischen Demokratie", *Staat und Recht*, 1/1986, pp. 11-19.

377. "Wissenschaftlicher Kommunismus: Sozialistische Lebensweise und demokratische Aktivität", *Informationsbulletin*, 1/1986. Berlin: Akademie für Gesellschaftswissenschaften beim ZK der SED, Institut für Wissenschaftlichen Kommunismus, 1986.

378. Karl A. Mollnau, "Sozialistische Demokratie und Persönlichkeitsentwicklung", *Einheit*, 2/1986, pp. 121-126.

379. Willi Büchner-Uhder/Rudolf Hieblinger/Eberhard Poppe, "Zur Erhöhung der Wirksamkeit der örtlichen Volksvertretungen und der Autorität der Abgeordneten", *Staat und Recht*, 1/1986, pp. 3-11.

380. *Spiegel*, 20 (12 May) 1986, p. 129; 27 (30 June) 1986, p. 47.

381. Erich Honecker, "Bericht des Zentralkomitees der Sozialistischen Einheitspartei Deutschlands an den XI. Parteitag der SED". Dresden: Verlag Bild im Zeit, 1986, p. 95.

382. *Ibid.*, p. 47.

383. *Direktiv des XI. Parteitages der SED zum Fünfjahrplan für die Entwicklung der Volkswirtschaft der DDR in den Jahren 1986 bis 1990*. Dresden: Verlag Zeit im Bild, 1986, p. 7.

384. *Ibid.*, pp. 12-35.

385. *Ibid.*, pp. 102-103.

386. Werner Gruhn, "Reaktionen der DDR auf Tschernobyl", *Deutschland Archiv*, 7/1986, pp. 676-678.

387. Karl Lanius/Günter Flach, "Sicherheit - oberstes Prinzip bei der friedlichen Nutzung des Atoms zum Wohl der Menschheit", *Neues Deutschland*, 2 May 1986, p. 2. (For how the GDR further reacted to Western reactions, see "Bemerkungen über die 'verrückten Bundis'. Wie die DDR mit der Katastrophe von Tschernobyl umgeht", *Frankfurter Rundschau*, 27 May 1986.)

388. *Neues Deutschland*, 3-4 May 1986.

389. Fernsehen der DDR, 14 May 1986, 1758 GMT.

390. Fernsehen der DDR, 21 May 1986, 1756 GMT.

391. *Kölner Stadt-Anzeiger*, 23 May 1986.

392. *Spiegel*, 27 (30 June) 1986, p. 50.

393. "Synode der EKU kritisiert Moskauer Informationspolitik", *Berliner Taggesspiegel*, 25 May 1986.

394. *Kirche im Sozialismus*, 3/1986, pp. 94-95.

395. *Spiegel*, op. cit. (fn. 392).

396. Stimme der DDR, 27 May 1986, 1200 GMT.

397. Harri Harrland, "Die Arbeit der Staatsanwaltschaft mit den Eingaben der Bürger", *Neue Justiz*, 6/1986, pp. 223-225.

398. Stimme der DDR, 4 June 1986, 1505 GMT.

399. Radio DDR 1, 5 June 1986, 1403 GMT.

400. *Frankfurter Rundschau*, 26 June 1986. (See also *Frankfurter Allgemeine Zeitung*, 24 June 1986.)

401. *Spiegel*, op. cit. (fn. 392), p. 50.

402. *Ibid.*

403. *Neues Deutschland*, 14-15 June, 1986.

404. Horst Schötzki, "Tschnerboyl und die politische Moral", *Horizont*, 6/1986, pp. 6-7.

405. Manfred von Ardenne, "Aufgabe unser Geisteswissenschaftler", *Sonntag*, 26/1986, p. 2

406. "Interview Erich Honeckers für *Dagens Nyheter*", *Neues Deutschland*, 25 June 1986.

407. While Honecker said nucler accounted for 3% and coal for 90% of the GDR's energy, other GDR assessments set the nuclear proportion at 10-12%. (See, for example, *Umweltschutz*, op. cit., fn. 332, p. 35.)

408. For an overall view of nuclear energy policy in Eastern Europe, see Henrik Bischof, "Nach Tschernobyl – zur Atomenergie-politik der RGW-Staaten", *DDR Report*, 8/1986, pp. 433-436.

409. *Frankfurter Rundschau*, 24 June 1986.

410. Radio DDR 1, 26 June 1986, 1703 GMT.

411. Radio DDR, 26 June 1986, 1430 GMT.

412. "Chronik", *Kirche im Sozialismus*, 4/1986, pp. 183-188.

413. *Ibid*.

414. *Spiegel, op. cit.* (fn. 392), p. 47.

415. Fernsehen der DDR, 8 October 1986, 1843 GMT.

416. Anita M. Mallinckrodt, "Political Communication", in *Politics in the German Democratic Republic* (coauthors John M. Starrels and Anita M. Mallinckrodt). New York: Praeger Special Studies Series, 1975, pp. 293-349.

417. Bathrick, *op. cit.* (fn. 99).

418. Karlheinz Lohs, "Woran man uns messen wird", *Die Weltbühne*, 49 (December) 1984, pp. 1537-1539.

419. Such views expressed at the 5th Social Science Environmental Colloquium, in December 1985, were summarized by Eckhard Gielow and Helga Horsch in their article, "Ökonomische Regelung zur Bewertung und Stimulierung von Umweltmaßnahmen", in *Wirtschaftswissenschaft*, 8/1986, pp. 1213-1222.

420. Günther Kurt Lehmann, "Ich wandere ja so gerne... Zusammenspiel von Ästhetik, Natur und Technik", *Sonntag*, 52/1984, p. 8.

421. Hans Koch. *Grundlagen sozialistischer Kulturpolitik in der Deutschen Demokratischen Republik*. Berlin: Dietz Verlag, 1983, p. 65.

INDEX

197

puts, Interest groups, Political culture, Political communication, Political opposition

Theses of study.
  See Study

Urania, 35, 104, 138

Wagner, Heinz, 126
Wasiak, K., 43
Weimann, Robert, 41
Weinholz, Erhard, 125
Wensierski, Peter, 52
Western media, 3, 40, 43, 60-61, 64-66, 87, 126, 130, 136, 137, 151, 152, 153
White, Robert A., 19
White, Stephan, 12
Whitebrook, Maureen, 1, 19
Wiatr, Jerzy J., 8
Woderich,Rudolf, 68
Wolf, Christa, 32, 68, 90
Wolf, Gerhard, 61
Wolter, Manfred, 115
Writers' Union, 4-5, 32, 53

Zimmermann, Hartmut, 29